T0213072

Lecture Notes in Artificial Intelligence 10512

Subseries of Lecture Notes in Computer Science

More information about this series at http://www.springer.com/series/1244

Claude Frasson · George Kostopoulos (Eds.)

Brain Function Assessment in Learning

First International Conference, BFAL 2017
Patras, Greece, September 24–25, 2017
Proceedings

Editors
Claude Frasson
University of Montreal
Montréal, QC
Canada

George Kostopoulos
University of Patras
Patras
Greece

ISSN 0302-9743   ISSN 1611-3349   (electronic)
Lecture Notes in Artificial Intelligence
ISBN 978-3-319-67614-2   ISBN 978-3-319-67615-9   (eBook)
DOI 10.1007/978-3-319-67615-9

Library of Congress Control Number: 2017952886

LNCS Sublibrary: SL7 – Artificial Intelligence

Printed on acid-free paper

This Springer imprint is published by Springer Nature
The registered company is Springer International Publishing AG
The registered company address is: Gewerbestrasse 11, 6330 Cham, Switzerland

Preface

This volume contains the refereed papers presented at the International Conference on Brain Function Assessment in Learning, BFAL 2017, held on September 24–25, 2017 in Patras, Greece. The conference is the first in a multidisciplinary domain that regroups specialists in neuroscience, computer science, medicine, education, human-computer interactions, and social interaction. It promotes a cross-disciplinary approach to better understanding how to use the brain's capabilities to improve cognition and learning. The benefits cover a large variety of applications and this conference opens the way to collaborative projects and research as the synergy of all these disciplines is important to strengthen the impact and scope of the results.

The convergence of cognitive studies, tools of artificial intelligence, neuroscience approaches, and health applications opens a new era of multidisciplinary research tracks. The emergence of new assessment devices allows new ways of experimentation in laboratories, with light, non-intrusive, and low-cost sensors. Industrial representatives of relative technology were also invited to present their tools and equipment.

The conference gives the participants the opportunity to examine multiple applications of brain function assessment in learning–mainly in the education and health fields–which are becoming more and more promising. For example, knowing the brainwave activity and the condition of a user, researchers can detect whether he/she is not concentrating, or is over busy, hyperactive, anxious, not motivated, and they can apply corrective methods to provide calm, relaxation, and better receptivity to allow a better transfer of knowledge and life conditions.

There were 28 submissions. Each submission was reviewed by at least 1, and on average 2.4, Program Committee (PC) members, according to a double-blind process. The PC decided to accept 22 papers. Sixteen of these were accepted as full papers, and 6 were accepted as posters. The program also included 2 invited talks from well known researchers.

We would like to thank all the 32 members of the multidisciplinary Program Committee for their constructive work in making suggestions and improvements to the papers, and all the authors for contributing to an innovative program. This conference would never exist without the strong involvement of Kitty Panourgia, the organization chair, and her excellent NEOANALYSIS team (Katerina Milathianaki, Isaak Tselepis, Natalia Kakourou, and Alexia Kakourou).

The conference was organized under the auspices of the University of Patras and we would like to thank the university authorities and administration for contributing to the emergence of this new multidisciplinary conference.

July 2017

Claude Frasson
George Kostopoulos

Organization

Program Committee

Herve Abdi	The University of Texas at Dallas, USA
Theodore Antonakopoulos	University of Patras, Greece
Paolo Avesani	Fondazione Bruno Kessler, Italy
Nicolas Avouris	University of Patras, Greece
Panagiotis Bamidis	Aristotle University of Thessaloniki, Greece
Anastasios Bezerianos	University of Patras, Greece
Tassos Bountis	Nazarbayev University, Kazakhstan
Stefano Cerri	University of Montpellier, France
Maher Chaouachi	University of Montreal, Canada
Sergio Cruces	University of Seville, Spain
Dominique Durand	Case Western University, USA
Deniz Erdogmus	Northeastern University, USA
Claude Frasson	University of Montreal, Canada
Irinni Giannopulu	Bond University, Australia
Jean Gotman	McGill University, Canada
Foteini Grivokostopoulou	University of Patras, Greece
Ioannis Hatzilygeroudis	University of Patras, Greece
Pengyu Hong	Brandeis University, USA
Andreas Ioannides	AAI Scientific Cultural Service Ltd, Cyprus
Nikola Kasabov	Auckland University, New Zealand
George Kostopoulos	University of Patras, Greece
Elmar Lang	University of Regensburg, Germany
James Lester	North Carolina State University, USA
Wentai Liu	Brain Research Institute, USA
Alessandro Micarelli	University of Rome, Italy
Adamentia Mitsacos	University of Patras, Greece
Karim Oweiss	University of Florida, USA
Kitty Panourgia	Neoanalysis Ltd., Greece
Costas Porpodas	University of Patras, Greece
Philippe Robert	CHU of Nice, France
Andrzej Skowron	Warsaw University, Poland
Stefan Trausan-Matu	Politehnica of Bucarest, Romania
Isaak Tselepis	Neoanalysis Ltd., Greece
Beverly Woolf	University of Massachussetts, USA

Organization Committee

Kitty Panourgia   Neoanalysis Ltd., Greece
Alexia Kakourou   Neoanalysis Ltd., Greece
Natalia Kakourou   Neoanalysis Ltd., Greece
Katerina Milathianaki   Neoanalysis Ltd., Greece
Isaak Tselepis   Neoanalysis Ltd., Greece

Intelligent Control and Cognitive Control: Issues and Challenges

Peter P. Groumpos

Department of Electrical and Computer Engineering Technology,
University of Patras, Greece
Groumpos@ece.upatras.gr

Round Table Discussion

Panel Members: Claude Frasson, Peter P. Groumpos, George Kostopoulos,
Kyriakos Sgarbas

Summary or Abstract

From the Call for Papers: The theme of conference is **Brain Function Assessment in Learning** and its multiple applications-mainly in the Education and Health Fields - which will become more and more promising. For example, knowing the brainwave activity and the condition of a user, we can detect if he/she is not concentrated, over busy, hyperactive, anxious, not motivated, and we can apply corrective methods to provide calm, relaxation and better receptivity to allow a better transfer of knowledge and life conditions.)

The proposed Round Table (RT)

Today the whole world is phasing with an unprecedented set of problems never had before. Challenging and difficult problems relating to the Energy and Environment, the Health and Ecology, the business and Economics and the ongoing process of Spiritual Decline. We stand at the Abyss, at the steadily approaching threshold of unimaginable chaos, calamity and destruction of our planet earth. IS THERE ANY SOLUTION? YES, there exists a lasting solution to these issues facing humankind. It derives from the notion of the power of ideas and an idea so powerful that its effect upon the World will be most profound. Ideas come from the human brain. The most powerful brain executives-attributes are Intelligence and Cognition.

Much has been written on Cognitive Control (CC) in the neuroscience and psychology literature. In contrast, from an engineering perspective, cognitive control is in its very early stage of development. Looking back on the history of the field of control engineering in the 20th century, we see a trend in the evolution of controllers from simple structures such as open-loop and proportional–integral–derivative (PID) controllers to much more sophisticated ones with features such as optimality, adaptivity, robustness, and intelligence to some extent.

Cognitive Control (CC) is defined as the ability to flexibly adapt behavior to current demands, by promoting task-relevant information and behaviors over temporally-extended periods and in the face of interference or competition.

On the other hand the area of "**Intelligent Control (IC)** is a fusion of a number of research areas in systems and control, Computer science and operation research among others, coming together, merging and expanding in new directions. By others **Intelligent control** (**IC**) is a class of *Control techniques* that use various artificial intelligence computing approaches like neural networks, Bayesian probability, fuzzy logic, machine learning, evolutionary computation and genetic algorithms. New control techniques are created continuously as new models of *intelligent behavior* are created and computational methods developed to support them ignoring completely that in most of these controls, human intelligence and cognition play a major and crucial role in developing all above controls and been called **Intelligent Control (IC)**.

In the RT the basic and fundamental question of how Intelligent Control and Cognitive Control can be related mathematically and what is the role of Learning and thus creating new Knowledge.Learning is the most important thing that living creatures do. As far as any living creature is concerned, any action that does not involve learning is pretty much a waste of time. This is especially so for a human one. An organism cannot properly animate itself without first learning how to. Humans, before they can satisfy their own needs, first have to learn these needs, to understand and carefully evaluate them before they decide how to satisfy them. Indeed not an easy task.

Knowledge is a familiarity, awareness, or understanding of someone or something, such as facts, information, descriptions, or skills, which is acquired through learning or experience by perceiving, observing, discovering, innovation, or all kind of education forms.

Knowledge can refer to a theoretical or practical understanding of a subject. It can be implicit (as with practical skill or expertise) or explicit (as with the theoretical understanding of a subject); it can be more or less formal or systematic. In philosophy, the study of knowledge is called epistemology; the Greek philosopher Plato famously defined knowledge as "justified true belief", though this definition is now thought by some analytic philosophers to be problematic while others defend the platonic definition. In Plato's *Theaetetus*, Socrates and his student, Theaetetus discuss three definitions of *knowledge*: knowledge as nothing but perception, knowledge as true judgment, and, finally, knowledge as a true judgment with an account. However today each of these definitions is shown to be unsatisfactory. Knowledge acquisition involves complex cognitive processes: perception, communication, and reasoning; while knowledge is also said to be related to the capacity of *acknowledgment* in human beings. However, several definitions of knowledge and theories to explain it exist. There are also many different categories of knowledge. Understanding the different forms that knowledge can exist in, and thereby being able to distinguish between various types of knowledge, is an essential step for knowledge management (KM).

The panelist will address the above concepts and present their views as how intelligence and cognition can indeed provide solutions to today's problems of the society. The need to combine Intelligence and Cognition to a Unified theory of **Intelligent Cognitive Control (ICC)** will become evident. This RT will address **ICC** and scientifically search mathematical foundation for the ICC in order to search, investigate, analyze and provide solutions to the problems that the world is facing. Advanced revolutionary new theoretical and computational methods will be needed for advancing all the scientific sectors: healthcare, energy and environment, engineering, manufacturing, ecology, psychology, business and economics, education, philosophy and human productivity.

Figure 1. Raphael, detail of Plato and Aristotle, *School of Athens*, 1509-1511, fresco (Stanza della Segnatura, Palazzi Pontifici, Vatican)

Contents

Affective Learning:
Principles, Technologies, Practice

Panagiotis D. Bamidis[1, 2]

[1] Aristotle University of Thessaloniki, Thessaloniki 54124, Greece
[2] University of Leeds, Leeds, UK
{bamidis@auth.gr}, {p.bamidis@leeds.ac.uk}

Abstract. Although the issues around emotions and learning are not new, the term affective learning has only recently been defined as the learning that relates to the learner's interests, attitudes, and motivations. In the digital age we live though, affective learning is destined to be technology driven or at least enhanced. Having overemphasised the cognitive and relatively neglecting the affective dimension in the past, technology enhanced learning is now enforced by new neuroscience findings that confirmed that affect is complexly intertwined with thinking, and performing important functions that may guide rational behaviour, assist memory retrieval, support decision-making and enhance creativity. To cope with personalised learning experiences in such models of learners though, intelligent tutoring systems must now contain "emotion, affect and context", in analogy to successful human tutors. However, measuring and modelling learners' emotional and affective states remains a difficult task, especially when real-time interactions are envisaged. In this paper, the concept of affective learning is furnished with case studies where the roles of technologies, neuroscience, learning and education are interwoven. Medical education is borrowed as a domain of reference. Neuroscientific emphasis is placed in the synergy of two perspectives, namely, the detection and recording of emotions from humans and ways to facilitate their elicitation and their subsequent exploitation in the decision-making process. The paper concludes with a visionary use case towards affective facilitation of training against medical errors and decision making by intelligent, self-regulated systems that could exploit scenario based learning to augment medical minds for tomorrow's doctors.

Keywords: emotion, learning, affective computing, affective learning, technology enhanced learning, self-regulation, scenario based learning, decision making, affective neuroscience, brain function, skill enhancement, MOOC, bullying

1 Introduction

According to Mosby's Medical Dictionary [1] affective learning is defined through learning skills and specifically as the "acquisition of behaviors involved in expressing feelings in attitudes, appreciations, and values". In attempts to uplift the value of affective learning in higher education [2] affective learning has been referred to as "learning that relates to the learner's interests, attitudes, and motivations". Surprisingly enough, the roots of this are not too recent. When taxonomies (classifications) of educational domains were attempted for the first time [3] as tools that may be used to establish curricula and initiate research on learning, the cognitive domain became

© Springer International Publishing AG 2017
C. Frasson and G. Kostopoulos (Eds.): BFAL 2017, LNAI 10512, pp. 1–13, 2017
DOI: 10.1007/978-3-319-67615-9_1

one of the most influential ones of those. Bloom [4] used that as a vehicle to drive curricular development and assessment strategies (), while, later, it was complemented with the addition of the psychomotor and affective domains of learning [5].

However, in the digital age, affective learning is destined to be technology driven or at least enhanced. It is true, that human as well as machine learning research have greatly benefited from the exchange of ideas between psychology and computation [6], but unaligned with the educational taxonomists' recognition of the affect dimension, in artificial intelligence or intelligent tutoring systems for that matter, this was done unequally in the beginning, by overemphasising the cognitive and relatively neglecting the affective dimension in technology enhanced learning (TEL). Unlike the inherent contradiction [7] of the term "affective computing" [1] which was argued to marry two opponent streams (computing i.e. rational and affect i.e. non-rational), the role of affect in learning cannot be denied by anyone. Although the extension of cognitive theory to explain and exploit the role of affect in learning was in its infancy a decade ago [6], new findings in neuroscience, psychology, and cognitive science have confirmed that affect is complexly intertwined with thinking, and performing important functions [9] that may guide rational behaviour, assist memory retrieval, support decision-making and enhance creativity. Certainly, teachers know that affect plays a crucial role, as an intuitive factor for probing motivation, increasing the interest, driving engagement, uplifting attention. It is hoped that in that way it could also maximise learning outcomes, as studies demonstrated that emotional skills can be more influential than cognitive abilities in personal and career success [10]. To this extent and beyond memory, empathy [11] and experience have been shown as desirable aspects of the affective interactions [8] of learners and they have been linked with uplifting learning capacity and effectiveness. In recent years, self-regulation has notably been discussed as one way of achieving this [12]. However, self-regulation involves cognitive, affective, motivational and behavioural components that drive learners to achieve their desired goals [13] within learning environments and conditions.

What is the role of technology in this? Undoubtedly, a substantial body of research in Artificial Intelligence in Education (AIE) is to create adaptive learning environments capable of deriving models of learners and providing personalised learning experiences. Intelligent tutoring systems (ITSs) have exploited several rigorous models to represent the knowledge or expertise necessary for performing meaningful tutoring [14]. To that extent, and beyond cognition, learner models for ITSs should contain "emotion, affect and context", in analogy to successful human tutors that adapt their teaching strategies not only to the learners' knowledge and intellectual capacity, but also to their emotional states and the context under which learning is attempted. However, emotion and affect are not yet typical components of the learner model in usual adaptive intelligent learning environments [14], as measuring and modelling learners' emotional and affective states remains a difficult task, especially when real-time interactions are envisaged.

Narrowing our education focus down to medical education, Mc Lean [15] has emphasised some decades ago the issue of the "brain in relation to empathy and medical

---

[1] Computing that relates to, arises from, or deliberately influences emotions [7, 8]

education". The implication here is that "behavioral medicine demands of the physician two opposite traits: a detached objectivity about human behavior, balanced against a capacity for deep empathy". The whole point is how to best train medical students to acquire suitable skills for clinical, or community in that matter, decision making. Thus, in analogy to the use of role-playing to evaluate affective skills in medicine [16], many medical schools use the notion of Virtual Patients (VPs) [17] to maximise the value of decision-making and clinical management through scenario based learning activities (SBL), as a teaching/pedagogic method of choice, that provides students with the opportunity to work, think, and take decisions collaboratively. Some others, exploit the contemporary concept of mixed reality educational constructs to increase engagement and facilitate knowledge retention through experiential modalities [18].

One way or another, empathy is central to ensuring the quality of human communication and personal development. Thus, if systems, methods or lab activities could in fact consider more carefully the processes and feelings involved in human interactions in teaching and learning, that may indeed promote higher quality support for learners [19]. So, the scope of this paper is to provide an overview of affective learning furnished with case studies where the roles of technologies, neuroscience, learning and education are interwoven. Medical education is borrowed as a domain of reference. Neuroscientific emphasis is placed in the synergy of two perspectives, namely, the detection and recording of emotions from humans, while technological focus is given to techniques and tools to facilitate the elicitation of emotions and their subsequent exploitation in the decision-making process.

2 Affective Learning: Technological Perspectives

2.1 Affective Sensors and Learning Services

Sensors in any contemporary affective learning based environment should adaptively support a) learners based on their enriched affective models and b) teachers to orchestrate and support the learning procedures more efficiently. The sensors and the relevant interfaces, together with new signal processing, pattern recognition, and reasoning algorithms [20] for assessing and responding to the affective state of the learner in real time should also support learners in face-to-face, distance and blended learning conditions both in formal, informal and even game-based learning scenarios. Real time affective state recognition may be based on text and video algorithms (i.e., non-intrusive), as well as, biosignals - brain electrical activity and peripheral body signals (i.e., intrusive). The main goal is to provide real-time updates to the student model to activate student support functions. Affective state recognition includes the extraction of raw data followed by interpretation of raw signals into different emotions, and their intensities allowing the system to sense a broad spectrum of information and applying techniques from signal processing, pattern recognition, psychophysiology and machine learning, to make inferences based on such data. To complete the state recognition, fusion of the interpreted emotions from the different sensors is usually envisaged.

2.2   Affective Ontologies, Metrics and Analytics

Student and group modelling could be approached via the perception of a functional system, where the identification of its components would unlock the internal and external causalities, giving access for adjustments and regulations according to Boulding's Typology [21], which aims at defining a system's components by uncovering the "hard" facts (e.g., laws in the "hard" natural sciences) of "soft" social systems (e.g., learning, collaborative settings). Contemporary efforts in affective learning also involve the development of technologies for semantic integration of the diverse multimodal information from the various sensors to enable reasoning for supporting decisions. Ontological frameworks and relevant reasoning processes are developed to this extent to semantically represent the extracted information from sensors. For example, the MFOEM ontology [22] of affective phenomena such as emotions, moods, appraisals and subjective feelings, has been designed to support such endeavour within the broader Mental Functioning Ontology (MFO) and the Basic Formal Ontology (BFO). Furthermore, the ImREAL project developed new intelligent means to allow situational simulated environments to exploit the connection between the experience in the virtual environment and the experience in the real world. Utilising a socio-technical approach for activity model ontology development, ImREAL developed an Activity Model ONtology(AMOn) which is computer-processable representation of the concepts from the activity model [23, 24]. Contemporary uses of these ideas allow the exploitation of learner interactions with the e-learning environments by enabling detailed registration and complex processing of learning data in the form of analytics [26].

2.3   Empowering clinical decision with MOOCs and Scenario-Based Learning

The best way to acquire knowledge and experience for actual clinical or community care work is for students to work through real patient scenarios. However, in many cases this is not practical nor scalable and may be overcome with interactive electronic scenarios in the form of virtual patients (VPs), an effective training tool for clinical reasoning and developing skills in patient management [26, 27]. In this kind of interaction, students can explore and clinically manage the VPs, make mistakes, and learn from them thereby enabling active management of a patient rather than passive learning. It is ideal for the challenges presented in cases where practitioners need to make rapid assessments, instantly take decisions, and prioritise efforts and enhance emotions and memory especially when scenarios embed realistic representations [28]. In that sense, such scenarios provide an opportunity not only to explore the impact of on learning of affected states, but also to use modification of affected states to produce an immediate impact on competency.

Finally, Massive Open Online Courses (MOOCs), have become a trend for higher education institutes around the globe. Easy access to learning through the elimination of geographical, temporal and cultural constraints, flexibility in the pace of learning, the diversity of the cognitive domains offered, and the creation of learning communities of common interest around a subject make them particularly promising [29]. Clinical problem solving through MOOCs, however, is simultaneously a promise and a threat [30].

3 Case Studies

Experience in various affective and/or education contexts – at the Aristotle University of Thessaloniki (AUTH) – enables us to indicate opportunities and challenges for exploiting affective learning scenarios.

3.1 Affective Neuroscience

In the last few years, our group has spent a considerable amount of research effort to investigate human emotions and the way these may be also advanced by technology [8, 31]. Central to these efforts has been our dedication to fuse the emerging field of affective computing and affective medicine with neuroscientific research, in an attempt to study the topography and neural sources of human emotions [32], their oscillatory and synchronisation mechanisms [33, 34], how these are affected by alcohol consumption [35], or aged decline [36, 37] or in stressed everyday situations [38] as well as how affective technology can be used to educate children with emotional deficits [39] . The backbone of our efforts and success so far is surely linked with a multi-disciplinary approach and the combination of experimental skills and analytical/theoretical and methodological capacities [40, 41].

3.2 Affective Measurements upon Medical Student Clinical Skills Training

Theories of affect in learning allow the use of measurable quantities from classical macroscopic observations [42]. Analytics technologies offer new ways for learning assessment through data collection. This exemplar case endeavours to bring together sensors and analysis tools to explore the viability of neurophysiological data during extra-curricular clinical skill training of undergraduate medical students. It was conducted during the 4th "Essential Skills in the Management of Surgical Cases" course, in 2016. Medical students, in rotating groups of 6, practiced suturing for 20 min approximately on pork tissue. No limit was put to the number of sutures, participants did not have a quantified goal of sutures to be reached. Rotating pairs were selected each time to focus the integrative affective environment on them, with each pair given a Fitbit activitytracker to wear on their non-dominant hand to measure heart rate; being in view of a Microsoft HD web-cam recording their faces (data for emotion facial extrapolation; and wore an EMOTIV EPOC unobtrusive EEG sensor to record 14-channel EEG and measure mental state conditions.

On average, 7 sutures (7.28) completed by participants, with a high variability though, while the mean time needed to complete a suture was 155 seconds. A learning curve was defined based on the mean time needed for a suture versus the order of the sutures, with a trend being a decrease in time needed for a suture, but not significantly. Furthermore, Z-scores of excitement and frustration during the course of completion of sutures versus the order of the sutures were also calculated, showing an excitement Z-score maximisation at the last 80% of the first suture and the fist 30% of the second; the next 4 sutures had lower Z-scores than the first two and had some increase at the end of each suture. The Frustration Z-score was maximized during the whole first suture and then was close to zero for the duration of the other sutures. Emotion states like sadness, happiness, fear and surprise were tested for fluctuations, with fear decreasing over the course of suturing for 8 out of 10 participants, sadness increasing in 7, happiness increasing in 6, while surprise was decreasing in 7 of them.

These first corroborations can only be the starting point for further research. Ongoing endeavour is currently focused on integrating more sensor data and incorporating validation methods in the experimentation process. to explore insights offered by these results, which nevertheless, demonstrate the breadth of potential of a fully evidence based validated affective analytics integrative environment and its promising role in medical education powered by neuroscience.

3.3   Affective approaches to evaluate educational tools against bullying

School bullying, i.e. the aggressive behaviour among school aged children and adolescents with the intent to hurt, is usually expressed in a pattern of unwanted, and unpleasant actions of no justification systematically repeated over long periods of time, with a negative impact on everyone involved. Numerous intervention programs have attempted to educate the members of the school community to reduce the negative impact. This case study has explored the affective responses of adolescents induced by multimedia content featuring school bullying, while it examined whether subjective perceptions and adolescent attitudes towards bullying phenomena are consistent with the results of objective (affective) measurements [43]. A cross media interactive educational tool created in the context of the project 'European – AntiBullying Campaign' [44] was used and allowed students to interact with short affective events (~ 20 seconds) featuring scenes of school bullying from a victim cantered perspective. During this viewing/interaction multimodal signals of their implicit and explicit affective responses to these events were recorded. The protocol also interrupted the sequence of these affective events for some 15 seconds and instructed participants to affectively rate the passively viewed short event. Peer Relations Questionnaires were used together with activity trackers (FitBit Charge HR, worn on the participant's non-dominant wrist to measure heart rate), a webcam to capture facial expressions (allowing categorisations into "happy, sad, angry or surprised", and estimations of the emotional dimensions of valence and arousal), as well as, a 14 electrode EEG device (Emotiv EPOC) providing affective metrics of frustration and excitement. A visual scale-tool, AffectButton was used as an intuitive way to define current emotions [45] by means of a timestamped vector of three dimensions, arousal, dominance, and valence.

Overall results from 14 adolescents of both genders (11-16 years old; with parental consents provided), based on these multimodal, objective measurements of emotional responses to bullying content, seem to be confirming the subjective perceptions of the adolescent (indicated by the administered questionnaire). Results extracted from heart rate measurements showed that the emotional responses of adolescents are positively related to scenes involving physical violence and collisions. Similar results were found in the measurements of emotional expressions of the face, as well as measurements with the portable electroencephalogram. More specifically, there was a marginally significant difference in the Facial Expression Arousal levels for Physical Abuse (M=.412, SD=.255) and Intervention (M=.345, SD=.220) conditions; t(12)= 2.020, p = .066. Additionally, there was a significant difference in the Affect Valence levels for Physical Abuse (M=-.408, SD=.297) and Intervention (M=.240, SD=.227) conditions; t(13)= -7.058, p <.001. Finally, EEG Frustration differed significantly between Physical Abuse (M=.434, SD=.092) and Intervention (M=.522, SD=.125) conditions; t(13)= -2.262, p = .041.

Moreover, a statistically significant relationship was found between the Facial Expression arousal for the Verbal Abuse (M=.459, SD=.287) and Intervention (M=.345, SD=.220) conditions; t(12)= 2.761, p = .017. Additionally, there was also a significant difference between the Facial Expression Valence levels for Verbal Abuse (M=.305, SD=.157) and Intervention (M=.310, SD=.135) conditions; t(12)= -5.495, p < .001. Moreover, EEG Frustration also differed between Verbal Abuse (M=.451, SD=.0962) and Intervention (M=.522, SD=.125) conditions; t(13)= -2.166, p = .049. The EEG Excitement was also significant differed between the Verbal Abuse (M=.381, SD=.141) and Intervention (M=.460, SD=.136) conditions; t(12)= -2.210, p = .047. Finally, there was also a significant difference in the Affect valence for Physical Abuse (M=-.348, SD=.313) and Intervention (M=.240, SD=.227) conditions; t(13)= -6.879, p < .001.

Concluding, it was found that facial expressions were more intense and less positive (in the case of verbal abuse scenes), while EEG emotional indices, showed that adolescents felt more stressed and aroused, while watching scenes, where peers and the school environment offered their help to the victim. Objective measurements of emotional responses were consistent with the subjects' subjective perceptions as expressed in the questionnaires, thereby adding sense to the neuroscience investigations of such educational encounters.

3.4 Affective approaches to evaluate MOOC content

It is true that the original enthusiasm and hype for the capabilities of MOOCs has been mitigated due to high drop-out rates. It is nowadays more often stated that to improve the learning experience in MOOCs, the student profile should be augmented to include information about her emotional state [46]. The aim of this experimental case study is to analyse the emotional content of MOOC videos, both through the self-reported emotional state of the participants and through the analysis of electroencephalographic signals [47]. Research in this experimental case study was conducted in two phases. During the first phase (n = 33), participants attended a series of five video lessons[2] and completed PANAS, a self-reported emotional status questionnaire [48], immediately after the completion of each of them (randomised viewing order across subjects). Based on the participant emotional evaluations of the videos in the first phase, two video tutorials were selected to compose the material of the second phase: (a) that with highest score for the excitement and the lower frustration and (b) the one with the lowest enthusiasm score the highest frustration score. These two videos were then used in phase two with a different group of participants (n = 17) who had an Emotiv EPOC EEG recordings during their watching of these two videos (randomised order of viewing across subjects).

In phase two, PANAS scores were shown to be higher in frustration (M = 1.97, SD = .95) and lower in enthusiasm (M = 2.06, SD= .98) for video (b) in comparison to video (a) (frustration: M= 1.37, SD= .41; enthusiasm: M= 3.29, SD= 1.01). EEG analysis for video (b) showed lower frustration (M = 47.2, SD= 28.84) when compared to video (a) (M= 61.38, SD= 40.74); and higher in enthusiasm (M= 46.71, SD= 22.98) as compared to video (a) (M= 43.6, SD= 27.07). This means that, the results about the EEG derived emotional status of the participants in this case is different from that given by the self-reported emotions. as it seems that EEG results show that video (b) caused the same frustration and enthusiasm as video (a). Thus, results show that the self-reported emotional state of the users during MOOC-video viewing does not correspond to their objectively estimated emotional state as it is derived from the EEG recorded brain signals.

4   Towards Affective Measurements during Training Against Medical Errors

Medical error is now, in the developed world, one of the leading causes of death and harm in patients, and this newly-recognised major issue needs to be addressed through changes in education. Most clinical training is carried out in the 'clinical years' through apprenticeship, an exploratory and experiential method which effectively means practicing on patients! This approach has been shown to severely compromise patient safety [49]. Safety training mechanisms are largely either reactive or systemic devices making erroneous actions difficult to take. To this extend Medical Schools are considering the introduction of MOOCs for training against medical error. Such a MOOC would be ideal for capitalising on affected state responses to exemplar scenarios and would create an opportunity for teachers and educators to learn how to implement interactive virtual patients as a virtual simulation exercises which will allow learners to practice safely and at the same time experience the consequences of their actions when they fail. Existing platforms for provision of Virtual Patients (e.g. Open Labyrinth [50]), modified to include integration of affective state monitoring and student support mechanisms. Learning Data collected as part of the study could include learning analytics describing student paths, actions and decisions through the

---

[2] Chosen from Coursera και Edx; edited with Camtasia to fix durations around 3min 16-20 sec.

learning scenarios, telemetric data collected from affective technology components measuring affective state, and observations of the group dynamic and individual responses (either in person or through video and audio captures). In addition, data describing student and tutor attitudes and perceptions could be collected through survey instruments and semi-structured focus groups. This scenario is based on the principles of the informal learning in the way of covers learning which arises from the activities and interests of individuals and groups (in the specific domain the medical students).

The scenarios may be based on common presentations, created and developed across some Affective, Learning Paradigm and Gamification axes. For example, scenario presentations can be tuned to present either "Affectively Neutral" elements in scenarios, or "Affectively Charged" scenarios in which students are presented with authentic opportunities to select option choices and patient management, and explore the consequences of making serious virtual errors 'virtually' to induce challenging affective states. Strategies for affect recognition may also be explored for their suitability in the above context, in order to give appropriate responses and feedback; these include brain-computer interfaces, eye-tracking systems, face-based emotion recognition systems, and sensors to measure skin conductance (arousal), posture, and finger pressure. Moreover, such educational content may be further furnished by means of semantic annotations and analytics provisions, so that they can be consumable by any learner support part of an ITS platform to suggest content and facilitate the learning process.

5   Towards Emotionally Augmented Learning Minds

Much of medical education is about experiential, hands-on training to prepare future doctors to create a portfolio of skillsets. Contemporary experiential technologies such as Virtual Patients, MOOCs or Virtual/Augmented/Mixed realities may offer simulated realistic but consequence free test-beds in which to interact safely and cope with emotional challenges pertaining to the real-life tasks [51]. For this hypothesis to work as a counterweight to technological hype fluctuations, these artefacts should be seen as part of contemporary learning environments. Ideally speaking, digital technologies must augment learning by supporting reflection, gathering of feedback and experiences, enable scenario-based learning driven by real problems and contextualised informal learning. Much of the challenge for these to become effective lies with the experience they may allow learners to attain. To this extent, emotional and affective learning becomes a central endeavour and vision for any ITS, as it may play a pivotal role for the vision of creating **emotionally augmented minds**: digitally empowered medical professionals who use technology to enhance their learning and professional development [52]. For this to happen, they should take advantage of the availability of a variety of technologies, personalise their learning by reflecting on their progress and identifying opportunities to learn anywhere and anytime, continuously improve in their profession. Key in this vision is the understanding of a learner's emotion and its smart and seamless exploitation during the learning process, through contemporary

ITS empowered by interactive contextualised nudges informed by methods in professional coaching [55].

What this paper has attempted to show, is to provide some neurophysiological evidence in support of the feasibility of the above vision. Obviously, neither all problems in the affective learning endeavour are solved by neurophysiological means, nor there is a clear understanding of the so far available results. Thus, the aforementioned vision should be taken with a caution, as here is a lot of value in the way that affective computing or e-learning systems are developed. However, there is a clear need for rigorous experimentation in educational neuroscience, while new ideas on affective learning are not fully developed and tested. We envisage various interdisciplinary projects in the following years to address this by engaging stakeholders, researchers and developers.

References

1. Mosby's Medical Dictionary, 9th edition. Elsevier. (2009).
2. Gano-Phillips, S. Affective learning in general education. Special Topic: Assessment in University General Education Program, 6(1), 1-44. (2009).
3. Bloom, B. S., Engelhart, M. D., Furst, E. J., Hill, W. H., & Krathwohl, D. R. Taxonomy of educational objectives, handbook I: The cognitive domain(Vol. 19, p. 56). New York: David McKay Co Inc. (1956).
4. Bloom, B. S. Taxonomy of educational objectives. Vol. 1: Cognitive domain. New York: McKay, 20-24. (1956).
5. Krathwohl, D. R., Bloom, B. S., & Masia, B. B. Handbook II: affective domain. New York: David McKay. (1964).
6. Picard, R. W., Papert, S., Bender, W., Blumberg, B., Breazeal, C., Cavallo, D., ... & Strohecker, C. Affective learning—a manifesto. BT technology journal, 22(4), 253-269. (2004).
7. Picard R W: 'Affective Computing', The MIT Press, Cambridge, MA. (1997).
8. Luneski, A., Konstantinidis, E., Bamidis, P.D. Affective medicine: A review of affective computing efforts in medical informatics. Methods of Information in Medicine, 49 (3): 207-218. (2010).
9. Cytowic, R. E. Synesthesia: A union of the senses. MIT press. (2002).
10. Goleman, D. Emotional intelligence. Bantam Books. (2006).
11. Paiva A., Dias, J., Sobral, D., Aylett, R., Woods, S., Hall, L., & Zoll, C. Learning by feeling: evoking empathy with synthetic characters. Applied Artificial Intelligence, 19:3-4, 235-266, DOI: 10.1080/08839510590910165. (2005).
12. Persico, D., & Steffens, K. Self-Regulated Learning in Technology Enhanced Learning Environments. In Technology Enhanced Learning (pp. 115-126). Springer International Publishing, (2017).
13. Zeidner, M., Boekaerts, M., & Pintrich, P. Self-regulation. Directions and challenges for future research. In M. Boekaerts, P. Pintrich, & M. Zeidner (Eds.), Handbook of self-regulation (pp. 749–768). New York: Academic Press. (2000).
14. Herder, E., Sosnovsky, S., & Dimitrova, V. Adaptive Intelligent Learning Environments. In Technology Enhanced Learning (pp. 109-114). Springer International Publishing. (2017).

15. MacLean, P. D. The brain in relation to empathy and medical education. The journal of nervous and Mental Disease, 144(5), 374-382. (1967).
16. Levine, H. G., & McGuire, C. H. The use of role-playing to evaluate affective skills in medicine. Academic Medicine, 45(9), 700-5. (1970).
17. Poulton, T. and Balasubramaniam, C. Virtual patients: a year of change. Medical teacher 33.11: 933-937. (2011).
18. Antoniou, P. E., Dafli, E., Arfaras, G., & Bamidis, P. D. Versatile Mixed Reality Educational Spaces-A Medical Education Implementation Case. In Ubiquitous Computing and Communications and 2016 International Symposium on Cyberspace and Security (IUCC-CSS), International Conference on (pp. 132-137). IEEE. (2016).
19. Cooper, B., Brna, P., & Martins, A. Effective affective in intelligent systems–building on evidence of empathy in teaching and learning. In Affective interactions (pp. 21-34). Springer Berlin Heidelberg. (2000).
20. Petrantonakis, P. C., & Hadjileontiadis, L. J. Emotion recognition from brain signals using hybrid adaptive filtering and higher-order crossings analysis. IEEE Transactions on Affective Computing, 1(2), 81-97. (2010).
21. Boulding, K. E. General systems theory-the skeleton of science. Management Science, 2(3), 197-208. (1956).
22. Hastings, J. The MFOEM Emotion Ontology. http://purl.bioontology.org/ontology/MFOEM. (2017).
23. Activity Model ONtology (AMOn); http://imash.leeds.ac.uk/ontology/amon/. (2017).
24. Thakker, D., Dimitrova, V., & Ediboglu, G. Introducing cultural prompts in a semantic data browser. In International Workshop on Intelligent Exploration of Semantic Data (IESD'12) in Conjuction with EKAW, Galway. (2012).
25. Arnold K. E. and Pistilli M. D. Course signals at purdue: Using learning analytics to increase student success. In Proceedings of the 2nd International Conference on Learning Analytics and Knowledge, pages 267–270. ACM, (2012).
26. Poulton, T. Hot topics in elearning & distance learning, In Proceedings of MEI2015, available though http://mei2015.camei-project.eu. Last Access June 2017 (2015).
27. Poulton, T., Ellaway, R. H., et al. Exploring the efficacy of replacing linear paper-based patient cases in problem-based learning with dynamic Web-based virtual patients: randomized controlled trial. J Med Internet Res, 16(11). (2014)
28. Antoniou, P. E., et al. Exploring design requirements for repurposing dental virtual patients from the web to second life: a focus group study. J Med Internet Res, 16(6). (2014)
29. Margaryan, A., Bianco, M., & Littlejohn, A. Instructional quality of Massive Open Online Courses (MOOCs). Computers and Education, 80, 77–83. http://doi.org/10.1016/j.compedu.2014.08.005. (2015).
30. Harder, B. Are MOOCs the future of medical education?. BMJ: British Medical Journal (Online), 346. (2013).
31. Bamidis P.D., Papadelis C., Kourtidou-Papadeli C., Pappas C., Vivas A., "Affective computing in the era of contemporary neurophysiology and health informatics", Interacting with Computers, 2004, 16(4):715-721
32. Lithari, C., Frantzidis, C.A., Papadelis, C., Vivas, A.B., Klados, M.A., Kourtidou-Papadeli, C., Pappas, C., Ioannides, A.A., Bamidis, P.D. Are females more responsive to emotional stimuli? A neurophysiological study across arousal and valence dimensions Brain Topography, 23 (1), pp. 27-40. (2010)
33. Styliadis, C., Ioannides, A. A., Bamidis, P. D., & Papadelis, C. Amygdala responses to valence and its interaction by arousal revealed by MEG. International Journal of Psychophysiology, 93(1), 121-133. (2014).

34. Klados, M.A., Frantzidis, C., Vivas, A.B., Papadelis, C., Lithari, C., Pappas, C., Bamidis, P.D., A framework combining delta event-related oscillations (EROs) and synchronisation effects (ERD/ERS) to study emotional processing. Computational Intelligence and Neuroscience, 2009, art. no. 549419. (2009)

35. Lithari, C., Klados, M.A., Pappas, C., Albani, M., Kapoukranidou, D., Kovatsi, L., Bamidis, P.D., Papadelis, C.L. Alcohol Affects the Brain's Resting-State Network in Social Drinkers PLoS ONE, 7 (10), art. no. e48641. (2012)

36. Ladas, A., Frantzidis, C., Bamidis, P., & Vivas, A. B. Eye blink rate as a biological marker of mild cognitive impairment. International Journal of Psychophysiology, 93(1), 12-16. (2014).

37. Frantzidis, C. A., Vivas, A. B., Tsolaki, A., Klados, M. A., Tsolaki, M., & Bamidis, P. D. Functional disorganization of small-world brain networks in mild Alzheimer's Disease and amnestic Mild Cognitive Impairment: an EEG study using Relative Wavelet Entropy (RWE). Frontiers in aging neuroscience, 6. (2014).

38. Klados, M. A., Kanatsouli, K., Antoniou, I., Babiloni, F., Tsirka, V., Bamidis, P. D., & Micheloyannis, S. A graph theoretical approach to study the organization of the cortical networks during different mathematical tasks. PloS one, 8(8), e71800. (2013).

39. Konstantinidis, E., Luneski, A., Frantzidis, C., Nikolaidou, M., Hitoglou-Antoniadou, M., Bamidis, P.D. Information and Communication Technologies (ICT) for enhanced education of children with autism spectrum disorders Journal on Information Technology in Healthcare, 7 (5), pp. 284-292. (2009).

40. Lithari, C., Klados, M. A., Papadelis, C., Pappas, C., Albani, M., & Bamidis, P. D. How does the metric choice affect brain functional connectivity networks?. Biomedical Signal Processing and Control, 7(3), 228-236. (2012).

41. Klados, M.A., Papadelis, C., Braun, C., Bamidis, P.D. REG-ICA: A hybrid methodology combining Blind Source Separation and regression techniques for the rejection of ocular artifacts (2011) Biomedical Signal Processing and Control, 6 (3), pp. 291-300.

42. Antoniou, P. E., Kartsidis, P., Xefteris, S., Arfaras, G., Konstantinidis, E., & Bamidis, P. D. Towards medical education neuroscience: pilot results of integrative affective analytics from clinical skills workshops. http://www.frontiersin.org/10.3389/conf.fnhum.2016.220.00035/event_abstract. (2016).

43. Billis, A., Styliadis, C., Baka, M., Arfaras, G., & Bamidis, P. D. Affective neuroscience/computing approaches in evaluating an interactive educational tool to counteract bullying. http://www.frontiersin.org/10.3389/conf.fnhum.2016.220.00091/event_abstract?sname=S AN2016_Meeting. (2016).

44. Alevizos, S., Lagoumintzi, I., & Salichos, P. The Interaction between Theory and Practice in Social Pedagogy□: A European Campaign and an Interactive Social Pedagogical Tool against Bullying in Schools. The International Journal of Social Pedagogy, 4(1), 55–64. (2015).

45. Broekens, J., & Brinkman, W. P. AffectButton: A method for reliable and valid affective self-report. International Journal of Human Computer Studies, 71(6), 641–667. doi:10.1016/j.ijhcs.2013.02.003. (2013).

46. Hadjileontiadou, J. S., Dias, B. S., Diniz, A. J.,& Hadjileontiadis, J. L. Fuzzy Logic-Based Modeling in Collaborative and Blended Learning, in Advances in Educational Technologies and Instructional Design (AETID). Hershey, PA: IGI Global. (2015).

47. Antoniou P.E. ... Bamidis P.D. Applications of Educational Neuroscience: the use of emotional estimators in three educational scenarios. Workshop on Aristotle University of

Thessaloniki Studies and the Globe in 21st Century. (In Greek). Available through http://studiestoday.auth.gr/ Last Access Jul 2017. (2016).

48. Watson, D., Clark, A. L., & Tellegen, A. Development and validation of brief measures of positive and negative affect: the PANAS scales. Journal of Personality and Social Psychology, 54(6), 1063–1070. http://doi.org/10.1037/0022-3514.54.6.1063. (1988).

49. Young, J. Q., Ranji, S. R., Wachter, R. M., Lee, C. M., Niehaus, B., & Auerbach, A. D. "July Effect": Impact of the Academic Year-End Changeover on Patient Outcomes. A Systematic Review. Annals of internal medicine, 155(5), 309-315. (2011).

50. Dafli, E., Antoniou, P., Ioannidis, L., Dombros, N., Topps, D., & Bamidis, P. D. Virtual patients on the semantic Web: a proof-of-application study. Journal of medical Internet research, 17(1). (2015).

51. P. E. Antoniou, E. Dafli and P. D. Bamidis, "Design of Novel Teaching Episodes in Medical Education Using Emerging Experiential Digital Assets: Technology Enabled Medical Education Beyond the Gimmicky," 2015 IEEE International Conference on Computer and Information Technology; Ubiquitous Computing and Communications; Dependable, Autonomic and Secure Computing; Pervasive Intelligence and Computing, Liverpool. pp. 1560-1565. doi: 10.1109/CIT/IUCC/DASC/PICOM.2015.360. (2015).

52. Bamidis, P.D., Dimitrova, V., Tresure-Jones, T., Poulton, T., and Roberts T.E. Augmented Minds: Technology's role in supporting 21st Century Doctors. EC-TEL workshop on European Technologies and workplace learning and professional development. (2017).

53. Piotrkowicz, A., Dimitrova, V., Treasure-Jones, T., Smithies, A., Harkin, P., Kirby, J., and Roberts, T. Quantified self analytics tools for self-regulated learning with myPAL EC-TEL. (2017).

Understanding how learning takes place with neuroscience and applying the results to education

Andreas A. Ioannides

Laboratory for Human Brain Dynamics
AAI Scientific Cultural Services Ltd., Nicosia, Cyprus
a.ioannides@aaiscs.com

Abstract. Human learning has been dramatically altered by the new situation that saw us climb down trees and out of the savanna to larger communities with great reliance on agriculture and more recently industry. Psychology appeared as a scientific discipline at a time that formal education for all was becoming accepted. From the very beginning psychology and education had a major influence on each other. Education is notoriously slow to change. As the ideas of developmental psychologists started influencing education policy, new paradigms for education emerge from a variety of disciplines including computer science, medicine and particularly neurosciences. Each of these disciplines has its own vocabulary and progress is often limited because there is no common framework to bring together specialists from different disciplines or to formulate common research. We provide such a framework through a generalization of key concepts of developmental psychology. In the new framework, these concepts are cloaked with what we might call the standard model of modern neuroscience. Here, we customize this framework for learning and education. Formal education is seen as a continuation of a process that begins with the mother and develops in pre-school play. The main goal of this process is to maintain and continually update an internal representation of the external world in the key brain networks while keeping intact the core representation of self. The first steps in a research program using this new framework are described with some results and conclusions about future actions.

Keywords: neural representation of self, self-evolution and education, midline self-representation core, (MSRC), sleep states, assimilation, accommodation, zone of proximal development (ZPD), mass screening of pupils

1   Introduction

Living is learning because learning is a prerequisite for survival. Our species was catapulted to the top of the evolutionary pyramid, primarily because of the changes in the anatomy and physiology of the brain that allowed an explosive increase in the capability of humans to learn. For millennia, human learning was perfected solely through the brutal laws of survival, which initially were confined to safe movement through space and fine control of body and its limbs [1]. The complexity of the new tricks to be learnt demanded a protracted childhood and the provision of guidance

© Springer International Publishing AG 2017
C. Frasson and G. Kostopoulos (Eds.): BFAL 2017, LNAI 10512, pp. 14–35, 2017
DOI: 10.1007/978-3-319-67615-9_2

shielded from the life and death scenarios lurking beyond; this was provided by the family. In the beginning of life outside the womb, the newly born infant was helped primarily by the mother to grasp the connection between organized sequence of motor actions and achieving a distant goal. This assignment of meaning to motor sequences constitutes the "ontogenesis of narrative" [2] and hence the start of the long road to language. As the infant grew to childhood, play with other children had become the way to accumulate more knowledge often in semi-protected environment where danger was never far away. As agriculture allowed the growth of sizable communities, learning through play was diminished with work in the fields becoming a priority from a young age. As populations grew more, another aspect of learning grew in importance: harnessing the effort of each individual to serve team goals related to work, social order and the protection of the community against external threats. This form of learning required community-wide participation using rituals, music and language [3]. The emergence of rituals can be thought of as the beginning of formal learning "in the society" culminating in ancient times in festivals, theatre performances and other public events that reinforced the social bond between citizens and allegiance to the rulers. Formal education is a relatively new innovation in evolution, even if one counts the early and mainly privately organized form that arose in many cultures soon after they adopted writing as a way of keeping records and augmenting the information stored and transferred between generations. For the vast majority of children, progress did not mean improvement in their education but squashing the happy urge to learn through play into submission of the young to serve the rulers either as servants in homes and fields or later with the industrial revolution as factory laborers. The concept of public education for the general population grew slowly during renaissance as part of humanism's challenge of the church dogmas for a divine social order that fixed people in their proper strata of society. Humanists instead argued that through education human beings can change dramatically and documented these views in books and practiced them in the schools they created [4]. Attitudes towards education changed in the last two centuries with society largely accepting that mass education is not only beneficial for every child, but also it has an added value for society at large, in both monetary and social terms. However, the methods adopted for education were influenced by the recent history. The enlightened people that pushed for the provision of education to all children could only come from the same part of society that introduced and maintained so successfully the new ways of commerce and industry. In these circles the notion of learning through play have long been abandoned and replaced by methods designed to force children from young age to work in homes of aristocracy as servants, or as laborers in farms, mines and factories. Since the early days of mass education in the late 17th century, children were herded into classes and what the top tier of society considered important at the time was to be stamped into the children's mind through forced repetition and testing, aided by plentiful punishment for failure or dissent.

Psychology from its early beginnings, in the late nineteenth century to today has been pre-occupied with education and almost every one of its founders have something important and new to say about how children should be educated. Many of these people, notably Sigmund Freud and William James, completed degrees in medicine and/or what we now call neuroscience and neurophysiology. Although at these times the neuroscientific method had not matured enough to be a powerful instrument on its own, it seems that these pioneers of psychology had powerful and positive influence from their studies of the human body and especially the brain and of course training in the exact sciences. The effect was to transform psychology to a science of measurements turning to varied degree away from introspection to objective and measurable quantities. Some of them, notably Edward Thorndike and Samuel Skinner based their approach on the effect of reward on learning stimulus – response contingencies. The rather sterile and mechanistic view of learning did little to challenge the format that slowly became established, a format that can be summarized as teacher-in-front of a classroom model. Far from it, this format of education was actively promoted "*A complete science of psychology would tell every fact about every one's intellect and character and behavior, would tell the cause of every change in human nature, would tell the result which every educational force - every act of every person that changed any other or the agent himself -would have. It would aid us to use human beings for the world's welfare with the same surety of the result that we now have when we use falling bodies or chemical elements. In proportion as we get such a science we shall become masters of our own souls as we now are masters of heat and light. Progress toward such a science is being made.*" [5]. If such is the nature of man, it seems logical and appropriate to manipulate through coercion and a combination of reward and punishment each child until he/she adopted the expected "correct form". The teacher-in-front of a classroom format is highly appropriate for such an indoctrination.

Other psychology pioneers emphasized more the individual characteristics of the child in terms of chronology when cognitive tasks can be tackled (William James and Jean Piaget) and the importance of the social context within education takes place (Lev Vygotsky). These pioneers moved away from the coercive approach to a more humane one, allowing for the complexity of the growing organism and the individuality of each child as an agent with unique characteristics and preferences. The last two, Piaget and Vygotsky re-introduced play as an important component of learning and developed their ideas for learning in the context of play. The thesis I will promote in this paper is that the emphasis on play was forced upon these pioneers because through play the development of a child evolves in the natural ways that evolution has shaped humans to learn. In section 2, I will focus on key concepts introduced by Piaget and Vygotsky that seriously challenged the educational system and began to change it fundamentally in the second half of the 20th century. In section 3, I will briefly outline the more recent ideas about learning influenced greatly by information processing ideas, the tsunami of data collected by neuroimaging methods and how this new era of educational psychology is poised to influence education practice and especially education evaluation. In section 4, I will return to main concepts of psychology as these were introduced by the pioneers of developmental psychology, and adapt them and generalize them in the light of recent findings from studies of brain function during awake state and sleep. These studies identify the self as an evolutionary end-point with a corresponding neural representation. Education is then seen as the accommodation of the self within the wider social context, pointing out the importance of early mass screening to determine the maturity of neural networks at the very start of school. In section 5, I will introduce the practical considerations that follow and sketch the efforts to develop an effective early mass-screening system outlining both the successes and some problems that slowed down progress.

2 Core psychology related to learning and education

Piaget defined assimilation and accommodation as the two key polar tendencies driving cognitive development. As a child gets older, his/her cognitive capabilities grow through the evolution and consolidation of cognitive schemas, internal representations of the world that are linked to each other and adjusted by assimilation and accommodation. Through assimilation, new experiences are fitted into existing schemata as representations of objects, situations or skills. Accommodation "happens" as the accumulated new information demands a major change to take place in one or more of the existing schemata or the creation of a new one. The balance between assimilation and accommodation is achieved through what Piaget defined as equilibration. In Piaget's framework, cognitive development follows a staircase course. Plateaus in cognitive development are characterized by assimilation-dominated periods when the child is in command of enough schemata to allow him/her to deal with new information through assimilation, with little need for drastic reorganization of existing schemata. As new information is accumulated however the equilibrium is upset because the existing schemata cannot cope any more. This creates a disagreeable state of affairs that drives the equilibration force through the generation of new schemata. Piaget defined four main stages of cognitive development, each one characterized by distinct qualitatively different kinds of learning. The driving force is an inner motivation to reach the equilibrium stages that is constrained by biological maturation and the exposure to different situations in the child's environment.

Although Piaget was aware of the contribution of social influences in cognitive development, he paid little direct attention to them in his later work. In contrast Vygotsky emphasized the importance of social and cultural elements in the development of children. Like Piaget, Vygotsky focused on what is happening during play, stressing the fact that in a game situation a child performs ahead of its current capabilities, but within what he called the "zone of proximal development" (ZPD), which Vygotsky defined as the area from the current actual developmental level and what a child is able to do, if guided by adults or more capable peers. It therefore follows that what a child achieves does not only depend on maturity and exposure to an arbitrary environmental influence but also on the societal and cultural messages and rituals that he/she constantly encounters. According to Vygotsky, the most effective learning is possible when the child is guided and challenged through ZPD, by individuals (teachers and peers), society and culture.

Piaget and Vygotsky and their many followers belong to the constructivism strand of psychology. This brand of psychology emerged partly as a reaction to the blinkered empiricism that conceived the mind as a passive "camera" of the external world and has driven education into a sterile format until the middle of the 20th century. In the second half of the 20th century, the ideas of Piaget and his followers began to influence policy makers and eventually came to dominate not only the field of developmental psychology but also, in the 1960s and 1970s, started to greatly influence educational programs. In the following years the ideas of Vygotsky and his followers have become increasingly more effective, introducing socio-cultural elements in the curriculum.

3   Recent developments related to learning and education

Education is now at a crossroad. Major advances bring opportunities from three directions but there is great uncertainty about which of the many ways ahead can best realize the anticipated improvements in quality and effectiveness of education delivered, ensuring smooth transition within educational systems that are slow and conservative.

The first direction is how the progress in psychology beyond the pioneering work of Piaget and Vygotsky and their followers can be incorporated in the educational system. Neo-Piagetian theories adopted Piaget's idea and pushed them forward along the explanatory models that were prominent at the time. The computer era provided two concepts, processing power and memory capacity. Juan Pascual-Leone proposed a mathematical framework that used the processing power and memory content as contributors to the "set measure M", representing the "maximum number of discrete chunks of information or schemes that can be controlled in a single act" [6]. The M measure starts with the value of 1 increasing after the age of 3 by one unit every two years reaching the maximum value of 7 by the age of 15-16 years. As the M measure increases it becomes possible to accomplish more difficult tasks and hence traverse the developmental path that Piaget originally traced. This theme was elaborated by other theorist who replaced the mainly linear development in information processing capacity with more complex structures and processes.

Case and colleagues postulated a central conceptual structure (CCS) as a networks of semantic nodes and relations that support the full range of tasks that any given domain entails [7]: major transformations take place in the CCS as a child enters a new developmental stage, acting as frames for supporting and organizing the new knowledge to be accumulated. Key to our later discussion is the observation that the self can be seen as a specialized CCS implemented in the brain through the neuro-anatomical structures that "support autobiographical self and extended consciousness" culminating achievement of ontogenesis [8] with a very precise neuroscientific definition of its key core neural elements [9]. Amongst the neo Piagetian theorists, Fischer integrated most effectively within the Piaget framework, not only the information processing elements but also paid due attention to the wider than the individual factors introduced by the environment and society. To achieve this he used the classic concepts of Vygotsky of internalization and ZPD and advocated the promotion of a new field of Mind, Brain and Education [10, 11].

While in psychology, theorizing was getting too detailed and finding applications in education was making slow progress, advances in in Information Communication Technology (ICT) and neuroscience were producing overwhelming volumes of new data and opportunities that specialists and educationalists alike have difficulty in following, let alone organize and use in the educational system. The progress appeared to be especially relevant in non-invasive neuroimaging [8, 12].

Progress in ICT has created a range of opportunities in education, at the level of classroom provision and supporting school-related work and individual unsupervised use of ICT resources by children. For example, the information volume now available in the internet surpasses what any school can provide in volume, breadth and quality. A child exposed early to ICT can use the internet effectively from the early years of elementary school. Depending how this knowledge is channeled by the middle and late years of the primary education the child can use the internet to enhance what the school provides or can have his/her brain addicted to computer games and pointless time wasting on trivialities. Serious Games (SG) are ideally suited to provide on-demand specialized learning and training [13]. Intelligent Tutoring Systems (ITS) provide formal learning in a digital format. ITS have separate models for the learner and tutor. Modern Learner models describe cognitive and emotional states [14] to adapt learning strategies to suit learners' needs, objectives and interests. The use of neuro-physiological measures during SG offers the possibility of evaluating other attributes of the learner and using them for improving ITS, as was done recently for gauging motivation levels [15]. Modern ICT provide the opportunity today to monitor individuals and entire classrooms; it is possible to record a huge amount of data about individual pupils, groups of pupils and entire classrooms (including teachers!) that can be very valuable for improving learning. However, such use of the technology is not likely to be acceptable because of objections for ethical reasons and personal privacy violation. It is technically feasible to collect such data in an automatic way, removing much of the personal data while retaining processed automated analysis that can be linked to performance (of individual pupils and classes) without revealing any information about individuals. Such technically challenging but yet perfectly feasible projects may be acceptable from the ethical point of view, given the impetus that it might give towards a better education provision.

The third direction is spearheaded by advances in neurosciences and specifically in different forms of non-invasive neuroimaging [16]. Neuroimaging has opened up numerous new windows on the working brain and scientists have been busy for the last few decades in collecting data, mainly for adults. For millennia, the working brain was an inaccessible territory only to be speculated upon. Just recently, in the last couple of centuries, the human brain could be studied after death or in animals with invasive electrodes, but with no parallel access to the linguistic communication channel that is only available with human subjects. All these changed in only a few decades; today, the working brain is accessible with non-invasive methods for human experiments. Using these methods we can study in detail how parts of the brain are activated in specific tasks and how the brain solves problems by combining the results of processing in individual areas into networks of transient character that adapt and learn to accomplish the goals set by the experiment design. It is beyond the scope of this paper to go through the enormous range of studies, ranging from responses to simple and complex stimuli, complex tasks probing different states of consciousness, including awake relaxed state (resting state), different types of attention, sleep and anesthesia. The explanatory framework for describing these results within neuroscience relies on brain anatomy to describe where in the brain activity takes place and how activity in different brain areas influences activity in other areas, what kind of activity takes place (unitary volley, or group of volleys of action potentials, oscillatory activity in the cell membrane potential and/or across wide parts of the brain). None of these concepts are directly relevant to educationalist and even many psychologists do not feel comfortable with the fundamentals of neuroscience yet. For most neuroimaging methods, it is easier (and takes less effort) to study right-handed adults for a variety of reasons that include control of movement, higher varia-bility in performance for children, even within the same age range, availability and handling issues. Although studies of children are on the rise, these usually focus on special populations and generally use protocols developed for neuroimaging with little attention paid to developmental questions and other factors that are fundamental for drawing conclusions for education.

The problems mentioned above are addressed at many levels in an effort to formu-late a more scientific basis for education, with some proposing the creation of a new science of Mind, Brain and Education [8]. At the level of neuroscience, a number of projects have been initiated for the systematic collection of neuroimaging databases across the developmentally interesting ranges with standardized protocols [17–19]. At the level of psychology studying how the brain functions is becoming more and more a necessity for new graduates of psychology; many prominent psychologists have embraced neuroscience and are key players in the neuroimaging community. The bridge established between psychology and education in the second half of the 20th century has helped ameliorate the sterile practices of early educational systems. The bridge between education and neuroscience seems to be a bridge too far at times, as educationalists find it difficult to relate to the neuroscience fundamentals, despite great efforts at the level of individual universities, national programs and international initiatives, with the Organization for Economic Co-operation and development (OECD) playing a leading role.

4   A wider and more neuroscientific definition of basic concepts

In this section we will adapt some basic concepts from developmental psychology as building blocks for a neuroscience-based framework for describing learning process-es. The new framework that I propose here will allow neuroscientists, psychologists and educationalists to use the same concepts and exchange ideas in a shared language. Although the terms will carry slightly different connotations in the details of how they are used in the practices of each discipline, they will nevertheless convey the same central meaning that can be understood by all concerned specialists. The new frame-work has the additional advantage that it can produce automatically the stages of de-velopment as defined by Piaget, Vygotsky and their followers when details about how the anatomy of the brain and its function changes as different brain areas and their connections with the rest of the brain mature with age, in principle from birth to old age. I deal in separate subsections in turn with the key neuroscience background, how the neuroscience concepts introduced can cloak key basic concepts, specifically assimilation, accommodation and ZPD and how the resulting new framework provides an evolutionary perspective on education.

4.1   Neuroscientific concepts

The neuroscientific basis of our new framework is what we might call the standard model of neuroscience as this emerges by the voluminous results of neuroimaging in the last few decades. The brain structures can now be imaged using a variety of techniques with magnetic resonance imaging (MRI) providing a non-invasive view of amazing detail. The basic anatomical organization of the brain consists of a few hundreds of distinct cytoarchitectonic areas (CA), with neighboring center to center separation of a few millimeters [20]. CAs are connected to each other by bundles of white matter that allow electrical and chemical communication between them [21]. These white matter bundles can be mapped non-invasively using Diffusion Tensor Imaging (DTI) or traced using wet anatomy. Measurements with indirect and direct correlates of regional brain activity provide details about changes in activity within cytoarchitectonic areas as time advances or between conditions. The most widely used indirect methods are functional MRI (fMRI) and positron emission tomography (PET). Magnetoencephalography (MEG) and electroencephalography (EEG) are the most widely used direct correlates of mass electrical activity. Using these methods the activity within CAs can be mapped with temporal resolution from as small as a fraction of a millisecond or a few milliseconds (with EEG and MEG) to a few seconds (with fMRI) or minutes (with PET). Some of these techniques, especially EEG and to lesser extent fMRI, can be applied repeatedly so the time scale can be extended to weeks, months and years or the entire life of an individual. From these measurements one can construct correlational measures indicating linkage of activity from different areas; different methods exists to identify linked activity of varying types and complexity and therefore care must be taken when such results are interpreted [22]. High precision, real-time reconstructions can be used to compute causal descriptions of influences from one area to another with resolution in milliseconds [23, 24]. Using detailed modelling of the underlying neural basis of the interactions within and between areas, elaborate models of neural activity and connectivity can be tested using data from one or more neuroimaging modalities [25]. Graph theory provides a natural description of such an organization, both at the structural and functional level, with a hierarchy of networks relating structural and functional levels [26]. The notion of specialized areas that dominated neuroimaging for many years is now superseded by the concept of specialized networks that in healthy brains retain their individuality during awake resting state [27, 28] and sleep [29, 30]. The changes in activity from healthy canonical networks can then be documented within specific conditions and between conditions [31–33]. The evolution of networks can be also mapped as they change during a task and descriptive measures of network properties derived as time proceeds, e.g. relative to stimulus onset [34].

For the interest of brevity I will only discuss two networks that are the ones most relevant to our discussion: the default mode network (DMN) and the saliency network. The DMN comprises of a set of brain areas that were found to reduce their activity when a subject is awake and engages in a task that demands attention to external stimuli. The key networks of the brain can also be identified in studies of resting state, with the areas belonging to each network showing consistent correlated variation of activity over time. The DMN emerges as one of the networks and shows an anti-correlated pattern of variation with the other networks [28, 35], although some technical questions about these anti-correlations remain [36].

We have recently demonstrated [37] the only principled trend in large scale brain activity that one can recognize as a nearly monotonic change from awake state through light and deep sleep and eventually rapid eye movement (REM) sleep: a rise in the gamma band activity in two well-circumscribed areas in the left paramedial dorsal brain. For reasons that will become apparent soon we collectively label these two areas as the midline self-representation core (MSRC) of the brain. The first area, MSRC1 is on dorsal medial prefrontal cortex (dMPFC) with its center at Talairach Coordinates (TC) in mm (x=-5, y=42, z= 31). The second area, MSRC2, is in the precuneus in the midline posterior parietal cortex (center at TC: x=-5, y=-62, z= 51). If we group together the centers of these two areas and the centers of other areas assigned to the DMN in other studies, we will see that they separate into clusters with the two main clusters close to the midline sagittal cut, one in the frontal and the other in the caudal part of the brain. Now, if we view two-dimensional projections of each one of the two main clusters of DMN areas, it will appear that MSRC1 and MSRC2 are respectively at the center of the anterior and posterior clusters. A more careful examination reveals that MSRC1 and MSRC2 actually fill a void at the center of each cluster. With this perspective in mind, the anterior and posterior clusters of the DMN are revealed as an onion structure with at least three layers: each MSRC areas occupies the center of its cluster, surrounded in the next layer by areas identified in experiments with (awake state) tasks related to introspection autobiographical memories and the final outside layer identified in experiments with (awake state) tasks related to background and maintenance activities taking place where no attention needs to be allocated to specific tasks or the environment. Another clue about the nature of the representations of the MSRC is provided when we focus on the networks contributing to the mental operations relating to the self, as described for example by Uddin and colleagues. Imagining our own self activates areas close to the midline, called the cortical midline structures (CMS), while imagining others activates more lateral areas of the so called mirror neuron system (MNS) [38]. On the basis of these and many other related findings, I suggest that the MSRC areas carry the core neural representation of self, and hence the name.

The second network to consider is the saliency network that plays a critical role in monitoring the environment and accordingly recruiting other networks into action, either for introspection and rest, or to actively monitor the environment and objects just detected, or to initiate action to deal with some imminent perceived threat or opportunity [39]. The saliency network can be identified from resting state analysis of healthy subjects [28, 40] and its aberrant activation is associated with pathology [41]. Our latest analysis of sleep data showed that this network also plays a key role during sleep, and specifically during the second stage of (light) sleep, NREM2. In the analysis, we considered separately the periods around the large graphoelements from what we call "core periods" of NREM2, which correspond to the quiet, shorter lasting "B" periods of the cyclic alternating pattern in NREM [42, 43]. We then compared directly the activity of core periods of NREM1 and NREM2 and the periods before and during spindles and K-complexes (KC), the two characteristic graphoelements of NREM2 sleep stage [9]. The changes in activity that we identified, map a most interesting variation in environmental monitoring, most clearly expressed in the changes of activity in the rostral anterior cingulate cortex (rACC), the key node of the saliency network. These changes show that with sleep onset the loss of consciousness is accompanied by an active inhibition of environmental monitoring as seen by high low frequency (delta band) activity in the frontal lobe and reduction in high frequency (alpha and higher frequencies) activity in posterior parietal areas [9]. The transition from NREM1 to NREM2 is accompanied by a return of activity in rACC amidst the general increase in the inhibitory low frequency activity, which suggests opposing tendencies between sleep maintenance and the return of some vigilance mechanism. This conflict is present in the core periods well away in time from KCs and spindles that can be considered as the common baseline for these two characteristic graphoelements of NREM2. The periods in the last few seconds before spindles and KCs we see a clear differentiation: activity during KCs is seen in the same areas and largely in similar frequencies as in the periods before their occurrence; the activity during KCs simply grows in strength and spreads more widely. The KC activity is consistent with alerting influences in the frontal executive and environment monitoring areas gaining control just before KCs with the actual KC emerging as a final cognitive effort to decide whether or not sleep will continue.

In the case of spindles, the comparison between the activity during NREM2 core period and the two seconds before spindles shows increases in delta and theta bands: these increases were localized in the sub-genual anterior cingulate cortex (sgACC) and frontal pole in the delta band only, and in the rACC and dMPFC, sixth Broadman area (BA), BA6 in both delta and theta bands. These changes are consistent with a complete blockade of external inputs. During spindles we see only increases in activity in the alpha and sigma bands. The increases are in the frontal pole (low sigma only), dMPFC (alpha and low sigma) and precuneus (BA7, sigma only) medially (Figure 5B in [9]) and some other frontal areas of the left hemisphere (for details see [9]). All the changes identified before and during spindles are consistent with continuation of preparations starting at sleep onset and continuing all the way until spindles begin for some important process that must have no interference from the environment. This process requires cooperative activity between ventral structures and basal forebrain and linked sigma band activity between dMPFC and posterior parietal areas. These observations are consistent with the memory consolidation role assigned by many researchers to spindles [44].

In interpreting the results of our earlier studies [9, 37], we follow Menon's triple network model with an emphasis on the clear separation of roles in the key networks [41]. On the basis of our recent analysis of data from sleep [9, 37], it seems that the DMN separates into sub-systems with its central and least observed component (during awake state) the MSRC that carries the core neural representation of self [9]. The details of the activity of rACC, the key node of the saliency system, before and during spindles, has all the hallmarks of acting as a mechanism for blocking all external in-puts and thus preventing interference with the operations to follow that involve MSRC. Adding to this the fact that the activity of the MSRC areas is reduced during awake state [37], it seems that evolution has invested a lot of effort on protecting the neural representation of self from interference in both awake state and sleep. The overall pattern of activity observed for this system begins to make sense from an evo-lutionary perspective and when they are viewed within a framework that borrows concepts from psychology with profound implications not only in pathology but also for education that I will explore a little later.

4.2   A wider definition and use for key concepts of developmental psychology

Before describing the basic concepts from psychology, we consider the sub-divisions of different states of awareness. The first major separation is in terms of states while we are awake and states while we sleep. We separate awake state into two parts. The first one allows free movement in the environment, which for this reason, makes it difficult to use in controlled experiments. The second one allows only limited or no movement and it is further divided into active states under a task or continuous inter-action with the environment and resting state. The resting state is further divided into eyes closed or eyes open states, with further sub-divisions if desired. Sleep is divided into the sleep stages and rather than tasks the system is "exercised" by the large and/or highly rhythmic events that characterize each sleep stage. For all the states, except the first one, it is perfectly feasible today, to record EEG and MEG time-locked to additional recordings of the physiological state of the subject external stimuli and/or continually changing conditions in the environment (e.g. using virtual reality headsets) [45]. From such MEG measurements, it is possible to extract quantitative descriptions of brain activity at the levels of CAs, networks and whole brain. With a little more effort, this may also be possible using EEG data (with a sophisticated con-ductivity model for each subject). For the purposes of this article, I also assume that it will be possible in the not-too-distant future to extract similar information from wearable EEG devices after constructing a detailed model for each subject, using possibly a more extensive set of measurements with expensive (e.g. MEG) instrumen-tation for the model definition, but only once every few years. Given such a capabil-ity, it is a relatively short step to characterize each awake and sleep state and thus define physiological and non-physiological conditions for all the states of conscious-ness and whatever range of tasks one might wish to employ. A canonical set of measures can then be defined from measurements made across sufficiently large number of people. The canonical set will describe the range of basic neural network measures (including measures of network interactions) that are within the expected range for a given subset of the population, defined by categorical properties like gen-der, handedness etc. and ranges e.g. age range. By allowing an age range we acknowledge that there will be some variability especially in the early years of life, when the trajectory of neural network properties will be as important as the values that describe them. The goal is to define for any one healthy individual from infancy to old age a measure of his/her normal physiological range of brain activity (n-

PRoBA). It is important to stress that n-PRoBA can be quantified in terms of activity and organization of the basic brain networks during operations that the subject is doing routinely, e.g. at rest (i.e. the activity of the DMN while resting), or in a set of simple and complex tasks.

I now proceed to the selection of basic concepts that I want to use for the new framework. I selected as core concepts the ones that have established themselves in developmental psychology: assimilation, accommodation and ZPD. I redefine each one of them in terms of the neuroscientific terms introduced above so that these definitions are not restricted to children but they are applicable to any age. We also consider Piaget's schemata as the products of operations carried out by the interconnected neural networks in the brain identified by neuroimaging.

We define as assimilation any interaction with the environment that corresponds to effortless use of existing skill/knowledge that therefore corresponds to a (partial) fit of the experience into the current internal model of the world as this is represented by the activity of the neural networks of the individual's brain. In operational sense, we can define as assimilation any brain operation that help us navigate through the environment and social engagements that does not push the key networks, and especially the MSRC of the brain beyond their canonical performance in the sense defined above. During routine assimilation brain activity remains within n-PROBA.

We define as accommodation the process which involves controlled excursions away from n-PROBA that allow a re-adjustment of the internal model of the world that may lead to (mild) alterations of our own self-image. Accepting that the two left paramedial sides, MSRC1 and MSRC2 identified during our sleep studies [9, 37] are the core neural representations of self, we postulate that their activation during sleep are key elements of accommodation through memory consolidation mechanisms in light sleep [9]. Other memory consolidation mechanisms in slow wave sleep and during REM are also key contributors to accommodation, but their precise role requires further investigation. Whenever major accommodation takes place the input from the environment must be completely eliminated because only at these times the core representation of self is open to influences. This ensures that the inclusion of new experiences is integrated all the way to the core representations of self but without altering this representation more than it is absolutely necessary.

We define as ZPD the activities that are outside n-PROBA, but only because they have never, or rarely, been attempted so far. These activities are possible to undertake with the existing neural systems under guidance by teachers or advanced peers, especially during play. In essence ZPD is what the existing neural networks can do but have not done so yet, and as such they are likely to require no change in the basic networks and specifically no change in the MSRC. It is important to stress that ZPD, as defined here, does not require the existence of fixed developmental stages, it can be defined for any age. For example, a weak chess player may decide on retirement to play chess more regularly and does so with a coach and/or attending his/her local chess club; in doing so he/she enters regularly in his/her ZPD. A tempting speculation is that dreaming is an exercise in the new ZPD that accommodation creates through the incorporation of new memories. Dreams are our evening plays to prepare us for likely and demanding tasks of the next day.

In this framework assimilation takes place during the day and night when we are not asleep. Accommodation takes place all the time and during much of the day it involves alterations that do not require changes in the MSRC, generated by events operating within n-PROBA. Events and experiences that are beyond n-PROBA but are still within the ZPD, are stored temporarily in the hippocampus and the surrounding areas. The main accommodation process during sleep is simply the processing of the accumulated traces of salient experiences during the evening after all input from the environment is blocked. This is probably because during the day the influences from the environment cannot be blocked as this would be an unacceptable risk for survival. Thus storing them as they happen might change unacceptably the MSRC.

We propose under this framework that events so dramatic that can penetrate the protecting shield of MSRC during awake state and modify it, or they require too much change to be accommodated during sleep lead to pathological conditions and will not be examined here. Problems may also arise when the individual works within his n-PROBA but with conflicting pressures from its physical and social milieu for a long time, or within its ZPD but with insufficient guidance from adults or more competent peers, a situation that often arises when a child or adult changes the daily routine in a significant way. For a child, such a critical change can be at the start of formal schooling. We will return to the problems that often arises when children enter elementary school at the end of the next subsection. In the next section, we will discuss our research efforts and the practical solutions that we were driven to develop for effective work within the school environment.

4.3   Education from an evolutionary perspective

The self is an evolutionary end-point signifying that the complexity of the inner representation of the external world has grown sufficiently complex to include a self-representation. Early in ontogenesis, the infant has no sense of self. The sense of self, in its complete form that includes innate and social dimensions, is acquired with the help of adult carers and the society at large, but first and foremost by the mother. In terms of our earlier discussion, the newly born baby is for much of the time beyond his/her ZPD, simply because in the absence of a clear boundary of self, there is no clear cut boundary for ZPD either. It is the mother's interaction with the baby that allows the self to emerge through judicial selection of components that are "already present in spontaneous expression" [46]. The mother accomplishes an incredible triumph in guiding the infant through and beyond an ill-defined ZPD using fast decoding of each and every body movement, facial expression and voice intonation at recognition speeds that are only a few tens of milliseconds [24]. Through the reciprocal interaction with the mother, the infant is able to do the decoding too, setting off along a road to become an expert in recognizing the emotions and intentions of others in non-verbal interaction, the ticket for success in social life. Until EEG came to the scene, this decoding of the intentions of others as part of non-verbal communication was the closest we came to map (albeit sub-consciously) the networks of the brain. By the end of the first year the infant has some awareness of self. In the preschool years cognitive development and social interaction force the child's self-image to be influenced by how others describe his/her behavior. There remains some exaggeration of his/her abilities, as the preschool child cannot yet make a clear distinction between how the child observes his/her performance through the eyes of others and how he/she wishes his performance to be. The child enters formal education at this preoperational level of development, as Piaget described it, so there is inevitably a large variation in the self-image and cognitive development level.

Formal education should be thought of as an extension of what the mother and early play have started; ideally education adds more layers of knowledge and skills while nurturing the individuality and uniqueness of the person, which in our framework implies consistency of the new knowledge with the self-image, as this is maintained by the DMN and in particular the MSRC. When a new pupil arrives in school, there is little to inform the educator about the newcomer and any special abilities or needs can go unnoticed for years that affect specific sensory systems and general personality traits handled by specialized networks, e.g. for attention and emotions. In the last subsection, I outlined a framework for the neural representation of self and the other key brain networks. As I have already indicated, with such a generalized framework in place, it is possible to apply the neuroimaging technology available today for the evaluation of the maturity of the key neural networks of a child along one or more canonical classifications, derived from a central database of measurements. I hasten to add that collecting the data for such a database, thousands of children need to be scanned with MRI and detailed EEG and/or MEG data to be recorded in a series of experiments. Last but not least, sophisticated analysis must be performed on the recorded data. The database must have enough children of different ages, separating gender, handedness and other attributes like socioeconomic background, previous exposure to linguistic material and education. Given the magnitude of the task, what is needed is an initiative like the Research Domain Criteria (RDoC) [47], an attempt to base the classification of psychiatric diseases on brain systems that can be imaged and from which regional measurements of activity and quantitative descriptions of structural and functional networks can be objectively extracted for populations and individuals. Creating a canonical database using a framework like the one I propose in the last subsection could provide education a powerful tool for objective evaluation of the maturity level of networks dealing with cognition, attention and emotions.

In conclusion, not all children are ready for school when they enter elementary school. In terms of the framework developed above, some of the new activities a child is asked to do when he/she starts elementary school may simply be beyond his/her ZPD. In the next section I will describe a practical way for mass screening pupils at the first year of elementary school that was developed in the last decade and the ongoing efforts and problems to overcome the difficulties we have encountered. This effort is only the beginning in the long road towards a truly useful classification of each child's neural network maturity as he/she starts formal education.

5   Practical considerations for Education evaluation

If a child on entering elementary school is forced to work deep into, or beyond his/her ZPD without sufficient guidance, is like a recruit in the army thrown into battle without any basic training. More damage can be done if the child's failure is criticized continuously, directly or indirectly, as the result of laziness and/or stupidity. The usual reaction from an emotionally wounded child to such hostile new environment is to either become the class clown or keep quiet and just stay below the teacher's radar. The double tragedy is that in cases where learning difficulties are a real risk, like in developmental dyslexia (DD), the longer the real problem remains unrecognized the more difficult it becomes to take remedial action fast enough to enable the child to catch up with his peers. The situation is analogous to the child coming to the platform of education as the train is starting to move away. There is little precious time for the child to run and get on board, and the longer he stays behind, the more difficult it becomes to catch up the accelerating train. If the problem remains unresolved till the middle of elementary school, as is very often the case, then the train is already too far. The outcome of such a scenario is misery and performance well below the child's true ability throughout primary and secondary education, even when considerable resources are provided for remedial lessons. Statistics of the percentage of DD children that end up in low salary positions and criminality show clearly the disadvantage these children face. The success of many DD survivors of the educational system also show that this need not be the outcome.

We undertook a program of research aiming to characterize in an objective way and with as simple tools as possible, the maturity of key neural networks in the preschool and first years of elementary education. We were motivated by what we claimed above, namely that the technology for an objective evaluation of the maturity of key brain networks is possible today, but at a high cost. Initially, we targeted the diagnosis of DD. Our long term aim is to provide a mass screening capability with general evaluation for every child and eventually appropriate intervention designed individually for every child. The aim is optimal education for all children, helping children with special needs to overcome difficulties before these become a problem and helping children with special abilities to fulfill their potentials. Three projects were completed so far (see acknowledgements).

In the first project, *Personalized Advanced Cognitive Diagnosis for Children* (ABΓΔΠ; December 2010 – February 2013) we assembled a set of non-linguistic visual tests to map basic neural networks using accuracy tests. Some of the tests were taken from the literature [48, 49], while others were developed especially for the project and they were based on results obtained in some of our earlier experiments [50–54]. These tests were tried with children in the age range from 4 to 8 years old in a longitudinal study with four measurements over a period of 3 years. The original test was part of a story-line woven in the lesson (e.g. in a mythology story). The children were asked to select the correct item from the ones shown on a screen as part of their effort to help the hero in the story (e.g. Hercules). The children indicated their response by marking the correct option on a multiple choice paper. The study showed clear differences, which correlated well with independent tests for each child using a subset of tests from the Wechsler Intelligence Scale for Children (WISC). The method was however deemed too cumbersome for the classroom environment and also limited as it only measured accuracy with no real measure for the speed of response. We therefore adapted the tests for use with personal computers (PC). This PC-based version of the tests used specialized software that allowed as to collect automatically the responses and the reaction time from each pupil. The results were promising, but using many PCs to do the tests in parallel, could only take place in schools with a dedicated ICT room. Even for these schools the occupation of the high demand ICT room for a few hours at a time made the approach unattractive.

These problems were addressed in the second project, *Prodromal Analysis of Noetic Difficulties with Individual Automated System*, (PANDIAS; September 2013 – May 2015). The main goal of PANDIAS was to develop a way for efficient testing an entire class to serve as the basis for a mass-screening program. The PANDIAS solution was a hand-held device that could be independently operated by each child [55]. With enough devices so that each child had one, it is possible to screen all the children in a classroom within one lesson period. The second project was completed in the spring of 2015 and the final prototype device was operating with four tests. The selection of the four tests was based on the results of the first project and it used the most informative collection of four tests for a complete session well within one lesson period. Responses for the set of four tests have been collected during the two projects from over three hundred children. The majority of data collected were from the excellent collaboration that we had with one private school (see acknowledgements). For most of the data collected, there are two and in some cases four measurements, with matched reports from the school teachers for each child, spread over a period of two to three years. The PANDIAS device can be interfaced with the EEG and combine behavioral data from PANDIAS and the EEG were recorded from a small number of children. In these measurements, the EEG was recorded in a protocol designed to probe specific neural networks, including sensory ones and the DMN. The EEG data analysis is ongoing using a newly developed method for tomographic analysis of EEG data developed under a third project by our team, *Dynamic Field Tomography* (DEFT; October 2012 – April 2015) and they will not be discussed further here.

The four tests provided in the final prototype device allow the collection of data with minimal disruption of the school program. The children respond well to these tests and they are happy to do them. The recording of reaction time provides significant and independent information to the accuracy results. The availability of data from all pupils in a classroom allows the data from each child to be contrasted with the data from his classmates, thus ensuring that the comparison is with peers with similar school experiences. Repeated tests can provide a particularly sensitive warning to changes in individual children. Indeed our preliminary longitudinal analysis of the data, collected from the projects ΑΒΓΔΠ and PANDIAS, suggests that while it is difficult to establish a level from the data of an individual child at any one point in time, the developmental trajectory one can trace when repeat data are available provides a much clearer picture of the progress achieved and where problems may exist. On the basis of the early results the minimum requirement is collection of data at the beginning and end of a school year, with some additional benefit obtained if one additional set is obtained half way through the academic year. We have also studied the evaluation of teachers with two independent evaluations per child. We found that the teacher evaluations from the middle years of the elementary school are more informative and confident and reasonably uniform across repeated periods and for different teachers in the same period. The evaluations of teachers in earlier years are less confident and judging from the divergence between teachers for the same child and same period, they are also less reliable.

I have presented a framework based on generalizations of key concepts of developmental psychology. This framework can serve as a common reference for neuroscience, psychology and education specialists. It can also support research programs by combining under one roof the knowledge about education accumulated over centuries with the latest neuroscience findings. Our limited efforts to start such a program of research has allowed us to adapt both the neuroscience knowledge and the approach to evaluation of entry level children to primary education. While teachers once engaged in the project were fascinated with the work and clearly saw its relevance to their work, the wheels of bureaucracy were often so slow to move and more often than not, made it difficult to exploit the results in the state schools. On the contrary the project colleagues from the private sector found it much easier to assimilate the knowledge and use it effectively in their school not only to help pupils but also to advance the careers and foster the enthusiasm of the teachers involved in the work.

Acknowledgments. The work reported here was co-funded by the EU Regional Development and structural Fund and the Research Promotion Foundation of Cyprus (enterprises/product/0609/076 and enterprises/product/0311/042 grants) and by PANDIAS project No.59 managed by the Ministry of Energy, Commerce, Industry and Tourism. Much of the work and longitudinal data were obtain at The Heritage Private School, Palodia, Limassol and the excellent support and enthusiasm for the project by the Director Dr. Kypros Kouris, the head teacher and teaching staff of the primary school directly involved in the project. The author acknowledges helpful discussions with Dr. Lichan Liu and Mr. Panagiotis Koulouris.

Abbreviations:

ΑΒΓΔΠ *Personalized Advanced Cognitive Diagnosis for Children*
ACC   Anterior Cingulate Cortex
CA   cytoarchitectonic areas
CCS   central conceptual structure
CMS   cortical midline structures
DD   developmental dyslexia
DEFT   *Dynamic Field Tomography (project)*
DMN   default mode network
dMPFC dorsal medial prefrontal cortex
DTI   Diffusion Tensor Imaging
EEG electroencephalography
fMRI functional MRI
ICT   Information Communication Technology
ITS   Intelligent Tutoring Systems

KC   K-complex
MEG   Magnetoencephalography
MRI magnetic resonance imaging
MSRC   midline self-representation core MSRC
n-PRoBA normal physiological range of brain activity
NREM non-REM
OECD   Organization for Economic Co-operation and development
PANDIAS *Prodromal Analysis of Noetic Difficulties with Individual Automated System*
PC   personal computer
PET positron emission tomography
rACC   rostral ACC
RDoC   Research Domain Criteria
REM rapid eye movement
SG   Serious Games
sgACC sub-genual anterior cingulate cortex
TC   Talairach Coordinates
WISC   Wechsler Intelligence Scale for Children
ZPD zone of proximal development

The three names in italics are completed research projects

References

1.   Llinas, R.R.: I of the Vortex: From Neurons to Self. MIT press (2001)
2.   Delafield-Butt, J.T., Trevarthen, C.: The ontogenesis of narrative: from moving to meaning. Front. Psychol. 6, 1157 (2015). doi:10.3389/fpsyg.2015.01157
3.   Merker, B.: The Vocal Learning Constellation. In: Music, Language, and Human Evolution (2012)
4.   Elias, J.L., Merriam, S.B.: Philosophical foundations of adult education. Krieger Pub. Co, Melbourne (1995)
5.   Thorndike, E.L.: The contribution of psychology to education. Educ. Psychol. 1, 5–12 (1910)
6.   Pascual-Leone, J.: A mathematical model for the transition rule in Piaget's developmental stages. Acta Psychol. (Amst). 32, 301–345 (1970). doi:10.1016/0001-6918(70)90108-3
7.   Case, R., Okamoto, Y., Griffin, S., Mckeough, A., Bleiker, C., Henderson, B., Stephenson, K.M., Siegler, R.S., Keating, D.P.: the Role of Central Conceptual Structures in the Development of Children's Thought. Monogr. Soc. Res. Child Dev. 61, 1–295 (1996)
8.   Ferrari, M., McBride, H.: Mind, brain and education: The birth of a new science. Learn. Landscapes. 5, 85–100 (2011)
9.   Ioannides, A.A., Liu, L., Poghosyan, V., Kostopoulos, G.K.: Using MEG to Understand the Progression of Light Sleep and the Emergence and functional Roles of Spindles and K-complexes. Front. Hum. Neurosci. 11, 1–24 (2017). doi:10.3389/fnhum.2017.00313

10. Fischer, K.: A theory of cognitive development. Psychol. Rev. 87, 477–531 (1980). doi:10.1037/018662

11. Stein, Z., Fischer, K.W.: Directions for Mind, Brain, and Education: Methods, Models, and Morality. Educ. Philos. Theory. 43, 56–66 (2011). doi:10.1111/j.1469-5812.2010.00708.x

12. Arsalidou, M., Pascual-leone, J.: Constructivist developmental theory is needed in developmental neuroscience. Nat. Partn. Journals , Sci. Learn. 1, 1–9 (2016). doi:10.1038/npjscilearn.2016.16

13. Prensky, M.: Digital Game-Based Learning. McGraw Hill, New York (2001)

14. Conati, C., MacLaren, H.: Empirically building and evaluating a probabilistic model of user affect. User Model. User-adapt. Interact. 19, 267–303 (2009). doi:10.1007/s11257-009-9062-8

15. Derbali, L., Chalfoun, P., Frasson, C.: A Theoretical and Empirical Approach in Assessing Motivational Factors: From Serious Games To an ITS. In: Proceedings of the Twenty-Fourth International Florida Artificial Intelligence Research Society Conference. pp. 513–518. Association for the Advancement of Artificial Intelligence (2011)

16. Bandettini, P.A.: What's new in neuroimaging methods? Ann. N. Y. Acad. Sci. 14, 260–293 (2009). doi:10.1111/j.1749-6632.2009.04420.x

17. Satterthwaite, T.D., Elliott, M.A., Ruparel, K., Loughead, J., Prabhakaran, K., Calkins, M.E., Hopson, R., Jackson, C., Keefe, J., Riley, M., Mensh, F.D., Sleiman, P., Verma, R., Davatzikos, C., Hakonarson, H., Gur, R.C., Gur, R.E.: Neuroimaging of the Philadelphia Neurodevelopmental Cohort. Neuroimage. 86, 544–553 (2014). doi:10.1016/j.neuroimage.2013.07.064

18. Schumann, G., Loth, E., Banaschewski, T., Barbot, A., Barker, G., Büchel, C., Conrod, P.J., Dalley, J.W., Flor, H., Gallinat, J., Garavan, H., Heinz, A., Itterman, B., Lathrop, M., Mallik, C., Mann, K., Martinot, J.-L., Paus, T., Poline, J.-B., Robbins, T.W., Rietschel, M., Reed, L., Smolka, M., Spanagel, R., Speiser, C., Stephens, D.N., Ströhle, A., Struve, M.: The IMAGEN study: reinforcement-related behaviour in normal brain function and psychopathology. Mol. Psychiat. 15, 1128–1139 (2010)

19. Brown, T.T., Kuperman, J.M., Chung, Y., Erhart, M., Mccabe, C., Hagler, D.J., Venkatraman, V.K., Akshoomoff, N., Amaral, D.G., Bloss, C.S., Casey, B.J., Chang, L., Ernst, T.M., Frazier, J.A., Gruen, J.R.,.: Neuroanatomical assessment of biological maturity. Curr. Biol. 22, 1693–1698 (2012). doi:10.1016/j.cub.2012.07.002.Neuroanatomical

20. Zilles, K., Schleicher, A., Palomero-Gallagher, N., Amunts, K.: Quantitative analysis of cyto- and receptor architecture of the human brain. In: Toga, A.W. and Mazziotta, J.C. (eds.) Brain Mapping: The Methods. pp. 573–602 (2002)

21. Caspers, S., Eickhoff, S.B., Zilles, K., Amunts, K.: Combining cytoarchitectonic atlas information with diffusion tensor imaging – detailed mapping of transcallosal fibres of the inferior parietal lobule. Front. Neuroinform. (2013). doi:10.3389/conf.fninf.2013.10.00035

22. Rubinov, M., Sporns, O.: Complex network measures of brain connectivity: Uses and interpretations. Neuroimage. 52, 1059–1069 (2010). doi:10.1016/j.neuroimage.2009.10.003

23.   Ioannides, A.A., Fenwick, P.B.C., Liu, L.: Widely distributed magnetoencephalography spikes related to the planning and execution of human saccades. J. Neurosci. 25, 7950–7967 (2005). doi:10.1523/JNEUROSCI.1091-05.

24.   Liu, L., Ioannides, A.A.: Emotion separation is completed early and it depends on visual field presentation. PLoS One. 5, e9790 (2010). doi:10.1371/journal.pone.0009790

25.   Friston, K.J.: Functional and Effective Connectivity: A Review. Brain Connect. 1, 13–36 (2011). doi:10.1089/brain.2011.0008

26.   Ioannides, A.A.: Dynamic functional connectivity. Curr Opin Neurobiol. 17, 161–170 (2007). doi:10.1016/j.conb.2007.03.008

27.   Damoiseaux, J.S., Rombouts, S.A.R.B., Barkhof, F., Scheltens, P., Stam, C.J., Smith, S.M., Beckmann, C.F.: Consistent resting-state networks across healthy subjects. Proc. Natl. Acad. Sci. 103, 13848–13853 (2006). doi:10.1073/pnas.0601417103

28.   Greicius, M.D., Krasnow, B., Reiss, A.L., Menon, V.: Functional connectivity in the resting brain: A network analysis of the default mode hypothesis. Proc. Natl. Acad. Sci. 100, 253–8 (2003)

29.   Watanabe, T., Kan, S., Koike, T., Misaki, M., Konishi, S., Miyauchi, S., Miyahsita, Y., Masuda, N.: Network-dependent modulation of brain activity during sleep. Neuroimage. 98, 1–10 (2014). doi:10.1016/j.neuroimage.2014.04.079

30.   Horovitz, S.G., Braun, A.R., Carr, W.S., Picchioni, D., Balkin, T.J., Fukunaga, M., Duyn, J.H.: Decoupling of the brain's default mode network during deep sleep. Proc. Nat. Acad. Sci., USA. 106, 11376–11381 (2009). doi:10.1073/pnas.0901435106

31.   de Haan, W., Pijnenburg, Y. AL, Strijers, R.L., van der Made, Y., van der Flier, W.M., Scheltens, P., Stam, C.J.: Functional neural network analysis in frontotemporal dementia and Alzheimer's disease using EEG and graph theory. BMC Neurosci. 10, 101 (2009). doi:10.1186/1471-2202-10-101

32.   Stam, C.J.: Modern network science of neurological disorders. Nat. Rev. Neurosci. 15, 683–695 (2014). doi:10.1038/nrn3801

33.   Dimitriadis, S.I., Laskaris, N. a., Simos, P.G., Micheloyannis, S., Fletcher, J.M., Rezaie, R., Papanicolaou, a. C.: Altered temporal correlations in resting-state connectivity fluctuations in children with reading difficulties detected via MEG. Neuroimage. 83, 307–317 (2013). doi:10.1016/j.neuroimage.2013.06.036

34.   Ioannides, A.A., Dimitriadis, S.I., Saridis, G.A., Voultsidou, M., Poghosyan, V., Liu, L., Laskaris, N.A.: Source space analysis of event-related dynamic reorganization of brain networks. Comput. Math. Methods Med. 2012, 452503 (2012). doi:10.1155/2012/452503

35.   Uddin, L.Q., Kelly, A.M., Biswal, B.B., Castellanos, F.X., Milham, M.P.: Functional connectivity of default mode network components: correlation, anticorrelation, and causality. Hum. Brain Mapp. 30, 625–37 (2009). doi:10.1002/hbm.20531

36.   Murphy, K., Birna, R.M., Handwerkera, Daniel Jonesa, T.B.A., Bandettini, P.A.: The impact of global signal regression on resting state correlations: Are anti-correlated networks introduced? Neuroimage. 44, 893–905 (2009). doi:10.1016/j.neuroimage.2008.09.036

37.   Ioannides, A.A., Kostopoulos, G.K., Liu, L., Fenwick, P.B.C.: MEG identifies dorsal medial brain activations during sleep. Neuroimage. 44, 455–468 (2009).

doi:10.1016/j.neuroimage.2008.09.030

38.   Uddin, L.Q., Iacoboni, M., Lange, C., Keenan, J.P.: The self and social cognition: the role of cortical midline structures and mirror neurons. Trends Cogn. Sci. 11, 153–157 (2007). doi:10.1016/j.tics.2007.01.001

39.   Menon, V.: Salience Network Introduction and Overview. In: Toga, A.W. (ed.) Brain Mapping: An Encyclopedic Reference,. pp. 597–611. Elevier (2015)

40.   Seeley, W.W., Menon, V., Schatzberg, A.F., Keller, J., Glover, G.H., Kenna, H., Reiss, A.L., Greicius, M.D.: Dissociable Intrinsic Connectivity Networks for Salience Processing and Executive Control. 27, 2349–56 (2007). doi:10.1523/JNEUROSCI.5587-06.2007

41.   Menon, V.: Large-scale brain networks and psychopathology: a unifying triple network model. Trends Cogn. Sci. 15, 483–506 (2011). doi:10.1016/j.tics.2011.08.003

42.   Terzano, M.G., Parrino, L., Sherieri, A., Chervin, R., Chokroverty, S., Guilleminault, C., Hirshkowitz, M., Mahowald, M., Moldofsky, H., Rosa, A., Thomas, R., Walters, A.: Atlas, rules, and recording techniques for the scoring of cyclic alternating pattern (CAP) in human sleep. Sleep Med. 2, 537–53 (2001)

43.   Wehrle, R., Kaufmann, C., Wetter, T.C., Holsboer, F., Auer, D.P., Pollmächer, T., Czisch, M.: Functional microstates within human REM sleep: first evidence from fMRI of a thalamocortical network specific for phasic REM periods. Eur. J. Neurosci. 25, 863–71 (2007). doi:10.1111/j.1460-9568.2007.05314.x

44.   Rosanova, M., Ulrich, D.: Pattern-specific associative long-term potentiation induced by a sleep spindle-related spike train. J. Neurosci. 25, 9398–405 (2005). doi:10.1523/JNEUROSCI.2149-05.2005

45.   Ciani, O., Federici, C., Tarricone, R., Bezerianos, A.: Current and Future Trends in the HTA of Medical Devices. Presented at the (2016)

46.   Trevarthen, C.: Communication and cooperation in early infancy: a description of primary intersubjectivity. In: Bullowa, M. (ed.) Before Speech: The Beginning of Interpersonal Communication. pp. 321–348. Google Books (1979)

47.   Insel, T., Cuthbert, B., Garvie, M., Heinssen, R., Pine, D.S., Quinn, K., Sanislow, C., Wang, P.: Research Domain Criteria (RDoC): Toward a New Classification Framework for Research on Mental Disorders. Am. J. Psychiatry. 167, 748–751 (2010). doi:10.1176/appi.ajp.2010.09091379

48.   Becker, C., Elliott, M.A., Lachmann, T.: Evidence for impaired visuoperceptual organisation in developmental dyslexics and its relation to temporal processes. Cogn. Neuropsychol. 22, 499–522 (2005). doi:10.1080/02643290442000086

49.   Facoetti, A., Zorzi, M., Cestnick, L., Lorusso, M.L., Molteni, M., Paganoni, P., Umiltà, C., Mascetti, G.G.: The relationship between visuo-spatial attention and nonword reading in developmental dyslexia. Cogn. Neuropsychol. 23, 841–855 (2006). doi:10.1080/02643290500483090

50.   Abu Bakar, A., Liu, L., Conci, M., Elliott, M. a, Ioannides, A. a: Visual field and task influence illusory figure responses. Hum. Brain Mapp. 29, 1313–26 (2008). doi:10.1002/hbm.20464

51.   Poghosyan, V., Ioannides, A.A.: Attention modulates earliest responses in the primary auditory and visual cortices. Neuron. 58, 802–13 (2008). doi:10.1016/j.neuron.2008.04.013

52.   Ioannides, A.A., Poghosyan, V.: Spatiotemporal dynamics of early spatial and category-specific attentional modulations. Neuroimage. 60, 1638–1651 (2012). doi:10.1016/j.neuroimage.2012.01.121

53.   Liu, L., Ioannides, A.A.: Spatiotemporal dynamics and connectivity pattern differences between centrally and peripherally presented faces. Neuroimage. 31, 1726–1740 (2006). doi:10.1016/j.neuroimage.2006.02.009

54.   Plomp, G., Leeuwen, C. van, Ioannides, A.A.: Functional specialization and dynamic resource allocation in visual cortex. Hum. Brain Mapp. 31, 1–13 (2010). doi:10.1002/hbm.20840

55.   Ioannides, A.A., Papageorgiou, G.: Effective and Affordable Ways of Capturing Reaction Time and EEG to Dedicated Stimuli Using Stand-Alone Devices. In: Frontiers in Human Neuroscience (2016)

Tracing and Enhancing Serendipitous Learning with ViewpointS

Stefano A. Cerri[1] and Philippe Lemoisson[2]

[1] LIRMM: University of Montpellier and CNRS, France
cerri@lirmm.fr
[2] UMR Territories, Environment, Remote Sensing and Spatial Information, CIRAD, Montpellier, France
philippe.lemoisson@cirad.fr

Abstract. This is a position paper describing the author's views on a potential new research direction for assessing, constructing and exploiting brain-founded models of learning of individual as well as collective humans. The recent approach – called ViewpointS – aiming to unify the Semantic and the Social Web, data mining included, by means of a simple "subjective" primitive – the *viewpoint* - denoting proximity among elements of the world, seems to offer a promising context of innovative empirical research in modeling human learning less constrained with respect to the previous three other ones. Within this context, a few phenomena of serendipitous learning have been simulated, showing that the process of *collective* construction of knowledge during free navigation may offer interesting side effects of informal, serendipitous knowledge acquisition and learning. We envision therefore an extension of the modeling functions within ViewpointS by adding measures of the emotions and mental states as acquired during experimental sessions. These brain-related components may in a first phase allow to describe and classify models in order to understand the relations among knowledge structures and mental states. Subsequently, more predictive experiments may be envisaged. These may allow to forecast the acquisition of knowledge as well as sentiment from previous events during interactions. We are convinced that useful applications may range, for instance, from Tutoring, to Health, to consensus formation in Politics at very low investment costs as the experimental set up consists of minimal extensions of the Web.

Keywords: Brain-aware individual and collective models of human learning, Serendipitous knowledge and sentiment acquisition, Informal Learning, Web-interactive Knowledge construction and exploitation, Unifying Semantic and Social Web.

1   Introduction

This position paper aims to contribute to the BFAL17 Conference by means of a description of potential research projects combining the state of the art of the disciplines reported in the Call. We adopt the BFAL17 view that the emergence of new assessment devices allows to foresee totally new experiments on various aspects of

© Springer International Publishing AG 2017
C. Frasson and G. Kostopoulos (Eds.): BFAL 2017, LNAI 10512, pp. 36–47, 2017
DOI: 10.1007/978-3-319-67615-9_3

human learning, enabling a better understanding of human brain's structure and behavior about the crucial function of learning.

In particular we will capitalize from the long experience in Intelligent Tutoring that paved the way to better interactive systems enhancing learning by starting from the construction of models or profiles of community members [1], [2]. Our experience has shown that modeling is crucial in order to understand the interacting human and therefore to personalize interactions. However, modeling is extremely difficult if not intractable [3]. We aim to *make model acquisition easier*, as well as try to widen this modeling practice to *generic interactive systems of free navigation* and deepen it by *adding a brain-aware component*.

These experiments, however, have yet to be conceived, financed, conducted and evaluated requiring in addition the contributions of experts in different domains, each one unable to encompass the whole challenge of the enterprise.

In the following we will present our position concerning:

1.   human learning "as a side effect of interactions" (informal learning [4], in particular serendipitous learning);

2.   the potential exploitation of a new, emergent mode of tracing and exploiting agent-to-world (including other agents) interactions, called ViewpointS [5,6];

3.   the assessment of serendipitous, informal learning effects within ViewpointS – based on interactive processes by means of neuro-physiological experiments such as those performed mainly within formal learning contexts -; and finally

4.   the envisaged potential applications to learning-scientific discovery, acquiring a political conviction and health-radicalization.

2   Serendipitous learning

The concept of serendipitous learning is usually denoting the result of an event of learning occurring in the absence of explicit will of the learner; however it does not explain *how* this event occurs. We report from [7] quoting [8] that: "Like all intuitive operating, pure serendipity is not amenable to generation by a computer. The very moment I can plan or program 'serendipity' it cannot be called serendipity anymore." We may adopt most if not all the conditions for serendipity reported, yet the phenomenon is hardly to be foreseen, like other human phenomena linked to creativity. By consequence, we limit our ambition to the *analysis* of processes enhancing events of serendipitous learning occurring possibly during free navigation on the Web as a consequence of the availability of new knowledge structures tuned to the user.

We assume that *Information access and acquisition enhances learning as a function of the learner's interest and commitment.* As a consequence, we claim that

a. the *proximity* of Information *relevant to the learner* may facilitate this kind of unexpected learning during free navigation;

b. the *learner's* motivation, commitment, emotions, shortly: *mental state* [1] may facilitate this kind of learning.

Usually, we consider "free navigation" to be a process of searching among resources that are available at one click distance in a document or either in a list resulting from a search triggered by a query expressed in words. The proximity of a link to follow is then structural: a link is near if it is positioned next to my gaze when I look at the page. This position is determined by structural, logical, objective reasons.

There are other types of free navigation, however. For instance, we may freely navigate on a map from Google Maps: in this case proximity is topological, not structural: a city or a museum is near if its position is near to my gaze that looks at a point topologically near to the city or museum; latitude and longitude being the rationale for distance, i.e.: the topology is metric.

There exist also dedicated maps: they may enhance the appearance of selected objects or events. For instance, historical maps may show territories or monuments or battlefields by colors or symbols that facilitate discovering, understanding and mastering the history of the map area. These maps include knowledge that is *subjective* with respect to the producer.

Maps may also show proximities even without a real corresponding metric topology, as it is the case of maps of transport networks: the Information coded in the map is not strictly related to the fact that a metro station is more or less distant from the next one, rather that it is simply "the next station". *Topology may thus be non metric but conceptual*; tuned to the passenger's interest: what is my next station?

Another example that we all know are maps of the US – originally from Saul Steinberg - that show – in perspective - very small entities on the horizon corresponding to Europe and cities such as London or Paris or Pisa; the association of Pisa being purely due to the fact that, even if much smaller and less important than Paris or London, it is famous for its tower as a symbol of Italy or even Europe. For these maps what counts are not only the consumer's interest, but also his/her knowledge. This kind of "geographic" representation is *topological, non metric* and *adapted* to the subjective user's interests and knowledge.

We will show how to construct semi-automatically models during the construction and exploitation of an Information "geographical" map – called Knowledge Map, based on subjective proximity – that may fit the learner's cognitive state thus may be relevant to the learner and adapted to his/her mental state. As a consequence, we conjecture that *this navigation may enhance serendipitous learning, discovery and acquisition*.

---

[1] For simplicity (and limited competence): in this paper we are not making a clear distinction among these time-dependent human properties: the word "mental state" will represent non rational aspects such as emotions, motivation, commitment, sentiment.

3   The interest of subjective proximity in human cognition

In the theory and practice of the last 60 year's psychology, Rorschach tests [9, 10], Personality Traits tests [11,12] and Principles of grouping or Gestalt laws of grouping [13] are all based on subjective evaluations, not objective classifications. In these psychological approaches to human cognition, the subjective assessment of "proximity" among elements seems to play an important role for estimating the human mental state: for instance a certain Rorschach picture "evokes" some concepts/documents/people.

Also in the foundational work of Edelman in Physiology [14] « image evokes concept » may be interpreted as « there are strong connections between neural area 1 (image reception) and neural area 2 (abstraction X) » therefore « close to each other» if we choose the appropriate distance.

Vygotsky's ZPD (Zone of Proximal Development) and his vision [15], similar to the one of Piaget, may be considered another witness of the importance of "proximity" in learning processes both in spontaneous development and at school.

This does not mean that we adopt any of the above quoted visions, just that we notice that many qualified psychologists and physiologists consider subjective proximity among human cognitive structures as an important element to exploit in order to understand human cognition. Therefore, we have committed ourselves to found our investigations on human informal learning processes, in particular serendipitous learning, by means of representing and using *subjective proximities* rather than *objective fits*.

It will be one of the subjects of our investigation to outline the correspondence of these human cognitive structures – the ones linked to proximities - with the world elements (Agents, Documents and Concepts) that we consider essentially distinguished for representation and reasoning, as outlined in the following section.

4   Proximity in ViewpointS: Agents, Documents and Concepts

ViewpointS is a conceptual framework, now implemented through a Web application [2], enabling to represent, construct and exploit collective knowledge and intelligence in a rather innovative fashion [5]. In ViewpointS, the authors attempt to integrate the Semantic and the Social Web, data mining included, at the same time preserving subjectivity both during the construction and the exploitation of the representation.

The essential component of the model and the platform are *viewpoints*, i.e.: triplets declaring the proximity of an element to any other element of the reduced world. Thus ViewpointS – the model and the platform – consists of many *viewpoints* as well as the

---

[2] http://viewpoints.cirad.fr/ViewpointsWebApp (accessed on July 21st, 2017)

processes necessary for constructing and exploiting [3] them embedded in the Web application.

By adopting this model, we assume the world to be reduced to 3 sets of elements, also called *knowledge resources* or *resources*:

1.   Agents (Human and Artificial): these are active elements in the sense that they are the only ones actively declaring the proximity of any two elements. However, they are also passive in the sense that an Agent (the active one) may declare the proximity of another Agent (the passive one) with an Agent, a Document or a Classifier. Since each Agent has the right to "declare *viewpoints*" the declarations produced are autonomous and *subjective*. This is the world representing Human and – as much as metaphorically possible – Artificial Intelligence. Agents declare and exploit knowledge exhibiting therefore intelligence[4]. Provenance is always respected and may be used in search;

2.   Documents - written, pictures, graphs, movies, real as well as virtual i.e.: numeric documents - are what the Web exhibits about the real world external to Agents and

3.   Classifiers, also called Concepts - classes, subjects of a discipline, names of emotions, mental states, descriptors, names of communities, religions -. This is the world constructed by culture, language, history, science.

Proximity may be declared between two among the three sets of elements; therefore: 3x2 = 6 types of (undirected) proximity may be declared: Agent-Agent, Agent-Document, Agent-Concept, Document-Document, Document-Concept, Concept-Concept.

The formalization of these heterogeneous semantics is illustrated in Fig. 1:

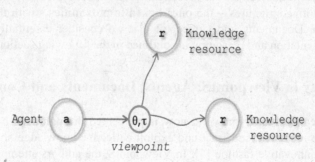

Fig.1: A "viewpoint". The straight arrow gives the provenance; 'θ' gives the semantics e.g., 'authorship', 'matches', 'similar'; 'τ' gives the time stamp

---

[3] In this context we prefer « construction and exploitation » to the terms « production and consumption » that are often popular within the description of network protocols.

[4] Notice that a significant part of this intelligence is due to the collective contributions by other Agents. One of the assumptions is that the crowd indeed shows a kind of wisdom.

Each Agent declares, constructs *subjective* proximities by emitting *viewpoints*.[5] Those are globally transformed into topological proximity within a graph – called: Knowledge Graph (KG). This graph KG can in turn be exploited by each Agent, according to his/her own subjectivity, the user's *subjectivity*, by means of transforming it into another Graph called Knowledge Map (KM) that is the result of a functional transformation called: *perspective*. The *perspective* may be considered like a rule-based filter that enters the KG and produces the KM on behalf of a single or collective Agent: proximities which are qualitatively declared in the KG by *viewpoints* are filtered and quantified on demand according to a *perspective* and transformed into subjective links between knowledge resources – called *synapses* – that form on turn the KM. This process is depicted in the simplified, yet detailed Fig.2 below.

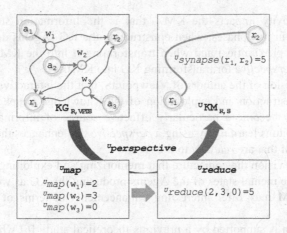

Fig. 2: The process of building a knowledge map ^{U}KM, where 'U' stands for the subjective perspective of the User specifying the ^{U}map and ^{U}reduce functions[6], i.e. the rules quantifying the viewpoints. In this example, the weights 2, 3 and 0 have been respectively assigned (^{U}map) to the viewpoints w_1 w_2 and w_3, and then these weights have been summed up (^{U}reduce) in order to produce a synapse weighting 5 between resources r_1 and r_2.

---

[5] The viewpoint (a_1, {r_2, r_3}, θ, τ) stands for: the agent a_1 believes at time τ that r_2 and r_3 are related according to the semantics carried by θ. Notice that *viewpoint* declarations may occur as side effects of other actions, such as clicking an URL. Artificial Agents (e.g.: mining algorithms or theorem provers from the Semantic Web) may also contribute to declare dynamically *viewpoints*.

[6] Notice that the Map-Reduce labels have been chosen with a view to the dataflow future implementation of the dynamic process. We believe that this implementation will be needed for performance, since the transformation KG->KM is in principle performed continuously for each Agent and dataflow processes are naturally concurrent. However, the conception of processes in terms of dataflow with the three classical operators (maps, accumulators = reducers, filters) is also an alternative to the classical object-oriented one. Dataflow concurrency may make explicit other interesting behaviors (and their corresponding interpretations) that may be more similar to the ones of the brain.

The following concrete points should be noted:

1. 'θ' takes currently values within a non-ambiguous and limited set (e.g.: 'matches', 'authorship' ,'similar') [7],
2. default functions for quantifying and aggregating the viewpoints according to 'θ' and other parameters have been defined, so that only expert users will possibly feel the need to tune them according to their needs ;
3. there is in principle no boundary in the choice of functions and rules for weighting and aggregating *viewpoints* in order to produce a perspective: we kept the current version simple, but more complex filtering processes may be conceived.

A perspective corresponds not only to the "once for all" user's profile; rather to a dynamic focusing lens that users exploit to interpret the Knowledge Graph evolving with the time.

So, the subjectivity impacts the KM - that is the Information structure where Agents navigate - in two phases: when constructing the KG (Agents declare autonomously subjective proximities) and when transforming it into the KM (Agents may define their own *perspective* for transforming KG into KM).

We adopt the vision of the authors of ViewpointS, that the interactive processes intertwining the construction and exploitation of the Knowledge Graph – Knowledge Map *may possibly* become a particularly effective source of informal learning, in particular serendipitous learning by using a *perspective* that enhances the proximity of elements in the KM that are *relevant* to the Agent.

We add to their vision the conjecture that memorizing and exploiting -by means of the *perspective*- the mental states of the Agents producing the KG as well as the ones consuming the KM may offer interesting enhancements in terms of serendipitous learning.

This assumption is supported by a previous theoretical study [6] where the ViewpointS authors have explored in a mock-up, simulated situation – called "the three princes of Serendip" - how they can graphically assess abstract concepts (i.e. colors) and promote serendipitous learning of these concepts. It was interesting to notice that such learning occurs as a consequence of free navigation in maps that have been influenced by other Agents on the basis of other Agent's competence, conviction, knowledge, without any explicit intention to teach. Once more: the external context influences learning even without any internal decision or intention.

5   Web Science: studying societies of Humans by tracing their behavior on the Web

A few years ago, a movement was launched about the notion of Web Science [16]. The main objective was to give a status of Science to the studies interested in understanding and predicting human individual and collective behavior, by means of dis-

---

[7] Practically: users may tune a limited number of sliders in order to define the filter concerning θ for building their own perspective.

tinguishing those initiatives from the very successful recent technical advances qualifying as Web Technologies.

The difference is certainly not a minor one: a science profits but does not coincide with its related techniques or technologies. In particular, a natural science looks into natural phenomena in order to understand and predict them as much as possible by iterating the cycle of conjectures and refutations [17]. One of the pillars of the process consists in the performance of Bayesian significance tests. However, before the formulation of a conjecture, one should have a *descriptive* idea about the phenomena at stake and the variables that may represent them in a significant way. This pre-study usually precedes inferential statistics.

The question then arises naturally: is the Web a "natural phenomenon"? Insofar the Web consists "only" of computers and telecommunication links, it is more a complex artifact as a natural phenomenon. However, IF the Web – as we assume to be the case – consists of a few billions of networked computers AND *humans* THEN it may be studied as a *natural,* social, complex *phenomenon.*

The metaphor of autonomous Agents helps: these entities may abstract autonomous behavior in societies of communicating humans and machines. These evolving behaviors may be studied in order to understand and forecast interesting individual and collective phenomena [8].

We assume that individual and collective knowledge construction and exploitation such as those occurring on the Web are interesting social processes, contributing significantly to our understanding of intelligence. We are also convinced that intelligence is not "all or nothing" but may only be evaluated differentially. Finally, we are convinced of the important influence of mental states and personality traits [9] in human individual and collective intelligence.

Activities on the Web are traceable as it is the case of search in Google, interactions in social media but *also construction and search within the ViewpointS environment.* Inferences about proximity made by ViewpointS are possible; a personalized Knowledge Map (KM) may be measured against one more generic.

Therefore, we conjecture that ViewpointS-based interactions suitably traced, studied and exploited may usefully contribute to the progress of Web Science, in the above outlined sense of the science of complex sociotechnical systems including humans.

---

[8] Notice that in distributed systems with *no centralized control* the closed world assumption does not hold for each Agent so that even a set of distributed communicating artificial Agents may be considered a collection of *autonomous* entities that present emergent phenomena similar to the natural ones.

[9] Personality traits are long-term properties of humans. Mental states are on the contrary ephemeral, time-related. In this paper we only consider mental states as consequences of emotions, motivation, commitment, sentiment.

6   The availability of new ways to measure brain mental states and their relations to learning

The concepts developed by Claude Frasson and his group at the University of Montreal about "measurable mental states" indeed pave new ways to assess brain behavior during human-computer interactions, in particular during (formal) learning sessions. Many preliminary results are available (for instance: [18]) confirming that physiological measures may be taken with relative ease. These enable to understand and forecast emotions and mental states so that a suitable feedback process may modify the foreseen plan of the learning session in order to better fit the learner's mental state. However, as much as we are aware, no previous investigation was done on learning as a side effect of *free* interactions, i.e.: informal and serendipitous learning.

In free interactions, there is no "plan of the learning session" as there is no explicit intention to learn or to teach when exploring the information space available. Therefore, if measurable mental states are made available, the only possible effect they may have on the learner's behavior is in *modifying the Information space, in our context: KM*. In the following, we outline shortly how the interplay between KG and KM may enhance the availability of particular elements in the KM as they are considered more "proximal to the user in his/her particular mental state" thus eligible for navigation and the consequent learning effects.

7   Exploiting the mental states of the internauts when analyzing the serendipitous knowledge acquisition processes

In the ViewpointS approach, exploiting the Knowledge Map issued from the *viewpoints* stored in the KG is done by choosing *perspectives*, i.e. valuation rules for these *viewpoints* according to their types, dates, provenance etc. Each *perspective* may fit the current needs or curiosities of a user (who can be viewed as "perspective rider") and leads to a specific KM (Knowledge Map).

The construction of the KG as well as the KM are dynamic: interactions of other Agents may update the KG and each user Agent may regularly update his/her KM by applying a filtering process adopting a *perspective*.

For instance, one may filter *viewpoints* in the KG by provenance: give more weight to the ones attributed to notorious personalities (high reputation), or either attribute a weight inversely proportional to the emission time, introducing a kind of forgetting.

Assuming that both criteria in the example have been applied in a *perspective*, *synapses* in the KM will possibly be reinforced by the most recent viewpoints declared by the personalities with high reputation.

Hereafter some very preliminary description of *how* to link viewpoints to Serendipitous Learning enhancement:

Let us suppose we have means for characterizing the mental state of the Agents at any time they interact with the KG (construction) or with the KM (exploitation).

If we assess and store the mental state of the *viewpoints* emitters by means of typing each viewpoint with an "emotional valence in construction[10]" embedded in the 'θ' parameter outlined in Fig. 1: we can exhibit, through the mechanism of *perspective*, which knowledge paths (i.e.: paths in the KM, *synapses*) emerge when a specific emotional valence is selected within the producers (of knowledge).

This representation of the knowledge produced by a single Agent or a society of Agents not only may reflect the beliefs of these Agents about the world's elements proximities, but also their emotions (or mental states) at the moment they have produced the beliefs. The advantage with respect to traditional profiling or modeling the user's state is that these representations do not necessarily require any particular action by the Agents or by the designer of the experiment, rather they are a simple side effect of interacting with the environment.

Reversely, if we assess and store the mental state of the users by means of typing each *perspective* with an "emotional valence in exploitation": we can exhibit which knowledge paths = *synapses* have been followed when a specific emotional valence is selected within the users. Typing perspectives with an emotional valence implies that perspectives become first class resources. This information (*perspectives* defined by a user when exploiting the KG) – together with the *viewpoints* emitted by the user within KG – may represent a powerful, dynamic model of the user's state.

The description of the evolution of KG and KM along the time, for single Agents as well as communities of Agents, may be a rich source of inspiration in order to understand the cognitive state of humans, combining rational – the resources concretely visited - and emotional aspects (mental states).

8   Examples of analysis of learning by observing human-web interactions

Serendipitous is an adjective that usually is associated to learning. Learning is usually linked to a "positive" event: changing the person's state from a state of ignorance to a state of competence with respect to a concept or a skill.

In our vision, we postulate that learning may be also associated to the events occurring in the framework of other processes modifying significantly human Agents, not necessarily in a positive way.

We postulate that all the times the "state" of a person is substantially modified by interactions with the environment *and there is no explicit intentions by the person,* the event may be qualified as serendipitous learning, by associating to the word learning the neutral connotation of "substantial modification of the state of the person", in particular the cognitive or the mental state of the person.

We propose therefore the conjecture that serendipitous learning is crucial in many situations essentially because it represent a very wide class of non-voluntary modifications of the person's state induced by interactions. Three examples – among many

---

[10] As it was noticed before, we are not yet able to specify exactly what we mean by emotional valence: it denotes some classification of a mental state.

possible ones - that we consider not only important but also adequate for investigation consist of:

1. a positive one: *science discovery* [11] (learning-discovering a new concept without an explicit intention);
2. a neutral one: *political adhesion* (learning-acquiring a significant political conviction);
3. a negative one: *radicalism* (learning-acquiring a new positive attitude-emotion toward facts that are associated to crime in general, for instance: mafia or islamistic criminal actions).

For each of these situations, we envision to perform free navigation experiments within the ViewpointS environment augmented by traces of the mental state of Agents, during both the phases of construction of the Knowledge Graph and of exploitation of the Knowledge Map. Since by definition serendipitous learning is not dependent on a purpose neither by the learner nor by the learning environment, the only way to measure it will be to analyze the KM before and after navigation. Resources (Agents, Documents, Concepts) available to the user have a certain distance with the user-Agent considered as a resource. The distance may change after an interaction, so we may use the distance of a user-Agent to one or more resources as a measure of proximity that evolves with time according to the Agent's rational and emotional state.

Let us consider the case n. 2, perhaps the easiest one: political adhesion. Part of the learners will be changing their sentiment and adhere to a candidate or a party (distance with the candidate or the party's key concepts will be reduced), or vice-versa will change candidate or move to a state of non adhesion as a result of the monitored navigation (distance with the initial candidate or party will increase).

9   Conclusion

In this position paper we speculate about the opportunity offered by current physiological measures of emotions and mental states to enrich significantly the construction and exploitation of human cognitive models by adding the emotional dimension. Both construction and exploitation are described within a new context of Agent interaction called ViewpointS, where a single primitive: subjective proximity seems sufficient to unify the Semantic and the Social Web. The major advantage of such an enrichment consists of the fact that the construction and exploitation of brain-enhanced models should come at no *specific* modeling costs except the necessary apparatus for acquiring the physiological signals and is used within free navigation where serendipitous learning seems to be a well established phenomenon.

---

[11] https://en.wikipedia.org/wiki/Role_of_chance_in_scientific_discoveries

References

1. Carbonnel, J.R.: AI in CAI: An Artificial-Intelligence Approach to Computer-Assisted Instruction. IEEE Transactions on Man Machine Systems 11(4), 190 - 202 (1970)
2. Self, J.A.: Student models in computer-aided instruction. International Journal of Man-Machine Studies, 6 (2), 261-276 (1974)
3. Self, J.A.; Bypassing the Intractable Problem of Student Modelling. In Frasson, C., Gauthier, G. (eds.), Intelligent Tutoring Systems: at the Crossroads of Artificial Intelligence and Education, Norwood (N.J.): Ablex, pp. 107-123 (1990)
4. Sefton-Green, J.; Literature Review in Informal Learning with Technology Outside School. NESTA FUTURELAB, report 7, https://www.nfer.ac.uk/publications/FUTL72 last accessed 2017/04/15
5. Lemoisson, P., Surroca, G., Jonquet, C. and Cerri, S.A. ViewpointS: When Social Ranking Meets the Semantic Web. In: Rus, V. and Markov, Z. (eds) FLAIRS 2017 The 30th International FLAIRS Conference, AAAI Press, Marco Island, Florida, USA (2017)
6. Surroca, G., Lemoisson, P., Jonquet, C. and Cerri, S.A. Preference Dissemination by Sharing Viewpoints : Simulating Serendipity. In: Fred, A., Aveiro, D., Dietz, J., Filipe, J., Liu, K. (Eds.) Proceedings of the 7th International Joint Conference on Knowledge Discovery, Knowledge Engineering and Knowledge Management, Volume 2: KEOD, IC3K (2) pp. 402–409 Lisbon, Portugal. (2015)
7. Corneli, J., Pease, A., Colton, S., Jordanous, A., Guckelsberger, C . Modelling serendipity in a computational context. CoRR abs/1411.0440 (2014), https://arxiv.org/abs/1411.0440 last accessed 2017/04/15
8. Van Andel, P.: Anatomy of the Unsought Finding. Serendipity: Origin, History, Domains, Traditions, Appearances, Patterns and Programmability. The British Journal for the Philosophy of Science 45, 2, 631–648 (1994)
9. Rorschach tests, https://en.wikipedia.org/wiki/Rorschach_test , last accessed 2017/04/15
10. Castrogiovanni P., Maffei G., Pasquinucci P.J., Lijtmaer N., Torrigiani G., Cerri S.A., Zampolli A. : Analisi linguistica delle risposte al test di Rorschach di schizofrenici e neurotici e dei rispettivi familiari. I. - Metodologia e primi risultati di un'analisi condotta mediante elaboratori elettronici. Neopsichiatria 34(4), Arti Grafiche Pacini Mariotti, Pisa, Italy, 810-837 (1968)
11. Personality Traits, https://en.wikipedia.org/wiki/Big_Five_personality_traits, last accessed 2017/04/15
12. Nunes, M.A.S.N., Cerri,S.A., Blanc,N. : Improving Recommendations by Using Personality Traits in User Profiles. International Conferences on Knowledge Management and New Media Technology, Graz, Austria, 92-100, (2008)
13. Principles of grouping or Gestalt laws of grouping, https://en.wikipedia.org/wiki/Principles_of_grouping , last accessed 2017/04/15
14. Edelman, G. Neural Darwinism: The theory of neuronal group selection. Basic Books, New York (1987)
15. VygotskyZPD, https://en.wikipedia.org/wiki/Zone_of_proximal_development last accessed 2017/04/15
16. Web Science, http://www.webscience.org/manifesto/ last accessed 2017/04/15
17. Popper, K .; Conjectures and Refutations. The Growth of Scientific Knowledge. Basic Books, New York (1962)
18. Chaouachi, M., Jraidi, I., Frasson, C.: Adapting to Learners' Mental States Using a Physiological Computing Approach. FLAIRS 2015, The 28th International FLAIRS Conference, AAAI Press, Hollywood, Florida, USA (2015)

Online Brain Training Programs for Healthy Older Individuals

Blanka Klimova

University of Hradec Kralove, Rokitanskeho 62, Hradec Kralove, Czech Republic
blanka.klimova@uhk.cz

Abstract. At present, there is a growing number of older population groups worldwide, which results in serious social and economic issues since some of these older people require special care. Therefore there is constant effort to maintain these older people active as long as possible. This might be done not only by pharmacological therapies, but especially by non-pharmacological approaches, among which brain training with the help of a computer seems a good solution. The purpose of this article is to explore available clinical studies implementing computer-based brain training programs as intervention tools in the prevention and delay of cognitive decline in aging, with special focus on their effectiveness. This was done by conducting a literature search in the databases Web of Science, Scopus, MEDLINE and ScienceDirect, and consequently by comparing and evaluating the findings of the selected studies. The findings show that that the exploited online brain (cognitive) training programs usually have a moderate positive effect on the delay of cognitive decline especially in the area of reasoning skills, working memory, and processing.

Keywords: brain training; computer; older people; randomized clinical trials; effectiveness

1   Introduction

At present, there is a growing number of older population groups worldwide. In 2000 the percentage of older individuals aged 65+ years reached 12.4%. In 2030, this number should rise to 19% and in 2050 to 22%. [1]. In Europe this population group aged 65+ represent 18% of the 503 million Europeans, which should almost double by 2060. [2] Aging is connected with a gradual decline of physical and mental activities. Therefore there is constant effort to maintain older people active as long as possible, improve the quality of their life [3-5] and enable them to stay socially and economically independent. [6] This might be done not only by pharmacological therapies, but especially by non-pharmacological approaches, among which brain training with the help of a computer seems a good solution since it can possibly delay a gradual decline of older people's cognitive functions such as processing speed, attention, working memory, or executive functions. [7]

Most recently, with the penetration of technologies in all spheres of human activities, technological devices have started to play a significant role in brain training since such training can be done at any time and accessed from anywhere. In addition, it can be personalized to people's own needs. [8-10] This approach is also more cost-

© Springer International Publishing AG 2017
C. Frasson and G. Kostopoulos (Eds.): BFAL 2017, LNAI 10512, pp. 48–56, 2017
DOI: 10.1007/978-3-319-67615-9_4

effective since people can do it at home. And such training programs can be more easily disseminated among a wide range of people. [6] Furthermore, research studies [11-12] have proved that older people in their 60s and 70s are nowadays much more digitally aware than they were ten years ago. Kueider et al. [13] also note that older people do not have to be necessarily technologically savvy to benefit from computer-based training programs.

Generally, there are three approaches to improve cognitive functions with the help of a computer and brain training programs are one of them. [14] The brain training programs are predominantly aimed at the enhancement of the speed and accuracy of perceptual processes, improved attention, episodic memory, executive function, reasoning, speech and language, or visual-spatial skills. Currently, there are five established brain training applications: Elevate – a cognitive training tool to build communication and analytical skills, [15] Lumosity – a series of online games that is targeted at the improvement of memory, speed, problem solving, attention, flexibility, which may help with remembering names and driving better, [16] Fit Brains – an application which focuses on the enhancement of mental performance through games and has a similar effect as Lumosity, [17] Brain HQ developed by Posit Science company, providing a series of training exercises, which can improve the ability to process visual scenes, working memory or cognitive flexibility, [18] and Brain workshop – an application which aims at the improvement of the short-term memory and fluid intelligence. [19] All these brain training programs are commercial and there has not been much academic research done on them to prove their efficacy independently on the companies which created them. In fact, there are just a few studies who have explored the issue of computer-based or online brain training programs.

Therefore, the purpose of this article is to explore available clinical studies implementing computer-based brain training programs as intervention tools in the prevention and delay of cognitive decline in aging, with special focus on their effectiveness.

2   Methods

The methodology of this review article based on [20] the method of a literature review of available sources on the research topic in the world's acknowledged databases Web of Science, Scopus, MEDLINE and ScienceDirect with special focus on clinical studies dating back to the period of 2015 until April of 2017. Nevertheless, older studies were also disucessed in order to compare and evaluate the findings from the selected studies and introduce the research topic. The search was based on the key words: *online brain training* AND *healthy aging*, *computer-based brain training* AND *healthy aging*. The period was limited to these recent years since several reviews on this topic had been written before. [21-22]

Majority of the studies were found in ScienceDirect – 7,514 studies. In the Web of Science only 12 studies were detected, in Scopus 3 studies and in MEDLINE 5 studies were identified. Thus, altogether 7,534 publications were detected in the databases. The titles of all studies as well as their duplicity were then checked in order to discover whether they focus on the research topic. 76 studies remained for further analysis. After that, the author checked the content of the abstracts whether the study examined the research topic. 35 studies/articles were selected for the full-text analysis, out of which the findings of 26 research studies were then used in the manuscript for the comparison of the findings in the part of Discussion, as well as in the Introductory part to discuss the topic, and only five studies could have been then used for the detailed analysis of the research topic.

The study was included if it matched the corresponding period, i.e., from 2015 up to April 2017; if it included healthy older individuals; if it focused on the research topic, i.e., on the use of online brain training programs for the delay of cognitive decline; and if the study was a clinical study, i.e., an intervention study or a randomized controlled trial; and if it was written in English. Therefore the studies, which included only people with mild cognitive impairment or dementia such as [23-24] or those who were outside the set covered period such as [25-26].

3   Results

Altogether five clinical studies were eventually included. Four studies were randomized controlled trials; three had active control groups [27-28, 31], one study a passive control, [29], and one study did not have any control group. [30] In all cases the brain/ cognitive intervention was delivered online. The main outcome measures consisted of a battery of tests such as the Wechsler Adult Intelligence Scale, Fourth Edition, or self-reported instrumental activities of daily living (IADL) test, or Swinburne University Computerized Cognitive Aging Battery. At the beginning participants were usually screened for dementia or other neurodegenerative diseases or depression with the help of the Mini Mental State Examination. The findings of these studies are summarized in Table 1 below according to the alphabetical order of their first author.

Table 1. Overview of the clinical studies exploring online brain training among healthy older adults

Study	Type of intervention	No. of subjects	Trial period	Findings	Limitations
Corbett et al. [27]	Cognitive training program, active control group	2,192 older subjects; mean age 65	Six months	Improved cognition, particularly the reasoning skills, which was evident already from week six.	Only people with computer access were included into the trial; people with higher levels of education; retention strategies need to be improved.
Murphy et al. [28]	Positive Imagery Training intervention active control group	77 older individuals; aged 60-80 years	four weeks (12 sessions)	Decreased negative affect and trait anxiety, and increased optimism across the three assessments.	A relatively small sample of the participants; a very short intervention period; methodology
Vaportzis et al. [29]	Tablet computer training intervention, passive control group	22 healthy older adults; aged 65-76 years	10 weeks	Participants in the intervention group improved their processing speed.	A small sample size; a short-term period; passive control group; prior computer experience.
Vermeij et al. [30]	Commercial working memory (WM) cognitive computerised programme (Cogmed) no control group	23 healthy older adults (mean age: 70.1 + 5.4); 18 patients with mild cognitive impairment (MCI) – (mean age: 68.4 + 6.3)	five weeks (25 sessions)	WM training may enhance WM performance and even induce improvement of WM processes that are impaired in MC. Participants also improved on figural fluency at group level, but not at individual level.	No untrained control group; a small sample size; a short-term period; limited statistical power; the study focused only on WM domain.
Walton et	Cognitive training	28 healthy older sub-	28 days	Improved performance in	A lack of the follow up

adfa, p. 4, 2011.
© Springer-Verlag Berlin Heidelberg 2011

al. [31]	program, active control group	jects (mean age 64.18)		multiple measures of processing speed; visual working memory can be enhanced over a short period of computerized cognitive training.	assessment; a small sample size; a short-term period.

Source: author's own processing

4 Discussion

The findings of this study show that the exploited online brain (cognitive) training programs usually have a moderate positive effect on the delay of cognitive decline especially in the area of reasoning skills which are needed for solving issues in their daily lives [27], working memory which reflects older people's capacity to retrieve and process new information, [30] and processing speed influencing daily life activities of older people. [29, 31] In addition, the findings indicate that computerized cognitive training may positively affect older people's behavior such as anxiety or mood. [28] Corbett et al. [27] and Vermeij et al. argue that online cognitive training is effective and feasible not only for healthy older individuals, but also for MCI patients. Kueider, Bichay, and Rebok [32] summarize the main benefits of cognitive trainings as follows: enhancement of cognitive abilities; healthcare costs cuts; non-invasive approach. However, they also claim that the cognitive training is mainly effective if it is targeted at multiple cognitive strategies.

As research [29] confirms it is the speed which is usually affected in early stages of aging and has an enormous impact on performing cognitive and motor skills. The results of this study indicate that through a relevant online training intervention with the help of a computer or a tablet, this processing speed may be enhanced. [29, 31] This has been also revealed by an Australian study [33] in which the Brain Fitness Program was implemented. The findings then showed that this program especially had contributed to the improved attention and concentration.

As far as the memory is concerned, the results from the reviewed studies indicate that working memory may be improved, however, only near transfer effects to other cognitive domains have been detected. Therefore there is no clear evidence for generalisations other than for working memory. [30-31] These outcomes have been also observed in a longitudinal clinical study by Rebok et al. [34] who claim that it is especially reasoning and speed, not memory, which result in improved targeted cognitive abilities for 10 years.

Furthermore, the findings indicate that older people are open to such online cognitive training programs since they can also meet their peers. For example, Rabipour and Davidson [35] report that compared to young adults, older individuals are far more optimistic about the brain training.

Recently, Zelinski and Reyes [36] have suggested that specific cognitive abilities such as memory or organizational skills might be improved through digital games whose mechanics can produce the experiences of presence, engagement, and flow, the subjective elements of game play that may keep interest and emotional investment in the skills practiced so that the play produces cognitive benefits.

The limitations of this study consists in a lack of studies on this topic and different methodologies, e.g., not all the studies were randomized controlled trials. Moreover, most of the analyzed studies except one [27] were short termed and contained a small number of subjects. According to Kurz and van Baelen [37], the intervention period should last 24 weeks at minimum. All these facts may affect the described findings.

5   Conclusion

Although the results of this review study indicate a positive effect of online brain training programs on the delay of cognitive decline, they must be treated with caution because they were predominantly short termed with small subject samples. Therefore more longitudinal clinical studies should be conducted to prove efficacy of these online brain training programs.

Acknowledgments

This review study is supported by SPEV project 2017/18 run at the Faculty of Informatics and Management, University of Hradec Kralove, Czech Republic. The author especially thanks Josef Toman for his help with data processing.

References

[1] Transgenerational Design Matters. (2009). Retrieved from
     http://transgenerational.org/aging/demographics.htm
[2] Patterson, I. Growing older. Tourism and leisure behaviour of older adults. Cambridge:
     Cabi (2006).
[3] Klimova, B., Kuca, K. Alzheimer's disease: Potential preventive, non-invasive, interven-
     tion strategies in lowering the risk of cognitive decline – A review study. J Appl Biomed
     13(4) (2015) 257-261
[4] Klimova, B., Maresova, P., Kuca, K. Non-pharmacological approaches to the prevention
     and treatment of Alzheimer's disease with respect to the rising treatment costs. Curr Alz-
     heimer Res 13(11) (2016) 1249-1258
[5] Klimova, B., Maresova, P., Valis, M., Hort, J., Kuca, K. Alzheimer's disease and language
     impairments: Social intervention and medical treatment. Clinical Interventions in Aging
     10 (2015) 1401-1408
[6] Klimova, B., Maresova, P. Elderly people and their attitude towards mobile phones and
     their applications – A Review Study. LNEE, 393 (2016) 31-36
[7] Naismith, S.L., Diamond, K., Carter P.E., Norrie, L.M., Redoblado-Hodge, M.A., Lewis,
     S.J.G., Hickie, I.B. Enhancing memory in late-life depression: The effects of a combined
     psychoeducation and cognitive training program. Am J Geriatr Psychiatry 19 (2011) 240-
     248
[8] Klimova, B., Simonova, I., Poulova, P., Truhlarova, Z., Kuca, K. Older people and their
     attitude to the use of information and communication technologies – a review study with
     special focus on the Czech Republic (Older people and their attitude to ICT). Educational
     Gerontology (2016) doi: 10.1080/03601277.2015.1122447
[9] Klimova, B., Maresova, P., Kuca, K. Assistive technologies in managing language disor-
     ders in dementia. Neuropsychiatr. Dis Treat 12 (2016) 533-540
[10] Maresova, P., Klimova, B. Supporting technologies for old people with dementia: a re-
     view. 13th IFAC and IEEE Conference on Programmable Devices and Embedded Systems
     — PDES. Poland: Cracow (2015) 129-134
[11] Hernandez-Encuentra, E., Pousada, M., Gomez-Zuniga, B. ICT and older people: Beyond
     usability. Educational Gerontology 35(3) (2009) 226-245

[12] Sayago, S., Sloan, D., Blat, J. Everyday use of computer-mediated communication tools and its evolution over time: an ethnographical study with older people. Interacting with Computers 23 (2011) 543-55

[13] Kueider, A.M., Parisi, J.M., Gross, A.L., Rebok, G.W. Computerized cognitive training with older adults: a systematic review. PLoS ONE 7(7) (2012) e40588

[14] Boot, W.R., Kramer, A.F. The brain-games conundrum: does cognitive training really sharpen the mind? 2014. (2014) Retrieved from: http://www.dana.org/Cerebrum/2014/The_Brain-Games_Conundrum__Does_Cognitive_Training_Really_Sharpen_the_Mind_/#sthash.affodbe5.dpuf

[15] Elevate. (2014) Retrieved from: https://www.elevateapp.com/#/about

[16] Lumosity. Retrieved from: http://www.lumosity.com/about

[17] Fit Brains. Retrieved from: http://www.fitbrains.com/

[18] Brain training. Retrieved from: http://www.brainhq.com/#

[19] Brain Workshop. Retrieved from: http://brainworkshop.sourceforge.net/

[20] Moher, D., Liberati, A., Tetzlaff, J., Altman, D.G. The PRISMA Group. Preferred reporting items for systematic review and meta-analysis: the PRISMA statement. PLoS Med 6(6) (2009) e1000097

[21] Kueider, A.M., Parisi, J.M., Gross, A.L., Rebok, G.W. Computerized cognitive training with older adults: a systematic review. PLoS ONE 7(7) (2012) e40588

[22] Lampit, A., Hallock, H., Valenzuela, M. Computerized cognitive training in cognitively healthy older adults: a systematic review and meta-analysis of effect modifiers. PLoS Med 11(11) (2014) e1001756

[23] Hyer, L., Scott, C., Atkinson, M.M., Mullen, C.M., Lee, A., Johnson, A., et al. Cognitive training program to improve working memory in older adults with MCI. Clinical Gerontologist (2016) doi: 10.1080/07317115.2015.1120257.

[24] Flak, M.M., Hernes, S., Skranes, J., Lohaugen, G.C.C. The Memory Aid study: protocol for a randomized controlled clinical trial evaluating the effect of computer-based working memory training in elderly patients with mild cognitive impairment (MCI). Trials 15 (2014) PMC4016674.

[25] Bozoki, A., Radovanovic, M., Winn, B., Heeter, C., Anthony, J.C. Effects of a computer-based cognitive exercise program on age-related cognitive decline. Arch. Gerontol. Geriatr. 57(1) (2013) 1-7.

[26] McAvinue, L.P., Golemme, M., Castorina, M., Tatti, E., Pigni, F.M., Salomone, S., et al. An evaluation of a working memory training scheme in older adults. Front. Aging Neurosci. 5 (2013) 20.

[27] Corbett, A., Owen, A., Hampshire, A., Grahn, J., Stenton, R., Dajani, S., et al. The effect of an online cognitive training package in healthy older adults: an online randomized controlled trial. JAMDA 16(11) (2015) 990-997

[28] Murphy, S.E., O'Donoghue, C.M., Drazich, E.H., Blackwell, S.E., Nobre, C.A., Holmes, E.A. Imagining a brighter future: The effect of positive imagery training on mood, prospective mental imagery and emotional bias in older adults. Psychiatry Res 230(1) (2015) 36-43.

[29] Vaportzis, E., Martin, M., Gow, A.J. A tablet for healthy ageing: The effects of a tablet computer training intervention on cognitive abilities in older adults. Am J Geriatr Psychiatry S1064-7481(16) (2016) 30319-0

[30] Vermeij, A., Claassen, J.A.H.R., Dautzenberg, P.L.J., Kessels, R.P.C. Transfer and maintenance affects of online working-memory training in normal ageing and mild cognitive impairment. Neuropsychological Rehabilitation 26(5-6) (2016) 783-809.

[31] Walton, C., Kavanagh, A., Downey, L.A., Lomas, J., Camfield, D.A., Stough, C. Online cognitive training in healthy older adults: a preliminary study on the effects of single versus multi-domain training. Translation Neuroscience 6 (2015) 13-19

[32] Kueider, A., Bichay, K., Rebok, G. Cognitive training for older adults: What is it and does it work? (2014). Retrieved from http://www.air.org/sites/default/files/downloads/report/Cognitive%20Training%20for%20 Older%20Adults_Nov%2014.pdf

[33] Walker, J.E., Thompson, K.E., Oliver, A.I. Maintaining cognitive health in older adults: Australians' experience of targeted computer-based training, using the brain fitness program. Physical & Occupational Therapy in Geriatrics 32(4) (2014) 397-413.

[34] Rebok, G.W. Ten-year effects of the ACTIVE cognitive training trial on cognition and everyday functioning in older adults. J Am Geriatr Soc 62(1) (2014) 16–24.

[35] Rabipour, S., Davidson, P.S.R. Do you believe in brain training? A questionnaire about expectations of computerized cognitive training. Behavioural Brain Research 295 (2015) 64-70.

[36] Zelinski, E.M., Reyes, R. Cognitive benefits of computer games for older adults. Gerontechnology 8(4) (2009) 220-235

[37] Kurz, A., van Baelen, B. Ginkgo biloba compared with cholinesterase Inhibitors in the treatment of dementia: a review based on meta-analyses by the Cochrane collaboration. Dement Geriatr Cogn Disord 18 (2004) 217–226.

Evaluating Active Learning Methods for Bankruptcy Prediction

Georgios Kostopoulos[1], Stamatis Karlos[1], Sotiris Kotsiantis[1] and Vassilis Tampakas[2]

[1]Educational Software Development Laboratory (ESDLab)
Department of Mathematics, University of Patras, Greece
[2]Technological Educational Institute of Western Greece
Department of Computer Engineering Informatics
kostg@sch.gr, stkarlos@upatras.gr,sotos@math.upatras.gr,
vtampakas@teimes.gr

Abstract. The prediction of corporate bankruptcy has been addressed as an increasingly important financial problem and has been extensively analyzed in the accounting literature. Over recent years, several machine learning methods have been effectively applied to build accurate predictive models for detecting business failure with remarkable results, such as neural networks (NNs) and ensemble methods. This paper investigates the effectiveness of the active learning framework to predict bankruptcy using financial data from a set of Greek firms. Active learning is an emerging subfield of machine learning exploiting a small amount of labeled data together with a large pool of unlabeled data to improve learning accuracy. From what we know so far there exists no study dealing with the implementation of active learning methodologies in the financial field. Several experiments take place in our research comparing the accuracy measures of familiar active learners and demonstrating their efficiency in contrast to representative supervised methods.

Keywords: Bankruptcy prediction, pool-based active learning, margin sampling query, unlabeled data.

1   Introduction

Corporate bankruptcy has been identified as an important financial problem and a well-studied task as reported in the accounting literature. The accurate identification of business failure, which is defined as the inability of a firm to repay its financial obligations [4] is vital for both investors and creditors. Moreover, banks and credit institutions are interested in quantifying the financial risk of a firm in a timely manner before they expand a loan [8].

Several approaches have been originally proposed for the prediction of corporate bankruptcy such as structural approach and statistical or empirical approach [3]. One of the most widely used statistical tools for bankruptcy risk analysis is the Multivariate Discriminant Analysis (MDA). Altman [2] was the first to adopt MDA for classifying firms into two classes, healthy and bankrupt, under the assumption that the two

© Springer International Publishing AG 2017
C. Frasson and G. Kostopoulos (Eds.): BFAL 2017, LNAI 10512, pp. 57–66, 2017
DOI: 10.1007/978-3-319-67615-9_5

classes are normally distributed with equal covariance matrices. A series of studies carried out later applying the MDA approach to predict bankruptcy with promising results. Odom & Sharda [24] compared the predictive accuracy of neural networks (NNs) and MDA in bankruptcy risk prediction, concluding that NNs performed better, since they are not subject to the normality limitation of variables. Following this, many studies have shown that NNs considerably outweigh classical statistical methods in terms of prediction accuracy [32, 34, 37]. Over the last few decades, a number of rewarding studies have been carried out leading to the implementation of several machine learning techniques for the prediction of the bankruptcy filing, while examining the factors influencing this phenomenon.

This paper investigates the effectiveness of the active learning methodology to predict corporate bankruptcy using financial data from a set of Greek firms. Active learning is an emerging subfield of machine learning exploiting a small amount of labeled data together with a large pool of unlabeled data to improve learning accuracy. Several experiments take place in our research comparing the accuracy measures of familiar active learners and demonstrating their efficiency in contrast to representative supervised methods. To the best of our knowledge there exists no study dealing with the implementation of active learning methodologies for the prediction of firms at risk, so this study is considered to be an initial step in this direction.

The rest of the paper is organized as follows: Section 2 provides a short review of studies dealing with the implementation of machine learning techniques to predict corporate bankruptcy. Section 3 presents the central points of the active learning theory, while section 4 provides a description of the dataset and the main study questions. In section 5 we present the experiments that were conducted, the results obtained and a thorough analysis of these results. Finally, the paper concludes by summarizing the main aspects of the current study and considering some thoughts for future research.

2   Literature Review

In recent years, a number of considerable studies examine the effectiveness of machine learning techniques to detect firms at risk using predictive models based on several quantitative and qualitative financial variables. NNs have been widely applied for this purpose, since they can effectively detect non-linear relationships and are robust to noisy examples [1]. Several ensemble methods have also emerged recently with promising results.

Deligianni and Kotsiantis [8] applied a set of supervised algorithms for the prediction of corporate bankruptcy. Moreover, they implemented an ensemble of classifiers based on RIPPER, a well-known rule-based algorithm, and Naïve Bayes (NB) classifier, since they prevailed in predicting the true positive bankrupt and non-bankrupt cases respectively. Most importantly, the prediction was made in a good time before the final bankruptcy. Karlos et al. [17] examined the effectiveness of Semi-Supervised Learning (SSL) methods on bankruptcy prediction using data from Greek firms. Familiar algorithms from KEEL [35] were tested using several financial ratio variables. The results were encouraging compared to well-known supervised algorithms. The Rel-RASCO algorithm with a C4.5 decision tree as base learner prevailed over the rest algorithms with an accuracy measure of 67.47% one year before the bankruptcy filing. Jardin [9] showed that the accuracy of a classifier can significantly be improved when the horizon of the corporate bankruptcy prediction is at least three years. Moreover, he introduced an additional step during an ensemble-based modeling process, in which the decision space is divided into subspaces that are subsequently re-divided into smaller ones where each rule is designed to fit. Finally, he proposed a promising time-modelling technique. Jones et al. [16] examined the performance of 16 classifiers for corporate bankruptcy prediction using a 27-year period sample of US corporate bankruptcy data. The classifiers were tested on several variations of the dataset involving cross-sectional and longitudinal test samples. AdaBoost, generalized boosting and Random Forests (RF) outperformed other advanced methods, such as NNs, Support Vector Machines (SVMs) and Linear Discriminant Analysis (LDA) using the ROC curve analysis and H scores. In the same context, Barboza et al. [5] evaluated the performance of SVMs, RF, bagging and boosting to predict bankruptcy one year prior to the event using data regarding North American firms from year 1985 to 2013. Moreover, they made use of new variables, such as operating margin, change in return-on-equity, change in price-to-book and growth measures related to assets, sales and number of employees. Mselmi et al. [22] aimed to predict the financial distress of French firms applying SVMs, Partial Least Squares (PLS), Artificial NNs and Logit model. The dataset used contained information about 106 distressed and 106 non-distressed firms for the accounting years 2010-2012. A hybrid method integrating SVMs with PLS was introduced with an overall accuracy of 94.28% in the case of two years prior to financial distress.

It is evident that machine learning models show improved bankruptcy prediction accuracy over traditional statistic techniques [5], such as MDA and logistic regression (LR). A thorough analysis of the studies concerning the financial field reveals that several supervised methods have been effectively applied for the business failure detection, but none of them employs active learning methods.

3 Active Learning

Learning predictive models from both labeled and unlabeled data has been the researchers' top concern in the past decade. In many scientific fields, unlabeled examples are abundant, while labeled examples are limited and it is hard to obtain. Moreover, labeling examples is difficult and costly, since it requires a lot of effort and experts. SSL and active learning constitute two growing subfields of machine learning trying to effectively combine a small set of labeled data along with a large set of unlabeled ones to improve performance [39] aiming to build accurate models with the minimum number of labeled examples at the least cost [18].

In active learning the model chooses the instances from which it learns posing queries. Specifically, the model carefully selects which unlabeled instances will be labeled and asks from a human expert (oracle) the labels of these instances [10]. The key point in active learning is to build a high accuracy classifier without making too many queries using a small labeled training set [7]. Three major scenarios have been applied for querying the label of an instance: Pool-based sampling, stream-based selective sampling and membership query synthesis [29]. In stream-based sampling, an unlabeled instance is sampled and the learner decides whether to query it or not in accordance to a query strategy, while in membership query, the learner may request the label for any instance in the input space generating a query de novo. In the present study we adopt the pool-based active learning scenario, one of the most commonly used and well-studied active learning scenarios. Given a small set of labeled instances L and a large set of unlabeled instances U, the active learner selects one or more examples from U and asks from an oracle to label them. The L is augmented with these examples and the process is repeated until a stopping criterion is met [27].

Several techniques have been proposed to select the most informative instances for labeling [15] to decrease the amount of labeling requests [36], which are defined as active learning strategies [33]. Uncertainty sampling, random sampling and query by committee (QBC) [27] have been effectively applied in various active learning problems. Uncertainty sampling is the most frequently utilized strategy querying the labels for instances about which the model is most uncertain, mainly for two reasons: there is insufficient evidence for the output classes, there is strong but conflicting evidence for either output class. For binary classification margin sampling query is the most popular strategy [31], while entropy sampling is appropriate for multiclass classification problems. The key issue in uncertainty sampling is the method employed to measure the uncertainty of the model. It is worth noting that this method is vulnerable to noisy examples and outliers [30] and often outweighs random sampling [27]. In random sampling, instances are randomly selected from the unlabeled pool U. Even though it is a simple strategy, it has shown impressive results in relation to other sampling strategies [27]. In the QBC strategy, a set of classifiers is formed and selects the instances on which the committee disagree the most using bagging on L [21]. The disagreement between committee classifiers is usually measured using vote entropy, margin of disagreement or average Kullback-Leibler (KL) divergence [27]. The pseudo-code description of a pool-based active learning scenario using uncertainty as sampling strategy is shown in Algorithm 1.

Algorithm 1. Pool-based Active Learning with Uncertainty Sampling

---
Input: labeled dataset L, unlabeled dataset U.
1. Initially, apply base learner B to the training dataset L to obtain classifier C.
2. Repeat until U is empty or until some stopping criterion is met:
3.   Apply C to unlabeled dataset U.
4.   From U, select m instances for which C is most uncertain.
5.   Ask the teacher for labels of the m instances.
6.   Add the m labeled instances to L.
7.   Re-train on L to obtain a new classifier, C.
8. Output the classifier that is trained on L.

---

4   Study Questions and Dataset Description

The main research question of this paper is to assess the performance of active learning techniques for predicting corporate bankruptcy. Moreover, we seek to investigate if such a prediction could be done in a timely manner. The dataset used for our study was provided from the National Bank of Greece and the International Carbon Action Partnership (ICAP) in Greece. For a time period of three years (2003-2005) financial data of 145 individual firms were collected covering the periods one to three years before the bankruptcy. 49 firms correspond to bankruptcy cases, while the rest 96 correspond to non-bankruptcy. A total of 435 instances part three datasets, one dataset per year. More specifically, the dataset "Year -i", i=1,2,3 corresponds to data gathered i years before the bankruptcy filing.

Table 1. Dataset Variables

Variable	Description
GRTA	Growth Rate of Total Assets
GRNI	Growth Rate of Net Income
SIZE	Size of firm
GIMAR	Gross Income divided by Sales
S/CE	Sales divided by Capital Employed
S/EQ	Sales divided by Shareholder's Equity
CE/NFA	Capital Employed to Net Fixed Assets
TD/EQ	Total Debt to Shareholder's Equity
EQ/CE	Shareholder's Equity to Capital Employed
WC/TA	Working Capital divided by Total Assets
COLPER	Average Collection Period for receivables
PAYPER	Average Payment Period to creditors
INVTURN	Inventory Turnover Ratio

Each dataset instance is characterized by the values of representative quantitative variables (Table 1) and corresponds to an individual firm. 13 familiar financial and economic ratios were used as inputs, while variables GRTA, GRNI are not included in the dataset "Year -3". The values of each variable have been divided into three intervals (<a, [a,b], >b). A short description of the variables used is given below [13]:

Growth Rate of Total Assets is calculating as GRTA=$(TA_t-TA_{t-1})/TA_{t-1}$ and shows the ratio change in the total assets of a company over a year. Growth Rate of Net Income (GRNI) ratio refers to the percentage change in the profits of a company over a year. The size of a firm (SIZE) is calculating as ln(TA/GDP price index). Gross Profit Margin (GIMAR) is a metric for assessing a company's financial stability and health and is calculated by dividing a company's gross income by its net sales. Sales to Capital Employed (S/CE) ratio is used to measure the potential of a business to generate sales revenue by utilizing its assets. Sales to Equity (S/EQ) ratio shows the amount of equity required from a company to generate sales. CE/NFA metric is calculated by dividing the Capital Employed by Net Fixed Assets. Total Debt to Shareholder's Equity (TD/EQ) ratio measures the financial leverage of a company and is calculated by dividing the company's total liabilities by its shareholders' equity. EQ/CE metric is calculated by dividing the Shareholder's Equity by the Capital Employed. Working Capital to Total Assets (WC/TA) is a metric evaluating the liquidity level of a company and is calculated by dividing a company's net working capital by its net total assets. Average Collection Period for receivables (COLPER) is the time that it takes for a company to convert receivables into cash. Average Payment Period to creditors (PAYPER) is an indicator measuring the average time (in days) taken by a company in making payments to its creditors. Inventory Turnover Ratio or Inventory Turns (INVTURN) shows how many times a company's inventory is sold and replaced over a period of time (usually a year), and is calculated by dividing a company's sales by the average inventory. The output nominal variable "Bankrupt" is used to classify firms in two distinct groups: bankrupt and non-bankrupt.

5   Experimental Setup and Results

Initially, the dataset was partitioned randomly into 10 folds of similar size using the cross validation procedure. One fold was kept to evaluate the predictive effectiveness of the model, while the rest 9 folds were used for the training process. In each fold, 6 instances of the training set formed the labeled set and the rest 124 formed the unlabeled set. A Pool-based sampling scenario with the margin sampling query strategy was used. We have defined a maximum number of 30 iterations as a stopping criterion, while we selected a single example for labeling at each of the iterations. On this basis, at the end of the learning process there were 36 labeled instances.

A set of five familiar classification algorithms from Weka [38] were used as base classifiers to form five respective active learners. These classifiers are: Bayes Net [25], representative of the Bayesian Networks, Logistic Regression (LR) [23], Multilayer Perceptrons (MLPs) [12], representative of NNs, Random Forest (RF) [6], a collection of tree-structured classifiers and Sequential Minimal Optimization (SMO) [26], a very effective SVMs algorithm.

The experiments were carried out in three steps using the JCLAL (Java Class Library for Active Learning) tool [28], an open source software appropriate for implementing common active learning strategies and integrating new developed ones. The 1st step includes 11 variables related to financial data of firms collected three years before the bankruptcy filing (Year -3). In the 2nd and 3rd step, variables GRTA and GRNI are added along with new information regarding the firms.

Table 2. Correctly Classified Instances (%) of Active Learners

Base Classifier	SMO	LR	MLPs	RF	Bayes Net
Year -3	66.57	60.05	66.29	67.62	66.86
Year -2	68.24	61.62	63.38	68.90	67.43
Year -1	70.14	72.29	66.71	70.19	68.19

In each step we measure the accuracy of active learners, which corresponds to the percentage of the correctly classified instances (Table 2). The experimental results indicate that the active learner using RF as base classifier takes precedence over the others, three and two years before the bankruptcy filing, with an accuracy measure ranging from 67.62% to 68.90%. In the final step, one year prior to the bankruptcy filing, the percentage of correctly classified instances exceeds 70% for three active learners using RF, SMO and LR as base classifiers, indicating that we can predict bankruptcy with sufficient accuracy.

Since the existing studies were principally implemented supervised methods, we compare the above mentioned active learners to their corresponding supervised algorithms. In supervised learning, all available data are used to train a classifier for the prediction of any incoming example. Table 3 presents the accuracy measures of these algorithms in each one of the three steps. In this case, three years before the bankruptcy filing LR and RF measure an accuracy of 66.20% and 65.50% respectively. One year later, LR and Bayes Net accuracy is 63.40%. Finally, RF prevails with 67.60% accuracy one year before the bankruptcy event.

Table 3. Correctly Classified Instances (%) of Supervised Algorithms

Algorithm	SMO	LR	MLPs	RF	Bayes Net
Year -3	62.80	66.20	60.00	65.50	62.10
Year -2	60.00	63.40	59.30	62.10	63.40
Year -1	62.80	61.40	56.60	67.60	62.10

Table 4. Friedman Aligned Ranks Test (significance level of 0.05)

Algorithm	Rank
Active Learner (RF)	4.33
Active Learner (SMO)	7.00
Active Learner (Bayes Net)	7.67
Active Learner (MLPs)	14.33
RF	15.33
Active Learner (LR)	16.00
LR	18.50
Bayes Net	20.83
SMO	22.33
MLPs	28.67

We evaluate the performance of the above active learners and supervised algorithms using the Friedman Aligned Ranks nonparametric test [14]. According to the test results (Table 4) the algorithms are ranking from the best performer to the lower one. All the active learners, except the one with LR as base classifier, are comparatively better than the supervised ones showing that active learning can be successfully applied to predict the bankruptcy potential of firms.

Table 5. AUC (RF base classifier)

Step	Year -3	Year -2	Year -1
Area	62.363	66.240	65.259

Regarding the active learner using RF as base classifier, and for each one of the three steps of the experiments we present a graph (Figure 1) illustrating the accuracy percentage rate related to the number of labeled instances during the iterative learning process and measure the area (Table 5) bounded by the accuracy curve and the x-axis

(AUC). AUC is a commonly used metric to evaluate the performance of a binary classifier [20].

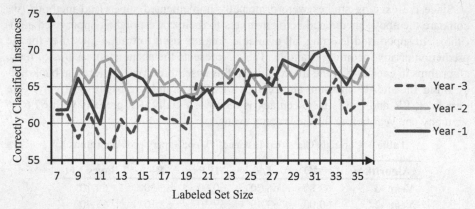

Fig. 1. AUC (Active learner with RF base classifier)

6   Conclusions

In this study, we assess several active learning algorithms for corporate bankruptcy prediction, using data from 146 Greek firms over a three year period time. Corporate bankruptcy is a financial phenomenon that has been extensively analyzed in the accounting literature over the last few decades. The accurate detection of failing firms has been an important research topic for financial institutions and is of a great concern to investors and creditors. Several statistical and machine learning models have been employed for financial distress prediction [11].

A number of experiments were conducted using several active learners and measuring the percentage of correctly classified instances in predicting firms' failure. The results show that the active learning methodology might be applicable to this problem. More specifically, the active learner with a RF as base classifier is the best performer with a prediction accuracy ranging from 67.62% to 70.19%. Furthermore, active learning and supervised learning have been compared, showing the supremacy of the active learning methods. A considerable advantage of the active learning framework is the limited number of labeled examples that are needed to train a model, achieving a predictive accuracy as if all examples were labeled. Since there is a lack of data in the financial field, active learning seems to be a promising predictive technique.

An important limitation of our study is that is based only on a relatively small number of firms. Furthermore, only quantitative variables were used. Perhaps the use of other quantitative variables, as well as qualitative variables such as reputation, leadership or the legal structure may improve the predictive accuracy. An interesting aspect is to combine SSL and active learning as presented in [19]. SSL has already been effectively used for bankruptcy prediction as presented in [17]. Finally, it is important to explore the efficiency of active learning methodology to other financial problems such as the prediction of fraudulent financial statements.

References

1. Alfaro, E., García, N., Gámez, M., & Elizondo, D.: Bankruptcy forecasting: An empirical comparison of AdaBoost and neural networks. Decision Support Systems, vol. 45(1), pp. 110-122 (2008)
2. Altman, E. I.: Financial ratios, discriminant analysis and the prediction of corporate bankruptcy. The journal of finance, vol. 23(4), pp.589-609 (1968)
3. Atiya, A. F.: Bankruptcy prediction for credit risk using neural networks: A survey and new results. IEEE transactions on neural networks, vol. 12(4), pp. 929-935 (2001)
4. Beaver, W. H.: Financial ratios as predictors of failure. Journal of accounting research, pp. 71-111 (1966)
5. Barboza, F., Kimura, H., & Altman, E.: Machine Learning Models and Bankruptcy Prediction. Expert Systems with Applications (2017)
6. Breiman, L.: Random forests. Machine learning, vol. 45(1), pp. 5-32 (2001)
7. Dasgupta, S.: Two faces of active learning. Theoretical computer science, vol. 412(19), pp. 1767-1781 (2011)
8. Deligianni, D., & Kotsiantis, S.: Forecasting corporate bankruptcy with an ensemble of classifiers. In Hellenic Conference on Artificial Intelligence, pp. 65-72. Springer Berlin Heidelberg (2012)
9. du Jardin, P. (2017). Dynamics of firm financial evolution and bankruptcy prediction. Expert Systems with Applications, vol. 75, pp. 25-43 (2017)
10. Dwyer, K., & Holte, R.: Decision tree instability and active learning. In European Conference on Machine Learning, pp. 128-139. Springer Berlin Heidelberg (2007)
11. Fallahpour, S., Lakvan, E. N., & Zadeh, M. H.: Using an ensemble classifier based on sequential floating forward selection for financial distress prediction problem. Journal of Retailing and Consumer Services, vol. 34, pp. 159-167 (2017)
12. Gardner, M. W., & Dorling, S. R.: Artificial neural networks (the multilayer perceptron)-a review of applications in the atmospheric sciences. Atmospheric environment, vol. 32(14), pp. 2627-2636 (1998)
13. Groppelli, A. A., & Nikbakht, E.: Barron's Finance (2000)
14. Hodges, J. L., & Lehmann, E. L.: Rank methods for combination of independent experiments in analysis of variance. The Annals of Mathematical Statistics, vol. 33(2), pp. 482-497 (1962)
15. Huang, S. J., Jin, R., & Zhou, Z. H.: Active learning by querying informative and representative examples. In Advances in neural information processing systems, pp. 892-900 (2010)
16. Jones, S., Johnstone, D., & Wilson, R.: Predicting Corporate Bankruptcy: An Evaluation of Alternative Statistical Frameworks. Journal of Business Finance & Accounting, vol. 44(1-2), pp. 3-34 (2017)
17. Karlos, S., Kotsiantis, S., Fazakis, N., & Sgarbas, K.: Effectiveness of semi-supervised learning in bankruptcy prediction. In Information, Intelligence, Systems & Applications (IISA), 2016 7th International Conference on, pp. 1-6. IEEE (2016)
18. Kremer, J., Steenstrup Pedersen, K., & Igel, C.: Active learning with support vector machines. Wiley Interdisciplinary Reviews: Data Mining and Knowledge Discovery, vol. 4(4), pp. 313-326 (2014)
19. Leng, Y., Xu, X., & Qi, G.: Combining active learning and semi-supervised learning to construct SVM classifier. Knowledge-Based Systems, vol. 44, pp. 121-131 (2013)
20. Ling, C. X., Huang, J., & Zhang, H.: AUC: a statistically consistent and more discriminating measure than accuracy. In IJCAI, vol. 3, pp. 519-524 (2003)

21. Mamitsuka, N. A. H.: Query learning strategies using boosting and bagging. In Machine Learning: Proceedings of the Fifteenth International Conference (ICML'98), vol. 1. Morgan Kaufmann Pub (1998)
22. Mselmi, N., Lahiani, A., & Hamza, T.: Financial distress prediction: The case of French small and medium-sized firms. International Review of Financial Analysis, vol. 50, pp. 67-80 (2017)
23. Ng, A. Y., & Jordan, M. I.: On discriminative vs. generative classifiers: A comparison of logistic regression and naive bayes. Advances in neural information processing systems, vol. 2, pp. 841-848 (2002)
24. Odom, M. D., & Sharda, R.: A neural network model for bankruptcy prediction. 1990 IJCNN International Joint Conference on, pp. 163-168. IEEE (1990)
25. Pearl, J.: Probabilistic Reasoning in Intelligent Systems. San Francisco, CA: Morgan Kaufmann (1988)
26. Platt, J.: Sequential minimal optimization: A fast algorithm for training support vector machines (1998)
27. Ramirez-Loaiza, M. E., Sharma, M., Kumar, G., & Bilgic, M.: Active learning: an empirical study of common baselines. Data Mining and Knowledge Discovery, pp. 1-27 (2016)
28. Reyes, O., Pérez, E., del Carmen Rodrıguez-Hernández, M., Fardoun, H. M., & Ventura, S.: JCLAL: a Java framework for active learning. Journal of Machine Learning Research, vol. 17(95), pp. 1-5 (2016)
29. Settles, B.: Active learning. Synthesis Lectures on Artificial Intelligence and Machine Learning, vol. 6(1), pp. 1-114 (2012)
30. Settles, B., & Craven, M.: An analysis of active learning strategies for sequence labeling tasks. In Proceedings of the conference on empirical methods in natural language processing, pp. 1070-1079. Association for Computational Linguistics (2008)
31. Shannon, C. E.: A mathematical theory of communication. ACM SIGMOBILE Mobile Computing and Communications Review, vol. 5(1), pp. 3-55 (2001)
32. Sharda, R., & Wilson, R. L.: Neural network experiments in business-failure forecasting: Predictive performance measurement issues. International Journal of Computational Intelligence and Organizations, vol. 1(2), pp. 107-117 (1996)
33. Sharma, M., & Bilgic, M.: Evidence-based uncertainty sampling for active learning. Data Mining and Knowledge Discovery, vol. 31(1), pp. 164-202 (2017)
34. Tam, K. Y., & Kiang, M. Y.: Managerial applications of neural networks: the case of bank failure predictions. Management science, vol. 38(7), pp. 926-947 (1992)
35. Triguero, I., García, S., & Herrera, F.: Self-labeled techniques for semi-supervised learning: taxonomy, software and empirical study. Knowledge and Information Systems, vol. 42(2), pp. 245-284 (2015)
36. Wang, J., & Park, E.: Active learning for penalized logistic regression via sequential experimental design. Neurocomputing, vol. 222, pp. 183-190 (2017)
37. Wilson, R. L., & Sharda, R.: Bankruptcy prediction using neural networks. Decision support systems, vol. 11(5), pp. 545-557 (1994)
38. Witten, I. H., Frank, E., Hall, M. A., & Pal, C. J.: Data Mining: Practical machine learning tools and techniques. Morgan Kaufmann (2016)
39. Zhou, Z. H.: Learning with unlabeled data and its application to image retrieval. In Pacific Rim International Conference on Artificial Intelligence, pp. 5-10. Springer Berlin Heidelberg (2006)

A Prognosis of Junior High School Students' Performance Based on Active Learning Methods

Georgios Kostopoulos[1], Sotiris Kotsiantis[1] and Vassilios S. Verykios[2]

[1]Educational Software Development Laboratory (ESDLab)
Department of Mathematics, University of Patras, Greece
[2]Hellenic Open University, Greece
kostg@sch.gr,sotos@math.upatras.gr,verykios@eap.gr

Abstract. In recent years, there is a growing research interest in applying data mining techniques in education. Educational Data Mining has become an efficient tool for teachers and educational institutions trying to effectively analyze the academic behavior of students and predict their progress and performance. The main objective of this study is to classify junior high school students' performance in the final examinations of the "Geography" module in a set of five pre-defined classes using active learning. The exploitation of a small set of labeled examples together with a large set of unlabeled ones to build efficient classifiers is the key point of the active learning framework. To the best of our knowledge, no study exist dealing with the implementation of active learning methods for predicting students' performance. Several assessment attributes related to students' grades in homework assignments, oral assessment, short tests and semester exams constitute the dataset, while a number of experiments are carried out demonstrating the advantage of active learning compared to familiar supervised methods, such as the Naïve Bayes classifier.

Keywords: Pool-based active learning, uncertainty sampling strategy, prediction, student performance, junior high school.

1 Introduction

Over recent years, there is a growing research interest in applying data mining techniques in education. Educational Data Mining (EDM) has become an efficient tool for teachers and educational institutions exploiting data stored in databases. Using a wide variety of machine learning methods and tools, EDM is trying to effectively analyze the academic behavior of students based on several characteristics and predict their progress, performance or dropout rates [18]. Recently, Slater et al. [23] reviewed 40 frequently used tools for data mining in education. Therefore, it is essential for educational institutions to support weak students and increase retention rates targeting to improve learning effectiveness and provide high quality education.

The main objective of this study is to predict junior high school students' performance in the final examinations of the "Geography" module using active learning. The exploitation of a small set of labeled examples together with a large set of unla-

© Springer International Publishing AG 2017
C. Frasson and G. Kostopoulos (Eds.): BFAL 2017, LNAI 10512, pp. 67–76, 2017
DOI: 10.1007/978-3-319-67615-9_6

beled ones to build efficient classifiers is the key point of the active learning framework. The students' examination grade has been classified into five pre-defined classes and is based on several quantitative assessment attributes, such as homework assignments, oral performance, short tests and semester exams that have been performed during the academic year. Moreover, we investigate the possibility to identify low performance students in a timely manner quite accurately. The accurate prediction of strengths and weaknesses of such students is beneficial for teachers, as well as for educational institutions. Students that are possible to fail in the final examinations need extra help and learning support. Well planned assignments and activities, additional learning material and supplementary lessons adapted to the different needs and knowledge levels of students may motivate them and enhance their performance. To the best of our knowledge there is no study dealing with the implementation of active learning methods in the educational field.

The rest of this paper is organized as follows: In Section 2 we present recent studies of machine learning technics for predicting students' performance in high school and especially familiar supervised methods. In Section 3 we briefly describe the active learning task. A description of the dataset is given in section 4 together with a detailed analysis of data attributes used. In section 5 we analyze the experiments carried out in this study and present their results while making a comparison to familiar supervised methods, such as the Naïve Bayes classifier. Finally, in Section 6 we conclude writing down some thoughts for future work.

2 A Recent Review of Data Mining Applications in Education

A number of very rewarding studies have been carried out in recent years, dealing with the implementation of familiar machine learning technics to evaluate high school students' performance in secondary education. Moreover, what all these studies have in common is the prediction (pass or fail) in the "Mathematics" module, confirming its importance for students, teachers and educational institutions. Some of these studies are analyzed below:

Cortez and Silva [2] parsed data originating from two secondary schools to predict students' performance (pass or fail) in "Mathematics" and "Portuguese language" modules in the final examinations at the end of academic year. Four familiar data mining methodologies, particularly Decision Trees, Random Forest, Neural Networks and Support Vector Machines (SVM), were tested in several demographic, social and school attributes showing a high predictive accuracy, especially in the case where the past school period grades were known.

Márquez-Vera et al. [13] implemented a Genetic Programming (GP) algorithm and recommended different classification technics from Weka [26] to predict high school students' failure in secondary education. More precisely, five rule induction algorithms, five decision tree algorithms and an evolutionary GP algorithm, named Interpretable Classification Rule Mining (ICRM), were used for successfully predicting students' final performance (pass or fail).

Stapel et al. [24] developed an online math learning platform in Germany with more than 100k interactive exercises grouped in series and arranged in digital books. The platform supports and guides students without teacher intervention, while teachers can be aware of students' performance through detailed reports. Data were collected during an academic year (2015) and included information related to students' activities in the platform 40 days before their first assessment attempt. Finally, an ensemble of classifiers was used to predict students' performance on specific learning objectives.

Livieris et al. [11] presented a user-friendly decision support tool for predicting high school students' performance in the final examinations of the "Mathematics" module. The tool incorporates familiar supervised algorithms from Weka and is based on several time-variant quantitative variables of students, such as written assignments, oral performance, short tests and exams. The notable results of the proposed tool show that it may be effectively used for the early identification of low performance students in high school.

In a recent study, Kostopoulos et al. [8] examined the effectiveness of semi-supervised methods to predict students' performance in distance higher education. Familiar algorithms from KEEL [25] (Self-training, Co-training, Tri-training, De-Tri-training, Democratic, RASCO and Rel-RASCO) were tested using several base classifiers. The experimental results were promising compared to familiar supervised methods, showing the predominance of the Tri-training algorithm with an accuracy measure exceeding 80% in the performance prediction (pass or fail) of students in the final examinations of a distance undergraduate course.

3 Active Learning

In many real world applications, there is often a lack of labeled data while unlabeled data can easily be obtained. Labeling unlabeled data may be a difficult and time consuming affair, as it requires a lot of human effort and experts. The need to utilize the hidden information in unlabeled data in order to build accurate predictive learning models has resulted into the development of significant machine learning approaches. Semi-supervised learning (SSL) and active learning are the two representative paradigms for learning from both labeled and unlabeled data [28].

In active or query learning the learning algorithm chooses the data from which it learns querying the labels of unlabeled examples from an oracle. These examples are usually the most informative ones. The essential aim of active learning is to minimize the number of queries posed, using a small number of labeled examples and build efficient predictive models at the lowest possible cost [3, 19]. Several scenarios have been proposed to ask queries such as pool-based sampling, stream-based sampling and membership queries synthesis [20]. In pool-based sampling, we consider that there are a small set L of labeled examples and a large set U of unlabeled ones. The best queries are selected from U, these examples are added to L and the iterative procedure is repeated until U is empty or a stopping criterion is met [16]. In stream-based or selective sampling an unlabeled example is picked for labeling by the oracle, and the active learner decides whether to query it or not, while in membership query synthesis the learner may request the label for any unlabeled example posing a query de novo.

A number of frequently used strategies [22] have been applied to evaluate the informativeness and representativeness of unlabeled examples and request their labels, such as uncertainty sampling, random sampling and query by committee (QBC) [12]. Uncertainty sampling is one of the most effective and simplest strategies querying the labels of the most uncertain to label examples. For binary classification margin sampling query is the most common strategy [21], while entropy sampling is used for classification problems with more than two class labels. Random sampling is another simple strategy in accordance with which, unlabeled examples are randomly selected from U. It is noteworthy that many studies have shown that random sampling often prevails over uncertainty sampling [16]. QBC queries the label of the most informative example, which is the one that a committee of classifiers disagree the most.

The pseudo-code description of a pool-based active learning scenario using uncertainty as sampling strategy is shown in Algorithm 1:

Algorithm 1. Pool-based Active Learning with Uncertainty Sampling

---

Input: labeled dataset L, unlabeled dataset U.
1. Initially, apply base learner B to the training dataset L to obtain classifier C.
2. Apply C to unlabeled dataset U.
3. From U, select m instances for which C is most uncertain.
4. Ask the teacher for labels of the m instances.
5. Add the m labeled instances to L.
6. Re-train on L to obtain a new classifier, C'.
7. Repeat steps 2 to 6, until U is empty or until some stopping criterion is met
8. Output a classifier that is trained on L.

---

4   Dataset Description

The present study is focused on the following two questions:

1. How do active learning techniques perform for predicting students' final performance in junior high school?
2. Can we predict the students that are going to fail or pass the final examinations in a good time?

The dataset used in our study was provided by a junior high school in Greece. For a time period of three years (2007-2010), data of 307 students (12-13 years) have been collected concerning the "Geography" module. Each instance in the dataset corresponds to an individual student and is characterized by the values of 15 performance attributes (Table 1). More specifically:

The assessment of students during the first semester consists of seven attributes: two 15-minute pre-warned tests, two oral examinations, several homework assignments, a 1-hour exam and the semesters' grade. The 15-minute tests (TEST_A1, TEST_A2) include short answer problems, while the 1-hour exam (EXAM_A) covers a wide range of the curricula. Several homework assignments and oral questions assess students' understanding of important concepts and topics in geography daily in the semester (HW_A, ORAL_A1 and ORAL_A2). Finally, the overall semester performance of each student corresponds to attribute GRADE_A. In the same way, the assessment of students during the second and third semester consists of five and three attributes respectively. The output nominal attribute "EXAMS" corresponds to the students' grade in the final examinations (2-hour exam) according to the following five-level classification: 0-9 (insufficient), 10-12 (poor), 13-14, (good), 15-17 (very good), 18-20 (excellent).

Table 1. Attributes Description

Attribute	Values	Description
TEST_A1	[1, 10]	1st semester's test1 grade
TEST_A2	[1, 10]	1st semester's test2 grade
EXAM_A	0-9, 10-12 ,13-14, 15-17, 18-20	1st semester's exam grade
HW_A	[0, 5]	1st semester's homework grade
ORAL_A1	[1, 10]	1st semester's oral1 grade
ORAL_A2	[1, 10]	1st semester's oral2 grade
GRADE_A	[1, 20]	1st semester's overall grade
TEST_B	[1, 10]	2nd semester's test1 grade
EXAM_B	0-9, 10-12 ,13-14, 15-17, 18-20	2nd semester's exam grade
HW_B	[0; 5]	2nd semester's homework
ORAL_B	[1, 10]	2nd semester's oral grade
GRADE_B	[1, 20]	2nd semester's overall grade
TEST_C	[1, 10]	3rd semester's test1 grade
ORAL_C	[1, 10]	3rd semester's oral grade
GRADE_C	[1, 20]	3rd semester's overall grade
EXAMS	0-9, 10-12 ,13-14, 15-17, 18-20	Grade in final examinations

In the following section we present the experiments that take place in our study and the experimental results.

5   Experiments

Initially, the dataset was partitioned into 10 folds of 276 instances using the 10-fold cross validation procedure. One fold was kept for assessing the predictive effectiveness of the model, while the rest 9 folds were used for the training process. In each fold, 21 instances of the training set formed the labeled set and the rest 255 formed the unlabeled set. A pool-based sampling scenario with the margin sampling query strategy was used. We have defined a maximum number of 30 iterations as a stopping criterion, while we selected a single example for labeling at each of the iterations. On this basis, at the end of the learning process there will be 51 labeled instances.

A set of five familiar supervised algorithms from Weka were used as base classifiers forming five respective active learners. These algorithms are:

- Bayes Net, representative of the Bayesian Networks [14]
- Multilayer Perceptrons (MLPs), representative of Neural Networks [6]
- Naïve Bayes [7], a very effective and simple classification algorithm [27]
- Random Forest (RF), a combination of tree-structured predictors [1]
- Sequential Minimal Optimization (SMO), a very effective SVM algorithm [15]

The experiments were conducted in two distinct phases of three sequential steps each time using the JCLAL tool. JCLAL is a computational tool for performing active learning methods for both researchers and programmers. JCLAL provides a friendly and high-level environment facilitating the implementation of existing active learning methodologies or the development of new ones [17]. It supports pool-based and stream-based sampling scenarios, as well as a variety of single-label and multi-label active learning scenarios, such as uncertainty and query by committee sampling. In each phase, the first step consists of the seven attributes (TEST_A1, TEST_A2, EXAM_A, ORAL_A1, ORAL_A2, HW_A, GRADE_A) referred to the assessment of a student during the first semester. The second step includes the attributes of both first and second semesters, while in the third step, all attributes are used.

Table 2. The Accuracy (%) of the Active Learners with the Margin Sampling Query Strategy

	Active Learner	1st step	2nd step	3rd step
Base algorithm	NB	59.84	66.73	68.99
	RF	61.56	64.08	67.04
	SMO	63.11	62.83	65.38
	MLPs	58.52	63.75	59.81
	Bayes Net	60.19	64.41	65.67

In the first phase of the experiments we evaluate the performance of the above mentioned active learners measuring the accuracy, which corresponds to the percentage of the correctly classified instances (Table 2). As Table 2 shows, the accuracy measure of the active learners ranges from 58.52% to 63.11% based on the attributes regarding the first semester's assessment. In the second step, the NB based active learner outweighs with 66.73% accuracy, while in the 3rd step the accuracy is 68.99%.

We evaluate the performance of the above active learners using the Friedman Aligned Ranks nonparametric test [5]. According to the test results the algorithms are ranking from the best performer to the lower one (Table 3). The NB based active learner prevails over the rest, followed by the SMO and RF based active learners.

Table 3. Friedman Aligned Ranks test (significance level of 0.05)

Algorithm	Rank
NB	5.33
RF	6.00
SMO	7.67
Bayes Net	7.67
MLPs	13.33

In the 2nd phase of experiments we make a comparison between the active learner using NB as the base classifier and the NB supervised classifier measuring the accuracy in each one of the experiments steps. The results (Table 4) indicate that active learning outweighs supervised learning in each of the three steps. It must be mentioned that supervised learning requires a large amount of labeled data to train the classifier (276 instances), while only a small amount of labeled data (51 instances) are needed for achieving better accuracy using active learning.

Table 4. Active Learning vs Supervised Learning (accuracy %)

Step	Active Learner (NB base classifier)	NB (supervised)
1st step	59.84	59.30
2nd step	66.73	61.60
3rd step	68.99	62.90

Regarding the active learner using NB as base classifier, and for each one of the three steps of the experiments we present a graph (Figure 1) illustrating the accuracy percentage rate related to the number of labeled instances during the iterative learning process and measure the area (Table 5) bounded by the accuracy curve and the x-axis (AUC). AUC is another common metric for assessing the performance of a binary classifier [10].

Table 5. Area Under the Accuracy Curve (NB)

Step	AUC
1st step	57.132
2nd step	64.614
3rd step	65.387

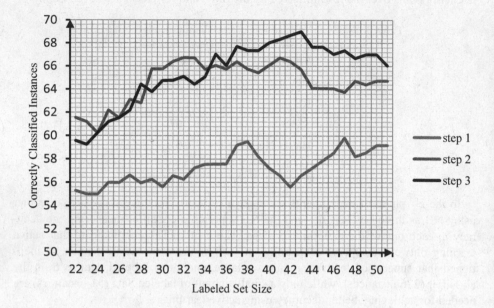

Fig. 1. Accuracy Curve of the NB based active learner

6   Conclusions

In the present study the effectiveness of active learning methodology is examined to predict the performance of junior high school students in the final examinations in the "Geography" module. Specifically, a pool-based sampling scenario was adopted making use of the margin sampling query strategy, while the dataset was based on several quantitative assessment attributes, such as homework assignments, oral performance, short tests and semester exams that have been performed during the academic year. To the best of our knowledge, no study exists, dealing with the implementation of active learning methods for the prediction of students' performance.

Several experiments were conducted measuring the accuracy of five active learners using familiar supervised algorithms as base classifiers. The experimental results indicate that it is possible to predict low performers with sufficient accuracy in a timely manner using a limited number of labeled examples as a training set. At the end of the first semester, the accuracy of the active learner using SMO as base classifier is 63.11%. At the end of the second semester the NB based active learner outweighs with 66.73% accuracy, while accuracy is 68.99% before the final examinations. Comparing the active learner using NB as base classifier and the NB supervised classifier, it is shown that active learning prevails over supervised learning in each one of the three experiment steps. It is worth noting that supervised learning requires a large amount of labeled data to train the classifier (276 instances), while only a small amount of labeled data (51 instances) were needed for achieving better accuracy using active learning.

An interesting aspect is to combine semi-supervised learning and active learning, since both methodologies aim to build effective predictive models exploiting a small labeled dataset together with a large unlabeled dataset. Studies in other domains have shown that such a combination may improve the predictive accuracy [4, 9, 29]. Further experiments and more research is needed using additional attributes (e.g. such as grades from previous years, the time of study, the number of school absences, parents education).

References

1. Breiman, L.: Random forests. Machine learning, vol. 45(1), pp. 5-32 (2001)
2. Cortez, P., & Silva, A. M. G.: Using data mining to predict secondary school student performance (2008)
3. Dasgupta, S.: Two faces of active learning. Theoretical computer science, vol. 412(19), pp. 1767-1781 (2011)
4. Hady, M. F. A., & Schwenker, F.: Combining committee-based semi-supervised learning and active learning. Journal of Computer Science and Technology, vol. 25(4), pp. 681-698 (2010)
5. Hodges, J. L., & Lehmann, E. L.: Rank methods for combination of independent experiments in analysis of variance. The Annals of Mathematical Statistics, vol. 33(2), pp. 482-497 (1962)
6. Hornik, K., Stinchcombe, M., & White, H.: Multilayer feedforward networks are universal approximators. Neural networks, vol. 2(5), pp. 359-366 (1989)
7. John, G. H., & Langley, P.: Estimating continuous distributions in Bayesian classifiers. In Proceedings of the Eleventh conference on Uncertainty in artificial intelligence, pp. 338-345. Morgan Kaufmann Publishers Inc. (1995)
8. Kostopoulos, G., Kotsiantis, S., & Pintelas, P.: Predicting Student Performance in Distance Higher Education Using Semi-supervised Techniques. In: Model and Data Engineering, pp. 259-270. Springer International Publishing (2015)
9. Leng, Y., Xu, X., & Qi, G.: Combining active learning and semi-supervised learning to construct SVM classifier. Knowledge-Based Systems, vol. 44, pp. 121-131 (2013)
10. Ling, C. X., Huang, J., & Zhang, H.: AUC: a statistically consistent and more discriminating measure than accuracy. In IJCAI, vol. 3, pp. 519-524 (2003)
11. Livieris I.E., Mikropoulos T.A., & Pintelas P.: A decision support system for predicting students' performance. Themes in Science and Technology Education, vol. 9(1), pp. 43-57 (2016)
12. Mamitsuka, N. A. H.: Query learning strategies using boosting and bagging. In Machine Learning: Proceedings of the Fifteenth International Conference (ICML'98), vol. 1. Morgan Kaufmann Pub (1998)
13. Márquez-Vera, C., Cano, A., Romero, C., & Ventura, S.: Predicting student failure at school using genetic programming and different data mining approaches with high dimensional and imbalanced data. Applied intelligence, vol. 38(3), pp. 315-330 (2013)
14. Pearl, J.: Probabilistic Reasoning in Intelligent Systems. San Francisco, CA: Morgan Kaufmann (1988)

15. Platt, J.: Sequential minimal optimization: A fast algorithm for training support vector machines (1998)
16. Ramirez-Loaiza, M. E., Sharma, M., Kumar, G., & Bilgic, M.: Active learning: an empirical study of common baselines. Data Mining and Knowledge Discovery, pp. 1-27 (2016)
17. Reyes, O., Pérez, E., del Carmen Rodriguez-Hernández, M., Fardoun, H. M., & Ventura, S.: JCLAL: a Java framework for active learning. Journal of Machine Learning Research, vol. 17(95), pp. 1-5 (2016)
18. Romero, C., & Ventura, S.: Data mining in education. Wiley Interdisciplinary Reviews: Data Mining and Knowledge Discovery, vol. 3(1), pp. 12-27 (2013)
19. Settles, B., & Craven, M.: An analysis of active learning strategies for sequence labeling tasks. In Proceedings of the conference on empirical methods in natural language processing, pp. 1070-1079. Association for Computational Linguistics (2008)
20. Settles, B.: Active learning. Synthesis Lectures on Artificial Intelligence and Machine Learning, vol. 6(1), pp. 1-114 (2012)
21. Shannon, C. E.: A mathematical theory of communication. ACM SIGMOBILE Mobile Computing and Communications Review, vol. 5(1), pp. 3-55 (2001)
22. Sharma, M., & Bilgic, M.: Evidence-based uncertainty sampling for active learning. Data Mining and Knowledge Discovery, vol. 31(1), pp. 164-202 (2017)
23. Slater, S., Joksimović, S., Kovanovic, V., Baker, R. S., & Gasevic, D.: Tools for Educational Data Mining A Review. Journal of Educational and Behavioral Statistics (2016)
24. Stapel, M., Zheng, Z., & Pinkwart, N.: An ensemble method to predict student performance in an online math learning environment. In Proceedings of the 9th International Conference on Educational Data Mining, International Educational Data Mining Society, pp. 231-238 (2016)
25. Triguero, I., García, S., & Herrera, F.: Self-labeled techniques for semi-supervised learning: taxonomy, software and empirical study. Knowledge and Information Systems, vol. 42(2), pp. 245-284 (2015)
26. Witten, I. H., Frank, E., Hall, M. A., & Pal, C. J.: Data Mining: Practical machine learning tools and techniques. Morgan Kaufmann (2016)
27. Zhang, H.: The optimality of naive Bayes. AA, vol. 1(2), pp. 3, (2004)
28. Zhou, Z. H.: Learning with unlabeled data and its application to image retrieval. In Pacific Rim International Conference on Artificial Intelligence, pp. 5-10. Springer Berlin Heidelberg (2006)
29. Zhu, X., Lafferty, J., & Ghahramani, Z.: Combining active learning and semi-supervised learning using gaussian fields and harmonic functions. In ICML 2003 workshop on the continuum from labeled to unlabeled data in machine learning and data mining, vol. 3 (2003)

The effects of working memory training on cognitive flexibility in man

Vasiliky Stavroulaki[1], Eleni Kazantzaki[1,2], Panagiotis Bitsios[1], Kyriaki Sidiropoulou[3] and Stella G. Giakoumaki[4]

[1]Medical School, [2]Forth institute of computer science, [3]Dept of Biology, [4]Dept of Psychology
University of Crete, Heraklion /Crete, 70013, Greece
medp2011781@med.uoc.gr

Abstract. In the present study we examined the effects of working memory training on cognitive flexibility in humans. Forty healthy male participants were divided into three groups (matched for demographic variables, schizotypy, impulsivity and baseline cognitive flexibility): a) fully adapted group (participants were fully trained with an executive working memory task for six consecutive days); b) partially adapted group (participants were partially trained with an executive working memory task for six consecutive days) and c) control group (participants did not receive cognitive training). Following training, participants were examined with a second cognitive flexibility task. We found that the fully adapted group had improved cognitive flexibility (they made fewer errors and needed fewer attempts to complete the test) compared with both the partially adapted *(all p values <0.005)* and the control *(all p values <0.05)* groups, who did not differ between each other *(all p values >0.2)*. These findings could have significant implications in the development of therapeutic approaches for the improvement of cognitive deficits in neuropsychiatric disorders.

Keywords: Working Memory, Cognitive Flexibility, LNS, ID/EDS, Transfer.

1 Introduction

The ability to flexibly adjust behavior in response to change is vital to everyday life. Cognitive flexibility is the ability to adapt cognitive processing strategies to face new and unexpected changes and is intrinsically linked to attentional processes [1,2]. Cognitive flexibility is significantly affected in several neuropsychiatric diseases, such as schizophrenia, depression and obsessive-compulsive disorders [3,4]. Since the development of drugs for improving deficits in cognitive functions has proven to be a very difficult and time-consuming process with extremely high costs [5], it is essential that alternative therapeutic methods are studied and cognitive training has been proposed to be one of them, in particular working memory training.

Working memory involves the temporary storage and manipulation of information by an attention based limited-capacity system [6,7] and thus underlies virtually most higher-order cognitive processes [7,8]. Working memory capacity can be measured with a wide variety of tests, which can be distinguished in two groups: the first set of

© Springer International Publishing AG 2017
C. Frasson and G. Kostopoulos (Eds.): BFAL 2017, LNAI 10512, pp. 77–87, 2017
DOI: 10.1007/978-3-319-67615-9_7

tests assesses transient, online maintenance functions that do not involve manipulation of the stored information [9] while the second set of tests involves maintenance plus manipulation of information, the so called "executive working memory." An example of this set of tests is the Letter-Number Sequencing task (LNS) [9]. Cognitive flexibility is typically measured in the laboratory using set shifting or task switching behavioral tasks [10], such as the Wisconsin Card Sorting Test (WCST) and the Intra-Extra Dimensional Shift task (IED). It is also important to note that working memory is also involved in these tasks, as participants have to retain two or more sets of rules for the successful completion of the test [10].

Research has shown that cognitive training can improve performance in a wide range of functions and that this improvement in performance is associated with neuronal changes ranging from the intracellular level to functional organization of the cortex [11-13]. It has, thus, been demonstrated that training of working memory results in performance transfer to untrained tasks in younger and older adults, as well as children [14-16]. There are also studies suggesting that cognitive improvements do not transfer to new tasks or transfer only to tasks with the same processing requirements as the trained tasks [17], with the effect sizes for a cognitive intervention being quite small [18,19]. Therefore, research results on the effects of transfer of cognitive training to humans are ambiguous. There are studies showing a positive effect of working memory training on other cognitive functions, but there are also studies that show no change between control and training groups [20]. It has also been suggested that transfer can occur if the training and transfer task engage not only similar processes but also identical brain regions [21]. This view is based on the fact that training a particular neural circuit can lead to the transfer of the training to other tasks and functions that are regulated by the circuit [13,21]. Therefore, in order to be effective, cognitive training must use a common neuroanatomic and neurophysiological background with the cognitive functions, which are controlled for transfer [21,22].

The aim of the present study is to investigate the possible improvement of cognitive flexibility after working memory training in humans. Our hypothesis was that participants who are "fully-trained" with an executive working memory task (i.e. the LNS which requires prefrontal activation for effective performance) will perform better in the ID/EDS test, compared to those who are "partially-trained" and those who are not trained at all. This hypothesis is based on the fact that there is common neuroanatomical substrate that supports the potential transfer of the training of working memory in cognitive flexibility, as these two processes share common brain regions [23,24].

2   Methods

2.1   Participants

Forty-five healthy male participants were recruited. Exclusion criteria included personal history of head trauma, medical or neurological conditions, current use of prescribed or recreational drugs and personal or family (up to second-degree) history of DSM-IV Axis I disorders. All participants underwent psychiatric assessment using the

Mini-International Neuropsychiatric Interview [25]. Two subjects were excluded due to axis I pathology and three subjects were excluded due to current use of recreational drugs; therefore the final sample consisted of 40 participants (age mean±SD: 33.20±5.240, age range: 25-43 years). The study was approved by the Research Ethics Committee of the University of Crete and the Bureau for the Protection of Personal Data of the Greek State. Following presentation of the study's methods, all participants received a detailed information sheet and gave written informed consent before participation.

2.2   Neuropsychological Assessment

Letter-Number Sequencing [LNS; 26]. The task assesses executive working memory. The Greek version of the task was used. The examiner reads to the participants, at an approximate rate of one item/second, strings of intermingled letters and numbers and they are required to store and recite these strings after re-ordering of the information (i.e. recite in numeric and alphabetical order). The strings are of increasing difficulty. The complete test consists of eight blocks with three trials each. Administration terminates if participants miss all three trials within a block. The outcome variable was the total number of correct strings.

Raven's Progressive Matrices [RPM; 27]. The task assesses abstract reasoning. It comprises five sets of 12 abstract patterns, each with one missing piece. Subjects are required to find the piece that best completes the pattern among a set of alternatives. Items within a set become increasingly difficult. The outcome variable was the total number of correct selections.

Wisconsin Card Sorting Test [WCST; 28]. The task assesses cognitive flexibility. We administered a computerized version of the task, consisting of four stimulus cards that vary along three dimensions (shape, colour and number) and a target card. Subjects have to match the target card with one of the four stimulus cards, according to one of the three categories. After each answer, feedback on the correctness of the selection is given to the examinee. After six consecutive correct responses, the sorting principle changes and participants are informed of the shift in the sorting rule. The test ends after six completed categories. The outcome measures were the number of completed categories, number of unrelated matched cards (i.e. the target card had nothing in common with the selected card), Milner-type and Nelson-type perseverative errors (Milner- type perseverative errors were defined as those that were correct on the immediately preceding stage of the test [29] and Nelson-type were all other perseverative errors [28]), Milner- and Nelson-nonperseverative errors and total number of errors.

Intra-Extra Dimensional Shift [ID/EDS; 30]. The test is part of the Cambridge Neuropsychological Test Automated Battery; it assesses cognitive flexibility and is administrated using a computer with a touch–sensitive screen [31]. Participants are presented with stimuli with only two visual dimensions (shape and line), and they are required to choose the one that is correct according to a rule. Starting with simple shape discrimination and reversal, subjects proceed to tests of distraction where irrelevant lines are introduced, first adjacent to the shapes and then superimposed on them. Once training to selecting the shape through several reversals is complete and the irrelevance of the lines has been established, one of two different types of shift takes place. Initially, there is an intra-dimensional shift, whereby novel exemplars of the stimuli are used, but with shape still the relevant dimension. When discrimination has been established to these new stimuli, an extra-dimensional shift occurs in which the line finally becomes relevant and the previously trained shape is irrelevant. Outcome measures were total errors (ID/EDS errors in extradimestional shift and ID Pre-ED errors in intradimensional shift), completed stage errors, completed stage trials and stages completed.

2.3   Personality Assessment

Schizotypal Personality Questionnaire (SPQ). We administered the Greek version of the scale [32]. The SPQ [33] can be used as a screening instrument in the general population for the identification of individuals with broad schizotypal traits and measures individual differences in schizotypal personality. It is a 74 dichotomous item scale organized into 9 subscales (ideas of reference, social anxiety, odd beliefs/magical thinking, unusual perceptual experiences, eccentric/odd behavior, no close friends, odd speech, constricted affect, and suspiciousness) that mirror the diagnostic criteria of Schizotypal Personality Disorder. These subscales are organized into four schizotypal factors, namely Negative (NegS), Paranoid (ParS), Cognitive-Perceptual (CPS) and Disorganized (DiS).

   Barratt Impulsiveness scale [BIS; 34]. The BIS is a 30-item, self-report scale that uses a 4- point Likert response scale purported to measure aspects of impulsivity. The items are organized into three non-overlapping high-order factors: non-planning (BISnp), motor impulsivity (BISm), and attentional impulsivity (BISa).

2.4   Procedure

Initially, all participants took part in a baseline assessment session. In this session, they completed the two personality scales along with RPM, WCST and LNS. Subsequently, they were divided into three groups (partially adapted group, fully adapted group, control group) according to their performance in the aforementioned tasks and scales, so that there were no differences between the three groups in any of these measures (i.e. all three groups were matched for these measures).

   Each group was treated as follows:

   1) Control group: Participants had no involvement in the study for six days following the baseline assessment session.

   2) Partially Adapted group: For six consecutive days following the baseline assessment session, participants were administered the LNS up to the strings with three digits.

   3) Fully Adapted group: For six consecutive days following the baseline assessment session, participants were administered the LNS up to the last string.

   One week after the baseline assessment session, all participants were administered the ID/EDS.

2.5   Statistical Analyses

Between-group differences were examined either with parametric (one-way ANOVA) or non-parametric (Kruskal-Wallis Test) analyses, according to normality of the distribution, as tested by with the Kolmogorov Smirnov test. Statistically significant differences between the groups were followed up with Bonferroni's post-hoc test or Mann-Whitney tests, accordingly.

3   Results

3.1   Demographic Data

There were no statistically significant differences between the three groups *(all values p> 0.08)* in any demographic, personality and baseline-cognitive variable *(Table 1)*.

Table 1. Demographic characteristics (Mean ±SD) and scores in the personality scales and neuropsychological tasks of the three groups

VARIABLES	CONTROLS n=14		PARTIALLY ADAPTED n=13		FULLY ADAPTED n=14		p-value
Age [a]	33.36 ±	1.455	32.38 ±	1.421	34.08 ±	1.508	>0.720
Education [a]	17.857±	0.7567	17.00 ±	0.4668	17.962 ±	0.8960	>0.600
Cigarettes/week [b]	22.93 ±	13.400	31.38 ±	12.567	11.54 ±	7.236	>0.420
Raven (raw score) [a]	51.00 ±	1.406	52.54 ±	1.796	55.46 ±	0.730	>0.081
SPQ total [a]	12.07±	1.629	12.08 ±	2.676	13.54 ±	3.341	>0.900
SPQ Cognitive Perceptual (4F) [b]	1.00 ±	0.378	1.38 ±	0.615	1.85 ±	0.619	>0.830
SPQ Negative (4F) [a]	6.43 ±	1.083	6.62 ±	1.408	6.31 ±	1.508	>0.980
SPQ Paranoid (4F) [a]	4.64 ±	0.935	4.77 ±	1.001	5.31 ±	1.429	>0.900
SPQ Disorganized (4F) [a]	3.29 ±	0.624	3.31 ±	0.827	3.69 ±	0.977	>0.920
BIS Higher Attention [a]	15.50 ±	0.761	15.46 ±	1.357	16.85 ±	0.953	>0.570
BIS Higher Motor [a]	20.79 ±	0.967	18.92 ±	1.083	19.85 ±	1.285	>0.490
BIS Higher Nonplanning [a]	24.14 ±	1.354	21.92 ±	1.211	23.23 ±	0.988	>0.420
WCST categories completed [b]	5.64 ±	0.289	5.69 ±	0.237	5.77 ±	0.122	>0.880
WCST total errors [a]	6.86 ±	1.515	4.92 ±	1.393	6.31 ±	1.140	>0.590
WCST unrelated cards [b]	1.50 ±	0.856	0.92 ±	0.560	0.31 ±	0.133	>0.450
WCST Nelson-perseverative errors [b]	1.71±	0.597	1.15 ±	0.296	2.31 ±	0.559	>0.140
WCST Milner-perseverative errors [b]	1.79 ±	0.381	2.08 ±	0.525	2.46 ±	0.538	>0.660
WCST Milner non-perseverative errors [a]	3.57 ±	0.768	1.92 ±	0.500	3.54 ±	0.704	>0.150
WCST Nelson non-perseverative error [a] [a]	3.64 ±	0.541	2.85 ±	0.732	3.69 ±	0.763	>0.620
LNS total score in the Baseline Assessment [a]	21.79 ±	0.853	21.62 ±	0.805	21.08 ±	0.655	>0,800

[a]: one way ANOVA
b: Kruskal–Wallis Test

3.2   Differences between the three groups in the ID/EDS test

There were significant differences between the groups *(Kruskal-Wallis $x^2 = 8.371$, p <0.05)* in the total number of errors in the nine stages of the test (Figure 1). Follow-up Mann-Whitney group comparisons revealed that the fully adapted group made fewer errors compared with both the partially adapted *(Mann-Whitney U= 31.5, p < 0.005)* and the control *(Mann-Whitney U= 47.00, p<0.05)* groups. The difference between the control and the partially adapted group, was not significant *(Mann-Whitney U= 77.00, p> 0.510)*.

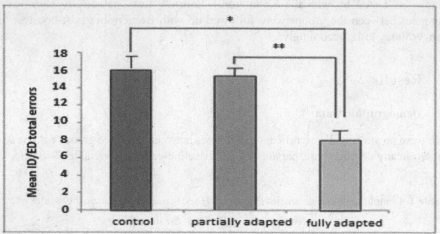

Fig. 1. Total number of errors (mean±SEM) made in the ID/EDS test for the three groups.*p <0.05; **p <0.005.

Participants who fail at any stage of the test are, by definition, less probable to make errors. Thus, the adjusted total errors (calculated by adding 25 trials for each stage not attempted due to failure) compensates for this. As previously, there were significant differences (Figure 2) between the groups *(Kruskal-Wallis x^2= 8.394, p <0.05)* and follow-up Mann-Whitney comparisons revealed that the fully adapted group made fewer errors compared with the partially adapted *(Mann-Whitney U= 31.5, p < 0.005)* and the control *(Mann-Whitney U= 47.00, p<0.05)* groups. The difference between the control and the partially adapted group was not significant *(Mann-Whitney U= 77.00, p> 0.510)*.

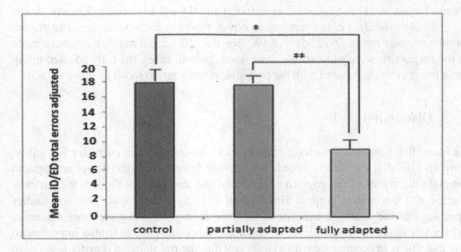

Fig. 2. Total number (mean±SEM) of adjusted errors made in the ID/EDS test for the three groups. *p <0.05; **p <0.005.

There were also significant differences between the groups *(Kruskal-Wallis x2= 9.303, p <0.05)* in the adjusted total number of trials completed in all attempted stages (Figure 3). Follow-up Mann-Whitney comparisons revealed that, in accordance to our previous findings, the fully adapted group made fewer attempts to complete the stages of the test compared with both the partially adapted *(Mann-Whitney U= 31.5, p <0.005)* and the control *(Mann-Whitney U= 44.50, p<0.05)* groups. The control group did not differ compared with the partially adapted group *(Mann-Whitney U= 65.50, p > 0.220).*

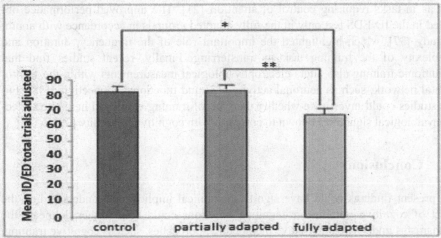

Fig. 3. Adjusted total number of trials completed at all attempted stages (mean±SEM) of the ID/ EDS test for the three groups. *p <0.05; **p <0.005.

Trends for statistical significance were found for ID–pre ED errors *(Kruskal-Wallis* $x^2 = 5.542$, *p=0.063)*, i.e. the number of errors made in intra-dimensional shift, and completed stage errors *[F (2,93) = 3,192, p= 0,053]*, i.e. the number of errors made on the stages that were successfully completed. In both cases, the fully adapted group made fewer errors compared with the partially adapted group *(both p values <0.05).*

4   Discussion

We found that training of working memory had a linear effect on cognitive flexibility. More specifically, the fully adapted group made fewer errors and fewer attempts to complete the stages of the cognitive flexibility task compared with both the partially adapted and the control groups. This finding is in agreement with previous studies reporting that the cognitive benefits of working memory training are more extensive and lead to improvements in a set of cognitive functions [14]. It is also important to note that this is in accordance with a) the view that the training and transfer tasks need to engage not only similar processes but also identical brain regions [21] in order for the transfer effect to be successful and b) the view that training a particular neural circuitry leads to the transfer of the training to other tasks and functions that are regulated by similar circuitry [21,13]. Thus, the processes examined in the present study (i.e. working memory and cognitive flexibility) are closely linked [35], since the LNS test evaluates executive working memory [9] and the ID/EDS test evaluates cognitive flexibility, which is largely correlated with working memory [36]. With regards to the neuroanatomical substrate of executive working memory and cognitive flexibility, it has been reported that both processes are mediated by a fronto-parietal network [23,24]. This is particularly important as changes in this fronto-parietal network (through training) are expected to improve performance in working memory tasks as well as in tasks requiring control of attention [21]. The improved performance observed in the ID/EDS test only in the fully adapted group is in accordance with another study [37], which highlighted the important role of the frequency, duration and complexity of the training task in transferring. Finally, recent studies find that mneumonic training also alters electrophysiological measurements within the fronto-parietal network, such as neuronal activity [13] and functional connectivity [38]. Future studies could investigate whether the type of training employed here alters electrophysiological signatures known to correlate with cognitive flexibility [39].

5   Conclusions

The present findings could have significant clinical implications: understanding the effect of cognitive training on cognitive functions could help further delineate the mechanisms underlying alternative therapeutic approaches, such as cognitive training, for the improvement of cognitive deficits in serious neuropsychiatric disorders. It is essential, however, that larger-scale studies are conducted and that related genetic and environmental factors are also studied.

References

1. Cañas, J. J., Quesada, J. F., Antolí, A., & Fajardo, I.: Cognitive flexibility and adaptability to environmental changes in dynamic complex problem-solving tasks. Ergonomics, 46(5), 482–501 (2007).
2. Moore, A., & Malinowski, P.: Meditation, mindfulness and cognitive flexibility. Consciousness and Cognition, 18, 176–186 (2009).
3. Boyle, P. A., Malloy, P. F., Salloway, S., Cahn-Weiner, D. A., Cohen, R., & Cummings, J. L.: Executive Dysfunction and Apathy Predict Functional Impairment in Alzheimer Disease. The American Journal of Geriatric Psychiatry, 11, 214 – 221 (2003).
4. Zgaljardic, D. J., Borodbc, J. C., Foldibd, N. S., Mattisa, P. J., Gordone, M. F., Feigina, A., & Eidelberga, D.: An Examination of Executive Dysfunction Associated with Frontostriatal Circuitry in Parkinson's disease. Journal of Clinical and Experimental Neuropsychology, 28, 1127 – 1144 (2006).
5. Paul, S. M., Mytelka, D. S., Dunwiddie, C. T., Persinger, C. C., Munos, B. H., Lindborg, S. R., & Schacht, A. L.: How to improve R&D productivity: the pharmaceutical industry's grand challenge. Nature Reviews Drug Discovery, 9, 203–214 (2010).
6. Baddeley, A.: Working Memory. Clarendon Press, Oxford (1986).
7. Honey, G. D., Fu, C. H., Kim, J. Brammer, M. J., Croudace, T. J., Suckling, J., Pich, E. M., Williams, S. C., & Bullmore, E. T.: "Effects of verbal working memory load on corticocortical connectivity modeled by path analysis of functional magnetic resonance imaging data". NeuroImage, 17, 573–82 (2002).
8. Jonides, J.: Working memory and thinking. In Invitation to Cognitive Science: Thinking (E. Smith and D. Osherson, Eds.), pp. 215–265. MIT Press, Cambridge, MA (2002).
9. Gur, R. E., Calkins, M. E., Gur, R. C., Horan, W. P., Nuechterlein, K. H., Seidman, L.J., Horan, W. P., Nuechterlein, K. H., Seidman, L. J., & Stone, W. S.: The Consortium on the Genetics of Schizophrenia: neurocognitive endophenotypes (2007).
10. Dajani, D. R., & Uddin, L. Q.: Demystifying cognitive flexibility: Implications for clinical and developmental neuroscience. Trends in Neurosciences, 38, 571 – 578 (2015).
11. Jolles, D. D., van Buchem, M. A., Crone, E. A., & Rombouts, S. A. R. B.: Functional brain connectivity at rest changes after working memory training. Human Brain Mapping, 34(2), 396–406 (2013).
12. Dresler, M., Shirer, W. R., Konrad, B. N., Müller, N. C. J., Wagner, I. C., Fernández, G., et al.: Mnemonic Training Reshapes Brain Networks to Support Superior Memory. Neuron, 93(5), 1227–1235 (2017).
13. Olesen, P. J., Westerberg, H., & Klingberg, T.: Increased prefrontal and parietal activity after training of working memory. Nature Neuroscience, 7, 75 – 79 (2004).
14. Morrison, A. B., & Chein, J. M.: Does working memory training work? The promise and challenges of enhancing cognition by training working memory. Psychonomic Bulletin & Review, 18, 46 – 60 (2011).
15. Klingberg, T., Fernell, E., Olesen, P. J., Johnson, M., Gustafsson, P., Dahlstrom, K., Gillberg, C. G., Forssberg, H., & Westerberg, H.: Computerized Training of Working Memory in Children With ADHD-A Randomized, Controlled Trial. Journal of the American Academy of Child & Adolescent Psychiatry, 44, 177 – 186 920 (2005).
16. Buschkuehl, M., Jaeggi, S. M., & Jonides, J.: Neuronal effects following working memory training. Developmental Cognitive Neuroscience, 2, 167–179 (2012).
17. Verghese, J., Mahoney, J., Ambrose, A. F., Wang, C., and Holtzer, R.: Effect of cognitive remediation on gait in sedentary seniors. Journal of Gerontology. A Biological Sciences Medical Sciences, 65A, 1338–1343 (2010).

18. Papp, K. V., Walsh, S. J., and Snyder, P. J.: Immediate and delayed effects of cognitive interventions in healthy elderly: a review of current literature and future directions. Alzheimers Dementia, 5, 50–60. (2009).

19. Shatil, E.: Does combined cognitive training and physical activity training enhance cognitive abilities more than either alone? A four-condition randomized controlled trial among healthy older adults. Frontiers in Aging Neuroscience, 5, 1- 12 (2013).

20. Persson, J., & Reuter-Lorenz, P.: Gaining control: Training executive function and far transfer of the ability to resolve interference. Psychological Science, 19(9), 881–888 (2008).

21. Klingberg, T.: Training and plasticity of working memory. Trends in cognitive Sciences, 14, 317-324 (2010).

22. Dahlin, E., Neely, A. S., Larsson, A., Bäckman, L., & Nyberg, L.: Transfer of Learning After Updating Training Mediated by the Striatum. Science, 320, 1510 – 1512 (2008).

23. Curtis, E. C., & D'Esposito, M.: Persistent activity in the prefrontal cortex during working memory. Trends in cognitive sciences, 7, 415 – 423 (2003).

24. Kim, C., Johnson, N. F., Cilles, S. E., & Gold, B. T.: Common and Distinct Mechanisms of Cognitive Flexibility in Prefrontal Cortex. The Journal of Neuroscience, 31, 4771– 4779 (2011).

25. Sheehan, D. V., Lecrubier, Y., Sheehan, K. H., Amorim, P., Janavs, J., Weiller, E., & Dunbar, G.C.: The Mini-International Neuropsychiatric Interview (M.I.N.I.): the development and validation of a structured diagnostic psychiatric interview for DSM-IV and ICD-10. Journal of Clinical Psychiatry, 59, 22-33 (1998).

26. Wechsler, D.: Wechsler Adult Intelligence Scale-Fourth Edition (WAIS-IV). San Antonio, TX: NCS Pearson Inc (2008).

27. Raven, J., Raven, J. C., & Court, J. H.: Manual for Raven's Progressive Matrices and Vocabulary Scales. Section 1: General Overview. San Antonio, TX: Harcourt Assessment (2003).

28. Nelson, H. E.: A modified card sorting test sensitive to frontal lobe defects. Cortex, 12(4), 313–324 (1976).

29. Milner B.: Effects of different brain lesions on card sorting. Archives of Neurology, 9(1), 90-100 (1963).

30. Fray, P. J., & Robbins, T. W.: Cantab battery: Proposed utility in neurotoxicology. Neurotoxicology and Teratology, 18(4), 499-504 (1996).

31. Robbins, T. W., James, M., Owen, A. M., Sahakian, B. J., Lawrence, A. D., McInnes, L., & Rabbitt, P M. A.: A study of performance on tests from the CANTAB battery sensitive to frontal lobe dysfunction in a large sample of normal volunteers: implications for theories of executive functioning and cognitive aging. Journal of the International Neuropsychological Society, 4(5), 474–490 (1998).

32. Tsaousis, I., Zouraraki, C., Karamaouna, P., Karagiannopoulou, L., & Giakoumaki, S. G.: The validity of the Schizotypal Personality Questionnaire in a Greek sample: tests of measurement invariance and latent mean differences. Comprehensive Psychiatry, 62, 51-62 (2015).

33. Raine, A.: The SPQ: a scale for the assessment of schizotypal personality based on DSM-III-R criteria. Schizophrenia Bulletin, 17(4), 555-564 (1991).

34. Patton, J. H., Stanford, M. S., & Barratt, E. S.: Factor structure of the Barratt impulsiveness scale. Journal of Clinical Psychology, 51(6), 768–774 (1995).

35. Takeuchi, H., Taki, Y., & Kawashima, R.: Effects of Working Memory Training on Cognitive Functions and Neural Systems. Reviews in the Neurosciences, 21, 427- 449 (2010)

36. Miyake, A., Friedman, N. P., Emerson, M. J., Wizki, A. H., Howerter, A., & Wager, T. D.: The Unity and Diversity of Executive Functions and Their Contributions to Complex "Frontal Lobe" Tasks: A Latent Variable Analysis. Cognitive Psychology 41, 49–100 (2000).
37. Schwaighofer, M., Fischer, F., & Bühner, M.: Does Working Memory Training Transfer? A Meta-Analysis Including Training Conditions as Moderators. Educational Psychologist, 50, 138 – 166 (2015).
38. Dresler, M., Shirer, W. R., Konrad, B. N., Müller, N. C. J., Wagner, I. C., Fernández, G., Czisch, M., & Greicius, M. D.: Mnemonic Training Reshapes Brain Networks to Support Superior Memory. Neuron, 93, 1227–1235 (2017).
39. Stokes, M. G., Kusunoki, M., Sigala, N., Nili, H., Gaffan, D., & Duncan, J.: Dynamic Coding for Cognitive Control in Prefrontal Cortex. Neuron, 78, 364–375 (2013).

Computers Cannot Learn the Way Humans Do – Partly, because they Do Not Sleep.

George K. Kostopoulos

Department of Physiology, Medical School, University of Patras, Rion Achaias, Greece

✉ gkkostop@upatras.gr

Abstract. One of the current frontier research themes in informatics relates to the extent to which computers and machines in general can become capable of learning and teaching each other. Hopes have been raised that their education could benefit from emulating mechanisms underlying learning in animal brains. An overview of these mechanisms will be briefly presented with a focus on the recently revealed fundamental role of sleep in memory consolidation and learning., Compared to brains, computers are found very much inferior when it comes to learning. Several road signs are suggested for enriching computers' repertory in the direction of increasing their capacity to learn by becoming more brain-like. However, the prospect of achieving such goal with state of art technology appears extremely dim.

Keywords: Learning; computers; machines; memory; sleep; Brain-like; Neuromorphic; Neuroscience; Artificial Intelligence

1 Computers are not brains

The once popular comparison of computers to brains has become meaningless – even comparing an animal brain to the entire internet -; the differences are fundamental. A comparison however, may be useful in identifying particular features of an animal brain which could inspire or even be realistically implemented in computer architecture in the frame of current artificial intelligence.

Modern day computers are clearly more powerful than humans in high-speed calculating, logical reasoning, and precise memorizing, but they still rely on humans to provide the knowledge they have. In brains, almost everything is potentially connected to everything else. For example, neurons simultaneously serving different sensory inputs deriving from a single experience interact; thus collectively constituting the memory of this experience. New impressions may interrupt and so modify every neural process. In this way brain manages to program itself and this is exactly what underlies learning: modify the preexisting model of particular actions and perceptions and make predictions, in a profitable to the organism and adaptive way [8]. However, for this process to be completed without bias, the brain has to be cut off from the environment from time to time. We humans, are especially adaptive and creative because we have built an internal world on which we base our modeling and extraction of meaning towards a coherent theory of the outside world.

C. Frasson and G. Kostopoulos (Eds.): BFAL 2017, LNAI 10512, pp. 88–97, 2017
DOI: 10.1007/978-3-319-67615-9_8

In contrast, mainstream computers execute the given rigid orders, which are strictly separated from the data. Thus, it is argued, computers are not "creative," do not "learn" and cannot "predict"; but can only be tasked with making inductive predictions based on past experiences – provided no dramatic changes take place - and seek complex correlations in the databases. However, correlation does not equal causation and only humans, because they have the ability to understand and grasp meaning, can distinguish between meaningful and meaningless correlations

To make computers learn, we use software that simulates neurons connected in networks like in a brain. These networks are trained with data until they can learn patterns or make predictions about what data might come next. Methods like these help computers recognize faces and understand speech, so in this respect computers can learn a little bit like humans. But humans are still much better – we can learn complex concepts and a vast number of different ideas. How we manage this will be reviewed below in sections 3 and 4

2 Why do we want machines capable of learning

In computers, it is now possible to have supervised learning, i.e. we pair an input with an output and teach a network to produce the output when it is presented with the input. Most supervised learning algorithms use a feedforward network architecture, taking the input at one end and processing it to produce the output at the other.

A fast-growing subfield of computer science, **machine learning**, strives to bestow to computers the ability to learn without being explicitly programmed [19]. Having evolved from the study of pattern recognition in artificial intelligence, machine learning advances algorithms which can learn from and make predictions on data through building models from sample inputs. In this way, they outperform algorithms based on following strictly static program instructions. Machine learning is already employed in a range of computing tasks where classical programming fails; learning to rank, optical character recognition, computer vision, email filtering etc.. It is obvious that learning machines will increasingly find application in industry and not only. If this is achieved, it will be comparatively easy to have one machine educate other machines with obvious runaway benefits.

Hopes have been raised for spearheading the development of learning machines through emulation of mechanisms underlying learning in animal brains; an endeavor promising further potential applications in the fields of education, robotics etc. a formidable, ambitious but also timely and most demanded task. The ability to learn appears particularly useful especially in robots which exploit their better than in humans ability to cooperate in absolute synchrony to solve common problems as in navigation through unexplored terrains. Equally important emerges machine learning in medical applications [23].

Obstacles in tackling this task start with (lack of) agreement on crucial definitions (of intelligence, memory, knowledge, the HW or SW nature of mind etc.) and end with ethical issues (isonomy of education for all, whether we should allow robots to become smarter than us? etc.) with all the hard to solve mysteries of neuroscience in between still unresolved. How realistic can therefore be any hopes of developing brain-like machines which would learn the way we do?

3 How we learn – from synaptic reorganization to changes in behavior

The constitution of a human being depends on her/his genes and on the influence of the environment. The later acts through learning (the process by which we acquire knowledge about the world) and through memory (the process by which that knowledge is encoded, stored, and later retrieved. For a thorough presentation of memory processes see chapters 65-67 in [18]. Advancing our understanding of brain mechanisms of learning is one of the primary frontiers in current neuroscience.

It is now well established that the synapses between the neurons in our brains have a remarkable capacity for plasticity and that changes in their weights (effectiveness) constitute the main mechanisms underlying all types of memory [4, 17, 18, 22]. Indicative of the advances being made at the reductionists' front of memory mechanisms is the recent demonstration that different forms of memory co-exist in the same neuron and each form can be manipulated separately [12]. At a psychological level memorization is a complex and dynamic process influenced by many extrinsic and intrinsic factors. Emotions, among other factors are strong agents in enhancing memories which have been associated with them either positively or negatively, It has been recently revealed that consolidation of memories is mainly accomplished offline and mostly during sleep. (Therefore, the provocative title of this article).

Decades of search for an "engram" of memories in the brain yielded little more than frustration [2] until the seminal observations of Brenda Milner [26], which lead to the current view that **there are several forms of learning and memory, each with its distinctive cognitive properties and mediated by specific brain systems** [17, 18]. First, they can be distinguished on the temporal axis. We perceive the existence of memory stages. i.e. that information processing goes through successive steps in time. **Working memory** of only few minutes seems to depend on sustained through reverberation firing of neurons and on dopaminergic neuromodulation in lateral prefrontal cortex [27]. Short-term functional changes (lasting hours) that increase or decrease the weight of specific synapses seem to underlie **short term memory**. It maintains transient representations of information relevant to immediate goals. Enduring functional changes (lasting days) lead to structural changes, including pruning of preexisting connections, and even growth of new connections during development and regeneration, and, most importantly, through experience and learning. This leads to selective consolidation into **long term memory**. It has been shown that long term storage of memories involves changes in chromatin structure and gene expression mediated by the cAMP-PKA-CREB pathway [18].

Second, based on the content of memories, we distinguish **explicit (declarative)** from **implicit (non-declarative) memory** [17, 18]. The former underlies the learning of facts and experiences (**episodic memory**) and it represents knowledge and concepts (**semantic memory**). Explicit memories are flexible, can be recalled voluntarily (by conscious effort) and can be reported verbally. The processes of the second include forms of perceptual and motor memory, knowledge that is stimulus-bound, is expressed in the performance of tasks without conscious effort, is not easily expressed verbally, develops earlier in infants, and perseveres better lesions and old age challenges. Medial temporal lobe structures are mainly involved in explicit memory;

while such localization of implicit memory differs according to the particular sub-type and the specific sensory and motor systems recruited for the task being learned. Thus, implicit priming depends on the particular cortical area involved in it and implicit procedural memories (of habits and skills) involve mainly the striatum. Implicit associative learning, classical and operant conditioning of emotional responses like fear depend on amygdala in the temporal lobe, while those of movements depend on cerebellum. Finally implicit non-associative learning like habituation and sensitization depend on the particular reflex pathways involved. [17-18]. It should be emphasized that for each task we identify the main among several brain areas, which usually form a functional network. Also, there is a redundancy of representation in brain areas and parallel processing – which explains in part why a limited lesion often does not eliminate any specific memory,

Finally, experimental brain lesions and human neuropsychology, allowed us to distinguish **retrograde** and **anterograde** processes of memory. Defect of the former type – often following a cortical lesion- presents with difficulty in recalling past events while a defect of the later presents with an inability to form new memories. The defect concerns the encoding of new explicit or declarative type of memories, while explicit learning remains intact [17, 18].

Recently a network of highly correlated and interacting brain areas has been revealed called default mode network (DMN [3], which is most commonly shown to be active when a person is not involved in any task, or focused on the outside world and the brain is at wakeful rest, such as during daydreaming and mind-wandering; but also when one thinks about others, (guessing their thoughts, emotions, and psychological motivations) or about themselves, (remembering the past, and planning for the future) [7]. Such non-task related activities take up as much as half of our wake time. The DMN has been shown to be negatively correlated with other networks in the brain such as attention networks. These correlations suggest some role of DMN in organizing past memories and creating the identity of the individual. "Our conception of the world around us is a creation of our imagination which happens to coincide with reality" [9]. This "coincidence" is achieved by learning. Our memory may be perceived as a film, but it is closer to a theatrical improvisation performance, with the actors producing every time a different play according to some very general instructions. The latter are very elementary structural elements of memory; abstractions of the perceived world. Such dynamic views of memory have been around and are gaining ground [8, 24].

In short, memory is a complex and very dynamic process comprising several distinct forms, each with distinct cognitive properties and underlying brain mechanisms. Each of these forms can be deconstructed into discrete encoding, storage, consolidation and retrieval processes. They can thus be classified into two dimensions: the time course of storage and the nature of the information stored. An alternative (or complementary?) to this prevailing view is that recalling a memory is recreation of a model aiming to predict the consequences of an action with each new relevant experience modifying the parameters of this model. Whichever way, human memory is notoriously inaccurate and vulnerable to many intrinsic and extrinsic factors; it is far from a faithful record of all details of an experience. However it is fast, creative and flexible, allowing us to adapt to the physical and social environment, while at the same time contributing in the biological basis of individuality

4. Sleep has a fundamental role in human learning.

Sleep is a universal, tightly controlled active process on which cognitive functions depend [29]. Far from being a break to rest, it is a sequence of very different situations during which the brain classifies the traces of the past, gets prepared for the work forthcoming and acquires knowledge. Different forms and stages of learning and memory might benefit from different stages of sleep and be sub served by different forebrain regions [11].

Although the exact mechanisms are still poorly understood, there is recently increasing evidence supporting the view of sleep as one of the main prerequisites for memory consolidation and therefore of learning [6, 25, 31].. Sleep deprivation has serious consequences on cognition and especially on learning. The reason why our brains need to disconnect from the environment for hours every day have been tentatively accepted to include (a) the need to conserve and replenish important for waking synaptic elements and (b) the need to reorganize brain synapses after the plastic changes underlying waking experiences (synaptic homeostasis or downscaling of synapses [32] and do it unbiased from ongoing environmental stimulation.

Furthermore during sleep, neurons involved in wakeful experiences are reactivated in multiple brain regions [16, 28], and neuronal networks exhibit various patterns of rhythmic activity [5] including spindles nested in slow oscillations [1]. All above findings are consistent with a role of sleep in modulating synaptic connections that are important for long-term memory formation and for preparing the brain for optimal memory encoding in the forthcoming wake period.

So, Tononi and Cirelli [32] suggest that sleep is the price the brain pays for plasticity, to consolidate what we already learned, and be ready to learn new things the next day. In support of a learning promoting role of sleep through enhancement of synapses, it has been recently shown in mouse motor cortex that sleep after motor learning promotes the formation of postsynaptic dendritic spines on a – task specific – subset of branches of individual layer V pyramidal neurons [34]. Neurons activated during learning of a motor task are reactivated during subsequent non–rapid eye movement sleep, and disrupting this neuronal reactivation prevents branch-specific spine formation..

But, can cognitive processes operate during sleep – especially in non REM sleep in the absence of consciousness ? Certainly, yes. Magnetoencephalographic studies in humans [14, 15], have provided evidence of local brain activations in specific midline cortical regions throughout sleep. These activations (gamma band power even greater than awake periods) arc consistent with cognitive processes during sleep. They appear most prominently in brain areas like precuneous lobule and anterior cingulate gyrus thought to be responsible for monitoring our internal environment and taking decisions accordingly. Electroencephalographic (EEG) studies during non-REM sleep provide indications for cognitive functions based on EEG K-complexes serving as sentinel for a safe sleep [10, 20, 21].

Anxiety associated experiences may be presented as a dream during REM sleep when the stress neurotransmitter Noradrenaline levels are lower. This may serve the purpose of disassociating these experiences from anxiety and therefor more tolerable to consciousness [33]. Emotions expressed during sleep either enhance or help overcome emotional weight of memories. Consistent with this is the finding of limbic system (amygdala and other areas) activations consistently preceding the start of rapid eye movements in REM sleep [13]. Stein [30] likens a memory which would hold only experiences and knowledge with a useless attic full of dusted books. The importance lies with evaluation of events and with interconnecting them. This process appears to take place in sleep. Dreams may be education for our future

5. Creating learning machines in brain's image and likeness?

Could the recent findings on the mechanisms underlying learning and especially sleep's contribution to human learning, help building more efficiently learning computers? Is it feasible to bridge any of the fundamental differences between brain and computer learning?. A ...wish list of exemplary changes in current state computers is attempted:
1...Computers should work much more offline in the way default system and sleep processes do for housekeeping, categorization, synaptic homeostasis, consolidating memories and modifying through rehearsal (equivalent to dreams) their association to emotions
2... Also, they should increase their on-line but task unrelated work embedded in a real environment, which they would continuously probe: make action-related hypotheses about the environment which will be modified by sensory feedback to this action [8].
3...Adopting the above norms computers would benefit from becoming much more personal by developing experience based biases (equivalent to emotions) to be used in the extraction of meaning from sensory inputs and in initiating movements (impetus)
4... as a corollary, learning should not rely on rigidly accurate information to be stored and retrieved, but rather on judiciously associational synthesis, aiming to extract meaning and improve the model of next relevant movement.
5... computers might benefit from developing a function equivalent to elementary consciousness i.e. awareness of the position in space and time of the frame of computing processes, which would take control of a limited part of tasks – actually focus on one at a time - and get periodically suspended for as long time as needed for the computer to work (see above examples 1-3) unbiased by changes in the environment
6....partly remove the watertight barriers between events, which were created by sequential appearance in time. Creative memories result from easy blending of old and new experiences.

It becomes clear that it does not suffice for a future learning machine to mimic the brain; it should mimic an organism surviving in a changing environment, a living robot. In my humble opinion, we are very far from achieving any of the above exemplary goals. A practical and modest approach could address less ambitious questions, but possibly supply foundational knowledge, i.e. (a) experimentally modeling sleep in brain slices and implement the main functions of sleep (replenishment and synaptic plasticity/homeostasis) in small networks; (b) long term network a computer to the brain of a living lower mammal

In any case, development of new learning machines would need evaluation criteria i.e. an unequivocal definition and testing process of intelligence. So far, this testing of a machine intelligence is based on how well it can handle human-made knowledge bases and rules and ultimately on its performance. The human analog of the latter, behavior, depends on so many external factors as to suggest that a better way of testing brain's intelligence is on the basis of its predicting ability.

6. Conclusions

As Moore's law nears its physical limits, a new generation of brain-like or neuromorphic computers are claimed to have come of age. Given that we still don't fully understand how brains work, computers are unlikely to be as good at learning as humans for perhaps hundreds of years. Again, such aphorisms may repeat the mistake experimental psychology was doing (above section 3, How we learn).: memory is not a single process but many different ones. Similarly, computers could become better at specific types of memorizing. Which one may be closer to their capabilities? We're making headway with artificial intelligence, but if we want computers to learn like us then both neuroscientists and computer engineers should think a lot harder. Several examples of new findings on the neuroscience of learning have been discussed in this article including some recent ones revealing that there is no learning without sleep. These examples illustrate the long and uncertain road, which science has to run before brain-like learning can be bestowed in what we call intelligent machines.

On a different vein, do we really want to make so good learners out of machines? Stephen Hawking wrote: "The development of full AI could spell the end of the human race." And Elon Musk: "AI is a greater threat to humans than nuclear weapons." When undoubtedly intelligent people are concerned about the threat of AI (see more in The Guardian, 27 July 2015), one can't help but wonder what's in store for humanity. My personal answer is: Not to worry... AI will not ask our permission. Like all basic science it will develop on its course and it cannot (and should not) be stopped. The scientists' responsibility is to make the scientific developments openly, timely and understandably known to the public, so they – the informed citizens - could intervene and legislate on how the research findings should (and should not) be applied.

Acknowledgments. The author's laboratory received support from the European Commission FP7 grant ARMOR, 2007-2013, agreement number 287720.

7...References

1- Aton SJ, Suresh A, Broussard C, Frank MG. Sleep promotes cortical response potentiation following visual experience. Sleep. 2014 Jul 1;37(7):1163-70. doi: 10.5665/sleep.3830. PubMed PMID: 25061244; PubMed Central PMCID: PMC4098801.

2- Bruce D. Fifty years since Lashley's In search of the Engram: refutations and conjectures. J Hist Neurosci. 2001 Dec;10(3):308-18. PubMed PMID: 11770197.

3- Buckner, R. L.; Andrews-Hanna, J. R.; Schacter, D. L. (2008). "TheBrain's Default Network: Anatomy, Function, and Relevance to Disease". Annals of the New

York Academy of Sciences. **1124** *(1): 1–38.* PMID 18400922. *doi:10.1196/annals.1440.011.*

4- Camina E, Güell F. The Neuroanatomical, Neurophysiological and Psychological Basis of Memory: Current Models and Their Origins. Front Pharmacol. 2017 Jun 30;8:438. doi: 10.3389/fphar.2017.00438. eCollection 2017. Review. PubMed PMID: 28713278; PubMed Central PMCID: PMC5491610.

5- Crunelli V, Hughes SW. The slow (<1 Hz) rhythm of non-REM sleep: a dialogue between three cardinal oscillators. Nat Neurosci. 2010 Jan;13(1):9-17. doi: 10.1038/nn.2445. Epub 2009 Dec 6. Review. PubMed PMID: 19966841; PubMed Central PMCID: PMC2980822.

6- Diekelmann S, Born J. The memory function of sleep. Nat Rev Neurosci. 2010 Feb;11(2):114-26. doi: 10.1038/nrn2762. Epub 2010 Jan 4. Review. PubMed PMID:20046194.

7- *Fox, Michael D.; Snyder, Abraham Z.; Vincent, Justin L.; Corbetta, Maurizio; Van Essen, David C.; Raichle, Marcus E. (2005-07-05). "The human brain is intrinsically organized into dynamic, anticorrelated functional networks". Proceedings of the National Academy of Sciences of the United States of America.* **102** *(27): 9673–9678.* ISSN 0027-8424. PMC 1157105 ③ PMID 15976020. *doi:10.1073/pnas.0504136102.*

8- Freeman WJ *How Brains Make Up their Minds.* Columbia University Press, New York, 2001, 180 p

9- Frith C Wie unser gehirn die welt erschafft. Auslage 2010 Heidelberg: Springer Spectrum

10- Halasz, P., and Bodizs, R. (2013). Dynamic Structure of NREM Sleep. SpringerQ12 Science & Business Media.

11- Hobson JA, Pace-Schott EF. The cognitive neuroscience of sleep: neuronal systems, consciousness and learning. Nat Rev Neurosci. 2002 Sep;3(9):679-93. Review. PubMed PMID: 12209117

12- Hu J, Ferguson L, Adler K, Farah CA, Hastings MH, Sossin WS, Schacher S.Selective Erasure of Distinct Forms of Long-Term Synaptic Plasticity Underlying Different Forms of Memory in the Same Postsynaptic Neuron. Curr Biol. 2017 Jul 10;27(13):1888-1899.e4. doi: 10.1016/j.cub.2017.05.081. Epub 2017 Jun 22. PubMed PMID: 28648820.

13- Ioannides AA, Corsi-Cabrera M, Fenwick PB, del Rio Portilla Y, Laskaris NA, Khurshudyan A, Theofilou D, Shibata T, Uchida S, Nakabayashi T, Kostopoulos GK. MEG tomography of human cortex and brainstem activity in waking and REM sleep saccades. Cereb Cortex. 2004 Jan;14(1):56-72. PubMed PMID: 14654457.

14- Ioannides AA, Kostopoulos GK, Liu L, Fenwick PB. MEG identifies dorsal medial brain activations during sleep. Neuroimage. 2009 Jan 15;44(2):455-68. doi:10.1016/j.neuroimage.2008.09.030. Epub 2008 Oct 7. PubMed PMID: 18950718.

15- Ioannides AA, Liu L., Poghosyan V and Kostopoulos GK, Using MEG to Understand the Progression of Light Sleep and the Emergence and Functional Roles of Spindles and K-Complexes Front. Hum. Neurosci., 16 June 2017 | https://doi.org/10.3389/fnhum.2017.00313

16- Ji D, Wilson MA. Coordinated memory replay in the visual cortex and hippocampus during sleep. Nat Neurosci. 2007 Jan;10(1):100-7. Epub 2006 Dec 17. PubMed PMID: 17173043.

17- Kandel ER, Dudai Y, Mayford MR. The molecular and systems biology of memory. Cell. 2014 Mar 27;157(1):163-86. doi: 10.1016/j.cell.2014.03.001. Review. PubMed PMID: 24679534.

18- Kandel, Eric R.; Schwartz, James H.; Jessell, Thomas M.; Siegelbaum, Steven A.; Hudspeth, A. J. (2013) Principles of Neural Science (5th ed.), New York: McGraw-Hill, ISBN 978-0071390118.

19- Kohavi R and Provost F. (1998), Glossary of terms" Machine Learning. 30: 271–274.

20- Kokkinos, V., and Kostopoulos, G. K. (2011). Human non-rapid eye movement stage II sleep spindles are blocked upon spontaneous K-complex coincidence and resume as higher frequency spindles afterwards. J. Sleep Res. 20, 57–72. doi: 10.1111/j.1365-2869.2010.00830.x

21- Kokkinos V, Koupparis AM, Kostopoulos GK. An intra-K-complex oscillation with independent and labile frequency and topography in NREM sleep. Front Hum Neurosci. 2013 Apr 26;7:163. doi: 10.3389/fnhum.2013.00163. eCollection 2013. PubMed PMID: 23637656; PubMed Central PMCID: PMC3636459.

22- LeDoux, J. Synaptic Self: How Our Brains Become Who We Are. Viking. Jan. 2002. c.400p. index. ISBN 0-670-03028-7.

23- Libbrecht MW, Noble WS. Machine learning applications in genetics and genomics. Nat Rev Genet. 2015 Jun;16(6):321-32. doi: 10.1038/nrg3920. Epub 2015 May 7. Review. PubMed PMID: 25948244; PubMed Central PMCID: PMC5204302.

24- Llinás, R. I of the Vortex: From Neurons to Self (MIT Press, Cambridge, MA. 2001). ISBN 0-262-62163-0

25- Maquet P. The role of sleep in learning and memory. Science. 2001 Nov 2;294(5544):1048-52. Review. PubMed PMID: 11691982.

26- Milner B. Psychological defects produced by temporal lobe excision. Res Publ Assoc Res Nerv Ment Dis. 1958;36:244-57. PubMed PMID: 13527787.

27- Petrides, M. (2000). The role of the mid-dorsolateral prefrontal cortex in working memory. Experimental Brain Research, 133, 44-54.

28- Ribeiro S, Gervasoni D, Soares ES, Zhou Y, Lin SC, Pantoja J, Lavine M, Nicolelis MA. Long-lasting novelty-induced neuronal reverberation during slow-wave sleep in multiple forebrain areas. PLoS Biol. 2004 Jan;2(1):E24. Epub 2004 Jan 20. PubMed PMID: 14737198; PubMed Central PMCID: PMC314474.

29- Siegel JM. Clues to the functions of mammalian sleep. Nature. 2005 Oct 27;437(7063):1264-71. Review. PubMed PMID: 16251951.

30- Stein S. Traume: Eine Reise in unsere innere Wirklichkeit. 2014 S. Fisher Verlag GmbH

31- Stickgold R. Sleep-dependent memory consolidation. Nature. 2005 Oct 27;437(7063):1272-8. Review. PubMed PMID: 16251952.

32- Tononi G, Cirelli C. Sleep and Synaptic Down-Selection. 2016 May 3. In: Buzsáki G, Christen Y, editors. Micro-, Meso- and Macro-Dynamics of the Brain [Internet]. Cham (CH): Springer; 2016. Available from http://www.ncbi.nlm.nih.gov/books/NBK435759/PubMed PMID: 28590688.

33- Walker MP The role or sleep in cognition and emotion. In Annals of new York Academy of Sciences 1156 (2009) Nr 1 168-197

34- Yang G. 2014 Sleep promotes branch-specific formation of dendritic spines after learning. Science 344: 1173-1178.

Modeling animal brains with evolutive cognitive schemas

Pierre Bonzon[1]

[1] Dept of Information Systems, Faculty of HEC, University of Lausanne, Switzerland

pierre.bonzon@unil.ch

Abstract. Very specifically, functional behavior assessment is a domain in developmental psychology looking at the reasons behind a child's observed behavior. More generally, it can be considered as the search for the explanation of human and non-human actions. Towards this goal, computational cognitive neuroscience offers a new range of possibilities that contrast with the usual statistical approaches. An attempt to assess brain functionalities in learning is illustrated here through the simulation of analogical inferences. As a main result of this paper, the mapping of evolutive cognitive schemas onto neural connection structures involving two types of cognitive transfer points out to a possible discontinuity between human and non-human minds.

Keywords: hebbian learning, neural process, cognitive schema, analogical infehrence, simulation.

1   Introduction

As early as in 1936, Piaget considered, and later defined [1], a cognitive schema as being "*a cohesive, repeatable action sequence possessing component actions that are tightly interconnected and governed by a core meaning*". According to this theory, cognitive schemas constitute the building blocks for knowledge acquisition. This concept has been first found incompatible (see e.g., [2]) with the then dominant paradigm of behaviorism, essentially because at that time the corresponding internal processes could not be observed nor measured. Since then, the statistical analysis of sophisticated experimental results and/or simulations [3] has led to the discovery of patterns of neuronal activations that could be identified with building blocks of perception [4]. Acquired memory and skills could thus rely on combining these elementary assemblies into higher-order constructs. These results, however, do not identify the processes relating perception and behavior. In other words, as pointed out by many commentators (see e.g., [5][6]), they do not allow for describing *algorithms* and underlying *circuits*. What is then needed, they conclude, is a "*middle-out*" approach that can identify plausible structures linking biology and cognition.

© Springer International Publishing AG 2017
C. Frasson and G. Kostopoulos (Eds.): BFAL 2017, LNAI 10512, pp. 98–107, 2017
DOI: 10.1007/978-3-319-67615-9_9

This need can be related to the general "*what*" and "*how*" questions of cognitive science as addressed by the historical Marr's "tri-level" hypothesis [7] that distinguishes *computational*, *algorithmic* and *implementation* levels. Adding on this, Poggio [8] argues that, in order to discover the representations used by the brain, one needs to understand "*how* an individual organism learns and evolves them from experience of the natural world", and that "learning algorithms and their a priori assumptions are deeper and more useful than a description of the details of *what* is actually learned". As a consequence, *evolution* and *learning* should be added to the levels in cognitive studies.

Towards this goal, a different approach to brain modeling has been proposed [9]. Defined by a logic program of about 300 lines, an experimental platform for this new type of modeling can be run on any PC. The corresponding formal framework stands out of the usual methods by focusing on *processes*. It relies for this on three concepts of computer science and mathematical logic i.e., the formal notions of:
- an *object in context* represented by expressions in a logical language
- *communicating processes* between *concurrent threads* that can be used to model the interaction of objects obeying various communication protocols
- a *virtual machine* interpreting virtual code that differs from a processor's native code.

In software engineering, a virtual machine constitutes the key mechanism that allows for interfacing high level objects i.e., software, with their low level physical support i.e., hardware. In a multi-level model of brain structures and processes, such a machine does function as an interface between the neural and cognitive levels, therefore allowing for grounded models of cognition to be formulated by relating perception and behavior at a *symbolic* level. This does not mean however that abstracting away physiological details detaches cognitive models from their supporting neural substrate: *quite to the contrary, as we shall briefly review below, communication protocols representing synaptic plasticity actually drive the hebbian learning of cognitive structures*.

2   Material and methods.

Our overall methodology can be described by the following sequence:
a) *micro scale* virtual circuits implementing synaptic plasticity through asynchronous communicating processes are first defined
b) *meso scale* virtual circuits corresponding to basic cognitive processes are then composed out of these micro scale circuits
c) both types of virtual circuits are finally compiled into *virtual code* to be interpreted by a virtual machine.

Communication protocols for *micro scale* circuits as well as the specifications of our virtual machine are given in open access in [9]. Examples of mesoscale circuits corresponding to cognitive software running on top of a simulated biological substrate are presented below for illustrative purposes. At the same time, they do constitute the building blocks of the developments to be presented in our Results section.

2.1 A case of classical conditioning

As a general evolution principle, organisms tend to devise and use "tricks" for their survival. The ability to evaluate a threat by learning predictive relationships e.g., by associating a noise and the presence of a predator, is an example of such tricks realized by *classical conditioning*.

Let us consider the classical conditioning in the defensive siphon and gill withdrawal reflex of *aplysia californica* [10]. In this experiment, a light tactile conditioned stimulus **cs** elicits a weak defensive reflex, and a strong noxious unconditioned stimulus **us** (usually an electric shock) produces a massive withdrawal reflex. After a few pairings of stimuli **cs** and **us,** where **cs** slightly precedes **us**, a stimulus **cs** alone triggers a significantly enhanced withdrawal reflex i.e., the organism has learned a new behavior. This can be represented by a wiring diagram, or *virtual circuit* (see Figure 1), adapted from [11] to allow for a one to one correspondence with symbolic expressions.

```
sense(cs)-*->=>-motor(cs)
         /|\
         ltp
          |
sense(us)-+->=>-motor(us)
```

Fig. 1. A virtual circuit implementing classical conditioning.

In Figure 1, the components **sense(us)** and **sense(cs)** are coupled with sensors (not shown here) capturing external stimuli **us** and **cs** and correspond to sensory neurons. The components **motor(us)** and **motor(cs)** are coupled with action effectors (also not shown) and correspond to motor neurons. Finally, the component **ltp** embodies the mechanism of long term potentiation and acts as a facilitatory interneuron reinforcing the pathway (i.e. augmenting its *weight*) between **sense(cs)** and **motor(cs)**. The interaction of these components are represented by the iconic symbols **->=>-** and **/|** that correspond to a synaptic transmission (i.e., **->=>-** represents a *synapse*) and to the modulation of a synapse, respectively. The symbols ***** and **+** stand for conjunctive and disjunctive operators (i.e., they are used to represent the convergence of incoming signals and the dissemination of an outgoing signal, respectively). Classical conditioning then follows from the application of hebbian learning [12] i.e., "neurons that fire together wire together". Though it is admitted today that classical conditioning in aplysia is mediated by multiple neuronal mechanisms [13] including a postsynaptic retroaction on a presynaptic site, the important issue is that the learning of a new behavior requires a conjoint activity of multiple neurons. This activity in turn depends critically on the temporal pairing of the conditioned and unconditioned stimuli **cs** and **us**, which in conclusion leads to implement the **ltp** component as a *detector of coincidence*.

2.2 A simple case of operant conditioning

The ability to assess and to remember the consequences of one's own actions is another example of associative learning providing survival advantages. In this case, *operant conditioning* [14] associates an action and its result, which can be *positive* or *negative*. Toward this goal, the organism will first receive either an *excite* or an *inhibit* feedback stimulus, corresponding for instance to a reward or punishment, respectively; it will then associate this feedback with an appropriate action.

Let us consider a simple thought experiment where a *pigeon* is learning to discriminate between grains and pebbles corresponding to two possible vectors **I** of external visual stimuli **[mat,smooth]** and **[shiny,smooth]**. The *circuit* given in Figure 2, represents the wiring of four components **sense(I)**, **learn(accept(I))**, **accept(I)** and **reject(I)**, together with two **ltp** and two opposite **ltd** (for long term depression) components. In addition to the external stimuli captured by component **sense(I)**, this circuit incorporates the two internal stimuli **excite(accept(I))** and **inhibit(accept(I))** that correspond to feedbacks from probing the food according to a set of *accepted* elements.

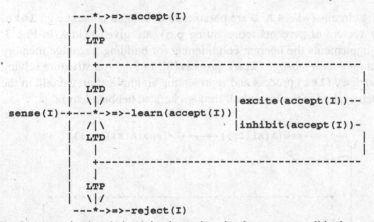

```
    ---*->=>-accept(I)
  |    /|\
  |    LTP
  |     |
  |     +------------------------------------------
  |     |                                         |
  |    LTD                                         |
  |    \|/                        |excite(accept(I))--
sense(I)-+----*->=>-learn(accept(I))|
  |    /|\                         |inhibit(accept(I))-
  |    LTD                          |               |
  |     |                                           |
  |     +------------------------------------------
  |     |
  |    LTP
  |    \|/
    ---*->=>-reject(I)
```

Fig. 2. A generic virtual circuit implementing simple operant conditioning

At the beginning of the simulation, the pathways from **sense(I)** to **learn(accept(I))** is open, while the pathways to both **accept(I)** and **reject(I)** are closed. After a few trials, the pigeon will have learned to close **learn(accept(I))** and to open either **accept(I)** or **reject(I)**. This process matches a fundamental principle in circuit neuroscience according to which *inhibition* in neuronal networks during baseline conditions allows in turn for *disinhibition*, which then stands as a key mechanism for circuit plasticity, learning, and memory retrieval [15]; this gives rise in turn to two populations of neurons that have opposing spiking patterns in anticipation of movement [16] as well as two eligibility traces with different temporal profiles, one corresponding to the induction of **ltp**, and the other to the induction of **ltd** [17][18].

3   Results

Following our previous results [9] on modeling the first three levels of animal awareness according to Pepperberg & Lynn (2000 [19]), the mapping of analogical inference schemas onto neural connection structures involving two types of cognitive transfer points out to a possible discontinuity between human and non-human minds.

3.1 Learning a simple analogical inference schema

Let us first consider a simple analogical inference schema involving two predicates **p** and **q** applied to objects **X1** and **X2**, i.e.

```
{p(X1)}                      {big(dog)}
{p(X2)}         e.g.,        {big(bear)}
 q(X1)                       strong(dog)
 q(X2)                       strong(bear)
```

where {**F**} represents a fact **F**, or proposition, that has been previously memorized. This schema can be viewed as first inducing an implication i.e., **p(X) -> q(X)**, where **x** is a variable, and then applying modus ponens i.e.,

```
p(X) -> q(X)
p(X)
q(X)
```

The corresponding circuits (where **A**, **B** are parameters defining a context e.g., **left**, **right**, and **I**,**J** vectors of percepts representing **p**,**q**) are given below. In Fig. 3, each half circuit implements the operant conditioning for building a storage memory trace relying on a *long term storage* (**lts**) process [9]. In Fig. 4, a structure relying on a *long term retrieval* (**ltr**) process and representing an implication is build in the upper half and then applied in the lower half through iterated hebbian learning.

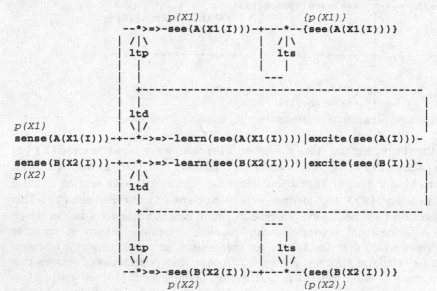

```
                     p(X1)                 {p(X1)}
            --*>=>-see(A(X1(I)))-+---*--{see(A(X1(I)))}
            | /|\                  | /|\
            | ltp                  | lts
            |  |                   |  |
            |  |                   | ---
            |  |                   |
            |  +----------------------------------------------
            |  |                                              |
            | ltd                                             |
   p(X1)    | \|/                                             |
sense(A(X1(I)))-+--*->=>-learn(see(A(X1(I))))|excite(see(A(I)))-

sense(B(X2(I)))-+--*->=>-learn(see(B(X2(I))))|excite(see(B(I)))-
   p(X2)    | /|\                                             |
            | ltd                                             |
            |  |                                              |
            |  +----------------------------------------------
            |  |                                 |
            |  |                                --- |
            |  |                                 |  |
            | ltp                               | lts
            | \|/                               | \|/
            --*>=>-see(B(X2(I)))-+---*--{see(B(X2(I)))}
                     p(X2)                 {p(X2)}
```

Fig. 3. Virtual circuit for memorizing perceptions

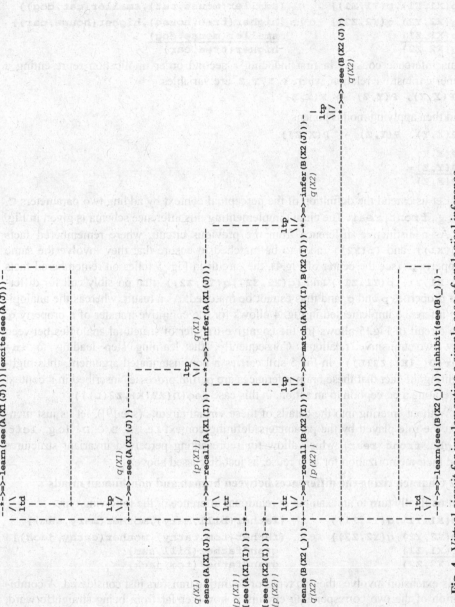

Fig. 4. Virtual circuit for implementing a simple case of analogical inference

3.2 Learning an analogical inference schema implementing transitive relations

Let us now consider a case of relational inference based on transitive relations i.e.,

```
{p(X1,Y1),p(Y1,Z1)}        {smaller(mouse,cat),smaller(cat,dog)}
{q(X2,Y2),q(Y2,Z2)}  e.g., {higher(tree,house),higher(house,car)}
 p(X1,Z1)                   smaller(mouse,dog)
 q(X2,Z2)                   higher(tree,car)
```

This inference consists in first inducing a second order implication representing a generic transitive relation, where `P,X,Y,Z` are variables

```
 P(X,Y), P(Y,Z) -> P(X,Z)
```

and then applying modus ponens

```
{P(X,Y), P(Y,Z) -> P(X,Z)}

 P(X,Y)
 P(Y,Z)
 P(X,Z)
```

Let us extend the definition of the perceptual context by adding two parameters `C`, `D` e.g., `front`, `rear`. The circuit implementing this inference schema is given in Fig. 5. As a distinctive difference from the previous circuit, where remembered facts `{p(X1)}` and `{p(X2)}` need to be matched to ensure that they involve the same property `p` (see the center of Fig.4), the circuit in Fig. 5 relies on remembered facts `{p(X1,Y1),p(Y1,Z1)}` and `{q(X2,Y2),q(Y2,Z2)}` that possibly call for different properties `p` and `q`, and thus cannot be matched. As a result, whereas the analogical inference implemented in Fig. 4 allows for the cognitive transfer of a property `q`, the circuit of Fig. 5 allows for the cognitive transfer of structural analogies between any two transitive relations. Consequently, the learning step leading to `infer(D(_(K),Z2(L)))` in Fig.5 still carries a non instantiated argument, thus highlighting the fact that these brain inferences are partial processes inscribed in a context D relating a perception to an action, in this case `see(D(X2(K),Z2(L)))`.

Without entering into the details of these virtual circuits (see [9]), let us just mention the role played by the parameters defining context i.e. , `A, B, C, D` (e.g., `left`, `right`, `front`, `rear`), which allow for representing perceived invariant structures and their memorization for later reuse, as just discussed above.

3.2 Characterizing the differences between human and non-human minds

Let us finally turn to an example of relational inference of the following type

```
{p(X1,Y1),q(Y1,Z1)}        {father(bill,mary),mother(mary,sam)}
{p(X2,Y2),q(Y2,Z2)}  e.g., {father(tom,cathy),mother(cathy,jack)}
 r(X1,Z1)                   grandfather(bill,sam)
 r(X2,Z2)                   grandfather(tom,jack)
```

This extension involves the two types of cognitive transfers just considered. A combination of the two corresponding circuits is however far from being straightforward, the difficulty being here the parallel matching of multiple interleaved properties. Whereas behaviors relying on simple analogical reasoning and transitive inference, as modeled by the circuits of Fig. 4 and 5, have been observed in non-humans animals, this more complex example is unarguably out of their reach. It is interesting to note that previous modeling approaches relying on substitutions [20] have led to similar conclusions [21]. On the other hand, further results [22] pertaining to a simple form of meta-cognition observed in animals, namely memory awareness, have been obtained

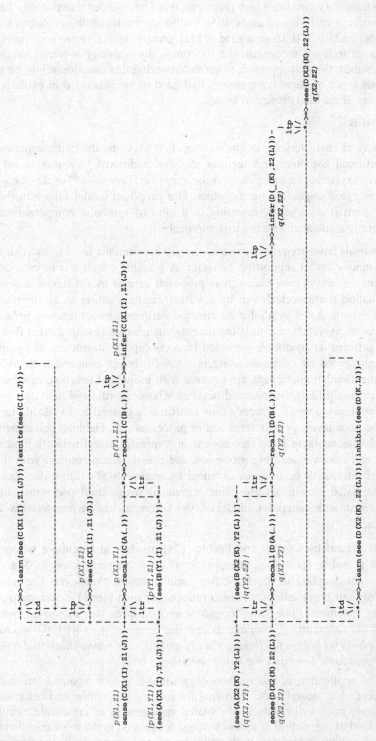

Fig. 5. Virtual circuit implementing transitive inferences

by combining elementary circuits (more precisely, this higher-order functionality can be reduced to successive layers of associative memories implementing *retrospective revaluation* as defined in [23]). If, as argued in [21], one of the challenges confronting cognitive scientists today is to explain the functional discontinuity between human and nonhuman minds, then an approach towards answering this question might be to study the various types of cognitive transfers that need to be embedded in evolutive cognitive schemas of the kind presented here.

4   Discussion

A common way of characterizing cognitive models is given by the two competing paradigms of artificial cognitive architectures i.e., the traditional *"sense-think-act"* cycle of cognitivist systems, on one side, and the simplified *"sense-act"* cycle of *embodied* and/or *emergent* cognition, on the other. Our proposed model falls into the second category, but it does so by resorting to a kind of symbolic computational framework generally associated with the first approach.

Various proposals have been made to close the gap between the level of individual neurons and symbolic levels supporting behavior. A possible solution is to consider group of neurons, or *neural assemblies*. It is proposed here to model neural assemblies in a simulation framework driven by a virtual machine acting as an interface between neural dynamics and symbolic information defining perceptions and behaviors. While the usual approach to simulating neural dynamics starts with current flows represented by differential equations, we opted for a conceptual abstraction of synaptic plasticity represented by communicating processes between concurrent *threads*. Whereas in some simulations threads are equated with individual neurons, in others they do represent multiple interconnected neurons whose coordinated activity converges into an aggregated result. Threads thus constitute a general and versatile tool for simulating various levels of structures and/or processes e.g., Hebbian cell assemblies. As a consequence, there is no reference to any specific neural network model. In order to try and discover learning processes, and thus in sharp contrast with the usual models of interactive brain areas obtained by quantitatively fitting data (i.e., where latent estimated parameters are being correlated with neural measures), the goal here is to construct a generative model of how behaviors can be interfaced with neural dynamics.

As forcefully argued by Cooper and Peebles [24], models in Cognitive Science cannot proceed at either level (i.e., computational or implementational in Marr's sense) without tight coupling to the algorithmic and representation level. The most important part of their argumentation (which reflects our own views) is summarized in the following statement: "*Integrated cognitive architectures that permit abstract specification of the functions of components and that make contact with the neural level provide a powerful bridge for linking the algorithmic and representational level to both the computational level and the implementational level*".

The successful application of this methodology could lead to a reconsideration of the whole concept of a "neural code" allowing for relating perception and behavior. Such a neural code may well reside in the spatial arrangement of mesoscale circuit patterns (i.e., a kind of population or sparse coding, as opposed to the more traditional rate or temporal coding associated with spike trains). More precisely, perception might be related to behaviors through the paths found by evolution via iterated hebbian learning.

References

1. Piaget, J.: Jean Piaget. In E. Boring, H. Langfeld, H. Werner, & R. Yerkes (Eds.), *History of psychology in autobiography* IV:.237-256. Clark University Press (1952).
2. Bruner, J.: *The Process of education*. Harvard University Press (1960).
3. Palmeri, T., Turner, M., Love B.: Model-based Cognitive Neuroscience. *J. of Math. Psychology* 76,B (2017).
4. Perin, R., Berger, T., Markram, H.: A synaptic organizing principle for cortical neuronal groups. *Proceedings National Academy Sciences of the USA (PNAS)* 108(12) (2011).
5. van der Velde , F., de Kamps, M.:The necessity of connection structures in neural models of variable binding. *Cognitive Neurodynamics* 9, 359–37 (2015).
6. Frégnac, Y., Bathellier, B. : Cortical Correlates of Low-Level Perception: From Neural Circuits to Percepts. *Neuron* 88 (2015).
7. Marr, D.: *Vision: A Computational Investigation into the Human Representation and Processing of Visual Information*. Freeman (1982).
8. Poggio, T.: The level of understandings framework. *Perception* 41, 1007-23 (2012).
9. Bonzon, P. Towards neuro-inspired symbolic models of cognition: linking neural dynamics to behaviors through asynchronous communications. *Cognitive Neurodynamics* 11 (4), 327-353 doi:10.1007/s11571-017-9435-3 (2017).
10. Kandel, ER., Tauc, L: Heterosynaptic facilitation in neurones of the abdominal ganglion of *Aplysia* depilans. Journal *of Physiology (London)* 181 (1965).
11. Carew, TJ., Walters, ET., Kandel, ER.: Classical conditioning in a simple withdrawal reflex in Aplysia californica, *The Journal of neuroscience* 1(12), 1426-1437 (1981).
12. Hebb, D.: *The organization of behavior. A neuropsychological theory*. J. Wiley (1949).
13. Antonov, I., Antonova, I., Kandel, ER., Hawkins, RD.: Activity-Dependent Presynaptic Facilitation & Hebbian ltp Are Both Required & Interact during Classical Conditioning in Aplysia. *Neuron* 37 (1) (2003).
14. Skinner, BF.: Are theories of learning necessary? *Psychological review* 57, 193-207 (1950).
15. Letzkus, J., Wolff, S., Lüthi, A.: Disinhibition, a Circuit Mechanism for Associative Learning & Memory. *Neuron*, 88(3), 264–276 (2015).
16. Zagha, E., Ge X., McCormick G.: Competing Neural Ensembles in Motor Cortex Gate Goal-Directed Motor Output. *Neuron*, 88(3), 565–577 (2015).
17. Huertas, M., Schwettmann, S., Kirkwood, A., Shouval, H.: Stable reinforcement learning via temporal competition between LTP & LTD traces. *BMC Neuroscience* 15(Suppl 1):O12 (2014).
18. He, K., Huertas, M., Hong, SZ, Tie, XX., Hell J., Souval H., Kirkwood, A.: Distinct Eligibility Traces for LTP & L.TD in Cortical Synapses. *Neuron* 88(3), 528–538 (2015).
19. Pepperberg, I, Lynn, S (2000). Possible Levels of Animal Consciousness with Reference to Grey Parrots (Psittaccus erithacus). *American Zoologist*, 40, 893-901.
20. Hummel, JE., Holyoak, K.: A Symbolic-Connectionist theory of Relational Inference and Generalization. *Psychological Review* 110 (2),220-264 (2003).
21. Penn, DC., Holyoak, K.J., Povinelli, D.J. Darwin's mistake: Explaining the discontinuity between human and nonhuman minds. *Behavioral and Brain Sciences*, 31, 109–178 (2008)
22. Bonzon, P. Beyond animal awareness: continuity vs discontinuity between human and non-human minds (*submitted*).
23. Holland, PC. Event representations in Pavlovian conditioning: image and action. *Cognition* 37, 105–131 (1990).
24. Cooper, R, Peebles, D. Beyond Single-Level Accounts: The Role of Cognitive Architectures in Cognitive Scientific Explanation, *Topics in Cognitive Science* 7, 243–258 (2015).

Neural Knowledge Tracing

Long Sha and Pengyu Hong

Computer Science, Brandeis University, Waltham, MA, USA
`longsha@brandeis.edu, hongpeng@brandeis.edu`

Abstract. Knowledge tracing aims to quantify how well students master the knowledge (tags) being tutored by analyzing their learning activities (e.g., coursework interaction data). It plays an important role in intelligent tutoring systems. In this paper, we cast knowledge tracing as a performance-prediction problem, which predicts the performances of students on exercises labeled by multiple knowledge tags, and propose to tackle this problem using Deep Learning techniques. We applied several Recurrent Neural Network architectures to model complex representations of student knowledge and predict future performances of students. Our experimental results demonstrate that the neural network architecture based on stacked Long Short Term Memory and residual connections give superior predictions on the future performances of learners. To model how a student answered a question that contains multiple knowledge tags, we explored three different variants to map knowledge states to prediction.

Keywords: Knowledge Tracing, Recurrent Neural Network, LSTM, Stacked LSTM, Residual Connection.

1 Introduction

Online intelligent tutoring systems have been booming in recent years because they offer opportunities for opening the best instruction resources, used to available to prestigious schools, to the whole world and help break down the barrier of education. It can also help dramatically reduce the time and financial cost in lifelong learning. There are several successful online educational platforms (e.g., Coursera, EdX, Khan Academy etc.) where students' learning activities can be recorded. Traditional 1-to-1 tutoring, which provides a so-called 'personalized education' from the instructor, has been proven to be very effective. This is because there are huge variances among students in terms of their knowledge backgrounds and capabilities of acquiring new knowledge. The instructor in 1-to-1 settings can provide personalized education based on the above differences in individual students. As the user base of online learning keeps growing at an unprecedented scale, it becomes crucial and beneficial to automatically model how well students master knowledge by analyzing their learning activities and then deliver personalized learning materials. In the meantime, online learning platforms have accumulated enough student learning activities that make it feasible to accurately and automatically model student knowledge.

© Springer International Publishing AG 2017
C. Frasson and G. Kostopoulos (Eds.): BFAL 2017, LNAI 10512, pp. 108–117, 2017
DOI: 10.1007/978-3-319-67615-9_10

Deep neural networks have recently been successfully used to significantly improve speech recognition, image-based object recognition/detection, machine translation, and many applications in other domains [1]. The multiple layer architectures of deep neural networks enable several levels of abstraction to represent complex observations, which can be used to model student knowledge states from their homework/coursework history. The data D used in this work is explained as the following:

$$D = \{S_1, S_2, \dots, S_N\}$$

$$S_i = \{x_{i1}, x_{i2}, \dots, x_{iM}\}$$

$$x_{it} = \{q_{it}, a_{it}\}$$

Where S_i represents the history of the i-th student and x_{it} is one Question-Answering (Q/A) interaction entry of the i-th student. The length of the interactions M varies among students. A Q/A entry contains a vector q_{it} labeling the question or exercise done by the i-th student at time t. The elements in q_{it} are binary representing if the corresponding knowledge tags are related to the question or not. a_{it} is using a binary value (1/0) to represent whether the question or exercise done by the i-th student at time t is correct or not. Our task is to model knowledge traces of students by analyzing the learning history data D, and use the results to predict the future performances of students.

Knowledge tracing has been an important task in intelligent tutoring [19,20]. Bayesian knowledge tracing (BKT) [4, 18] uses Hidden Markov Models to learn the student knowledge states as a set of binary variables representing if a student understands the corresponding concepts or not. Extensions were later added to BKT to handle contextualization of guessing and slipping estimates [21]. Recently researchers combined Item Response Theory (IRT) [22] and Learning Factor Analysis (LFA) [23] to achieve competitive results with BKT. Piech et al. [2] applied deep learning (more specifically, recurrent neural network) to knowledge tracing (DKT) and delivered a significant improvement over BKT. The input representations used in [2,3] are very different from ours. They decompose each Q/A entry x_{it} in our representation into multiple ones, each of which has only one knowledge tag. This setting can greatly inflate the reported prediction performance because one correct prediction was counted multiple times in evaluation. In addition, the order of their converted single-tag entries was set based on some undisclosed principle, which makes it hard to digest.

2 Models

In this work, we also adopt recurrent neural networks (RNNs) to model student knowledge states and predict student performances. RNNs have been successfully applied to model time series data, such as text, audio, and so on. RNNs allow gradient propagation through time to model the time series data with a different length of input and output [5]. The structure of a simple Recurrent Neural Network is shown in **Fig. 1**. The computational flow is as follows:

$$h_t = \tanh\left(W_{hx}x_t + W_{hh}h_{t-1} + b_h\right)$$

$$k_t = \sigma \left(W_{kh} h_t + b_k \right)$$

Using backpropagation through time, we can train such a simple RNN to trace student hidden knowledge state using the learning history data D.

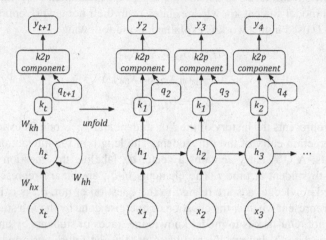

Fig. 1. The architecture of the simple recurrent neural network. Left is the concise representation, and right is the unrolled version along in time dimension. The variable h_t represents the hidden state of the model at time t, and k_t is a vector with a size of the knowledge tags to represent the mastery of knowledge/skills by a student at time t. The K2P component models the mapping from student knowledge states to student performances, which will be discussed later in section 2.1. The variable y_t predicts student performance. Note that each student has an RNN. We drop the student index for conciseness (same in the following figures).

While accessing student performances with their interactions, it can be decomposed to modeling long term dependencies and short term dependencies among interactions. It is well known that simple RNNs have a vanishing/exploding gradient problem making it very difficult to learn long-range dependencies [6, 7]. Long Short Term Memory (LSTM) [7] is an improvement over simple RNNs and is more capable of handling long-range dependencies. LSTM (see **Fig. 2**) contains several internal gates that are updated dynamically to control information flows. The additional complexity provided by those internal gates makes LSTM well-suited learning from time series data when there are time lags of unknown size and bound between relatively long-range important events [10, 24]. The computational flow of an LSTM shown in **Fig. 2** is as follows:

Three internal gates (input, forget, and output):

$$i_t = \sigma \left(W_i [x_t, h_{t-1}] + b_i \right)$$
$$f_t = \sigma \left(W_f [x_t, h_{t-1}] + b_f \right)$$
$$o_t = \sigma \left(W_o [x_t, h_{t-1}] + b_o \right)$$

The input is combined with the hidden state:

$$c\_in_t = tanh(W_{c\_in} [x_t, h_{t-1}] + b_{c\_in})$$

Inter-state update:

$$c_t = f_t \odot c_{t-1} + i_t \odot c\_in_t$$
$$h_t = o_t \odot tanh(c_t)$$
$$k_t = \sigma\,(W_{kh}h_t + b_k)$$

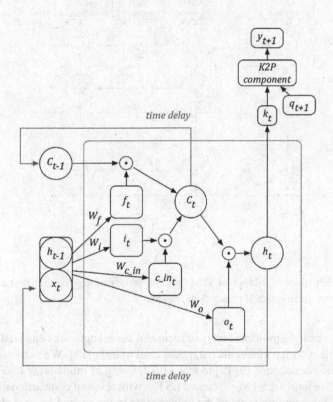

Fig. 2. The illustration of an LSTM module inside the recurrent structure at a single time step t, i_t is the input gate, f_t is the forget gate and o_t is the output gate. The dashed lines represented a $tanh$ function.

Although LSTM has a certain capability of learning relatively long range dependency, it still has trouble remembering long-term information [11]. It was demonstrated in [8] that stacking layers of RNNs can provide a way to ease the hardship of learning the long-term dependencies in LSTM. We, therefore, developed a two-layer stacked LSTM (s-LSTM, see **Fig. 3**). The computation flow of our s-LSTM is defined below:

$$h_{1,t} = f_{LSTM-1}(h_{1,t-1},\, x_t)$$

$$h_{2,t} = f_{LSTM-2}(h_{2,t-1},\, h_{1,t})$$

$$k_t = \sigma\,(W_{kh}h_{2,t} + b_k)$$

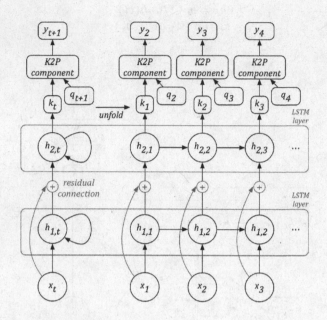

Fig. 3. The architectures of 2-layer s-LSTM (without green residual connections) and 2-layer s-LSTM-r (with the green residual connections) models.

However, stacking multiple layers of recurrent neural networks can lead to the *degradation* problem which makes such a model hard to train [12]. We explored the adoption of residual connections [9, 12] to make the training of multi-layer LSTM network easier, which we term s-LSTM-r (stacked LSTM with residual connections, **see Fig. 3**). In s-LSTM-r, the computational of the hidden state in the second layer is changed to:

$$h_{2,t} = f_{LSTM-2}(h_{2,t-1}, h_{1,t} + x_t)$$

2.1   Knowledge to Prediction (K2P) Component

Here we explain the K2P components used in the models described earlier. Since only the student answers in the data can be used as the output, we add a K2P component to each model to predict student performance given student knowledge states and a question. Basically, we trained the models to predict the student answer to the next question and implicitly model student knowledge states, and used the negative log likelihood of y_{t+1} with the true student answer at time step $t+1$ as the objective function. The following three K2P variants were explored.

Averaging Method. We predict student performance y_{t+1} by taking the element-wise dot product between the knowledge tags of the next question (q_{t+1}) and the k_t output of an RNN, and then taking the mean of the non-zero products. This method assumes that the probability of a student answering a question correctly can be captured by the average of his/her mastery of knowledge appeared in the question.

Minimum Method. Different from the above Averaging method, the Minimum method assumes that the probability of a student answering a question correctly can be captured by one knowledge item, which appears in the question and he/she masters the worst.

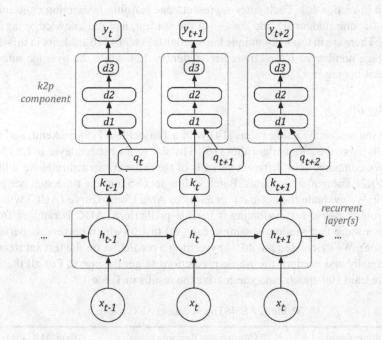

Fig. 4. The illustration of the Multi-Dense-Layer method, d1 and d2 are dense layers that set to be a size of 100 and d3 is a layer that densely connected with d2 with a size of 1. The upper green box represents the K2P component and the bottom green box is recurrent layer (in this figure we only show the simple RNN structure, the other 3 variants we discussed in section 3.1 also fit here).

Multi-Dense-Layer Method. There can exist complex relationships between how well a student understands individual knowledge items and his/her capability of answering a question correctly. We, therefore, investigated using a multi-dense-layer neural network to model such complex relationships (see **Fig.4**).

3   Experiment Results

3.1   Dataset

We evaluated our method on the ASSISTtment 2009-2010 'skill builder' benchmark dataset [13], which was the largest public benchmark dataset to our knowledge. The dataset was collected using the ASSISTment online tutoring platform, which allows K-12 students to complete homework and classwork online. We used an 80% / 20% split on the dataset for training and testing as suggested in [2]. The dataset consists of 346,860 unique QA entries after we preprocessed it into the dense multi-tag version as described in section 1.2. Each entry represents one learning interaction containing the question ID, one student ID, the answer of the student, and the knowledge tags of the question. There are in total 124 unique knowledge tags and 4216 students in this dataset. The average number of interactions per student is 124 while the average number of interactions per tag is 4238.

3.2   Results

We built the models by using Keras [14] with a TensorFlow [15] backend, and trained the models using the Adam algorithm [16]. The size of the hidden layer in LSTM is set to 200. We compared four different variants of the recurrent structure along with three different K2P component variants. Batch size is set to 5 and the time step per batch is set to 100. We evaluate the accuracy in terms of Area Under Curve (AUC) which provided a robust metric for evaluating 0/1 value predictions. AUC is ranging from 0.5 (which is a score that randomly sample can get) to 1.0 (which represents perfect discrimination). We calculated the AUC by getting a prediction on the test set treating all entries equally and used all the whole predictions to get the curve. For all the experiments, we train 100 epochs and summarize the results in Table 1.

Table 1. ASSISTment dataset AUC results.

Recurrent Structure	K2P Component Variant	Best AUC (%) (mean ± std)
sRNN	Averaging	69.53 (69.22 ± 0.27)
	Minimum	66.68 (66.18 ± 0.34)
	Multi-Dense-Layer	69.98 (69.92 ± 0.05)
LSTM	Averaging	73.20 (72.98 ± 0.15)
	Minimum	72.23 (72.07 ± 0.17)
	Multi-Dense-Layer	75.11 (75.03 ± 0.06)
s-LSTM	Averaging	74.74 (74.57 ± 0.10)
	Minimum	72.60 (72.51 ± 0.07)
	Multi-Dense-Layer	77.10 (76.96 ± 0.09)
s-LSTM-r	Averaging	75.28 (75.22 ± 0.05)
	Minimum	72.52 (72.48 ± 0.04)
	Multi-Dense-Layer	**77.87** (77.77 ± 0.10)

It should be noted that the performances listed in Table 1 are quite different from those reported in DKT [2] because we used a very different evaluation method. Using our evaluation method, the result of the original DKT method would be close to that of LSTM + Averaging K2P component in **Table 1.** We run it 5 with random partitions and report the AUC in the 'best (mean ± std)' format. We observed in our experiments that the enhanced recurrent models, which is more capable of dealing with the long-range dependency produced better results. Also, by adopting the residual connections, the network tackles the degradation problem and made it easier to train. The stacked LSTM with residual connections outperformed simple RNN by a significant margin. We also observed that better results were obtained when using a more complex K2P component (multiple-dense-layers versus average/minimal pooling layer). Using our trained model, we can visualize (see **Fig. 5**) to trace a student knowledge states change over a series of interactions.

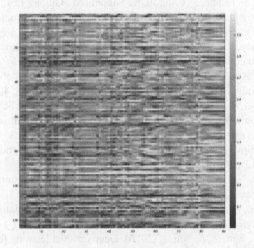

Fig. 5. Knowledge states of a typical student changing over 90 sequential interactions. The vertical axis represents different knowledge tags (124 total in the figure) and the horizontal axis represents the 90 sequential interactions. The values range from 0 (lowest) to 1 (highest) representing how well a student master the corresponding knowledge.

4   Conclusion and Discussion

We developed an LSTM-based knowledge tracing neural network model and demonstrated its power of tracing student knowledge from student learning history and using the tracing results to predict future performances of students. We learned from our experiment results that the capability of modeling long-distance dependency is essential. A close examination of the data revealed that some knowledge tags are closely related to each other. This explains why the results of using Multi-Dense-Layer K2P component are better than other K2P components. The multiple dense layers allow the model to capture dependencies between knowledge tags. We plan to investigate better methods for simultaneously tracing student knowledge and modeling interactions between knowledge tags in exercises, which can be explored to deliver better prediction results and more insights into student knowledge states. Recently, Convolution Neural Network (CNN) was shown to deliver promising results in analyzing time series data [17]. We plan to explore the possibility of replacing RNN by CNN or combining them in our knowledge tracing models.

References

1. LeCun, Y., Bengio, Y., & Hinton, G. (2015). Deep learning. Nature, 521(7553), 436-444.
2. Piech, C., Bassen, J., Huang, J., Ganguli, S., Sahami, M., Guibas, L. J., & Sohl-Dickstein, J. (2015). Deep knowledge tracing. In Advances in Neural Information Processing Systems (pp. 505-513).
3. Khajah, M., Lindsey, R. V., & Mozer, M. C. (2016). How deep is knowledge tracing?. arXiv preprint arXiv:1604.02416.
4. Corbett, A. T., & Anderson, J. R. (1994). Knowledge tracing: Modeling the acquisition of procedural knowledge. User modeling and user-adapted interaction, 4(4), 253-278.
5. Graves, A., Liwicki, M., Fernández, S., Bertolami, R., Bunke, H., & Schmidhuber, J. (2009). A novel connectionist system for unconstrained handwriting recognition. IEEE transactions on pattern analysis and machine intelligence, 31(5), 855-868.
6. Pascanu, R., Mikolov, T., & Bengio, Y. (2013). On the difficulty of training recurrent neural networks. ICML (3), 28, 1310-1318.
7. Greff, Klaus, et al. "LSTM: A search space odyssey." IEEE transactions on neural networks and learning systems (2016).
8. Bahdanau, D., Cho, K., & Bengio, Y. (2014). Neural machine translation by jointly learning to align and translate. arXiv preprint arXiv:1409.0473.
9. He, K., Zhang, X., Ren, S., & Sun, J. (2016). Deep residual learning for image recognition. In Proceedings of the IEEE Conference on Computer Vision and Pattern Recognition (pp. 770-778).
10. Paszke. 2015. LSTM Implementation Explained: apaszke.github.io/lstm-explained.html, 2016-07-15
11. Rocktäschel, T., Welbl, J., & Riedel, S. (2017, February 15). Frustratingly Short Attention Spans in Neural Language Modeling. arXiv.org.
12. He, K., Zhang, X., Ren, S., & Sun, J. (2016, October). Identity mappings in deep residual networks. In European Conference on Computer Vision (pp. 630-645). Springer International Publishing.
13. Feng, M., Heffernan, N., & Koedinger, K. (2009). Addressing the assessment challenge with an online system that tutors as it assesses. User Modeling and User-Adapted Interaction, 19(3), 243-266.
14. Chollet, François. "Keras." (2015).

15. Abadi, M., Agarwal, A., Barham, P., Brevdo, E., Chen, Z., Citro, C., ... & Ghemawat, S. (2016). Tensorflow: Large-scale machine learning on heterogeneous distributed systems. arXiv preprint arXiv:1603.04467.

16. Kingma, D., & Ba, J. (2014). Adam: A method for stochastic optimization. arXiv preprint arXiv:1412.6980.

17. Kim, Y. (2014). Convolutional neural networks for sentence classification. arXiv preprint arXiv:1408.5882.

18. Pardos, Z. A., & Heffernan, N. T. (2011, July). KT-IDEM: introducing item difficulty to the knowledge tracing model. In International Conference on User Modeling, Adaptation, and Personalization (pp. 243-254). Springer Berlin Heidelberg.

19. Cohen, G. L., & Garcia, J. (2008). Identity, belonging, and achievement: A model, interventions, implications. Current Directions in Psychological Science, 17(6), 365-369.

20. Corbett, A. (2001, July). Cognitive computer tutors: Solving the two-sigma problem. In International Conference on User Modeling (pp. 137-147). Springer Berlin Heidelberg.

21. D BAKER, R. S. J., CORBETT, A. T., AND ALEVEN, V. More accurate student modeling through contextual estimation of slip and guess probabilities in bayesian knowledge tracing. In Intelligent Tutoring Systems (2008), Springer, pp. 406–415.

22. Khajah, M. M., Huang, Y., González-Brenes, J. P., Mozer, M. C., & Brusilovsky, P. (2014). Integrating knowledge tracing and item response theory: A tale of two frameworks. In Proceedings of Workshop on Personalization Approaches in Learning Environments (PALE 2014) at the 22th International Conference on User Modeling, Adaptation, and Personalization (pp. 7-12). University of Pittsburgh.

23. Khajah, M., Wing, R., Lindsey, R., & Mozer, M. (2014, July). Integrating latent-factor and knowledge-tracing models to predict individual differences in learning. In Educational Data Mining 2014.

24. Olah, C. (2015). Understanding lstm networks. GITHUB blog, posted on August, 27, 2015.

Game Experience and Brain based Assessment of Motivational Goal Orientations in Video Games

Mohamed S. Benlamine, René Dombouya, Aude Dufresne, Claude Frasson

University of Montreal, Department of computer science, Heron Lab, Montreal, Canada
(ms.benlamine,rene.lacine.doumbouya, dufresne)@umontreal.ca,
frasson@iro.umontreal.ca

Abstract. The current study aims to measure the goal orientations motivation in different scenes of a video-game. The evaluation of player experience was done with both subjective measures through questionnaire and objective measures through brain wave activity (electroencephalography - EEG). We used GameFlow questionnaire to characterize the player's mastery goal in playing video game (Master or Performant). In terms of brain activity, we used the Frontal alpha asymmetry (FAA) to assess the player approach/withdrawal behavior within a game scene. Using game scene's design goal (defined by OCC variables) and player personality traits (using Big Five questionnaire), the resulting machine learning model predicts players' motivational goal orientations in order to adapt the game. In this study, we address player's motivation in game scenes by analyzing player's profile, his situation in scene and affective physiological data.

Keywords: Motivation, Video Games, Goal orientations, Player Model, EEG

1 Introduction

The ultimate question that a game designer is always trying to answer is: "how to make the game more attractive for the player and hold his attention more and more?" This question is all about the **Motivation of the player** in playing the game. Motivation has been extensively studied in psychology and social science. Motivation is defined as: "*The willingness to put effort into achieving goals*" [1]. Several researches suggest that goal-directed approach and withdrawal behaviors are regulated by two basic motivational systems: avoidance system and approach system [2]. As a result of nature selection, Approach-avoidance motivation is deeply embedded in our mind because it is crucial for survival to discriminate between pleasurable and rewarding stimuli that we can approach, and dangerous stimuli that we should avoid [3]. Many studies from neuroscience [4, 5] have proven the existence of approach-related motivation in neural circuity. In fact, behavioral approach is localized in the left anterior cortical regions, and behavioral withdrawal is in the right anterior cortical regions using Functional magnetic resonance imaging (fMRI). Moreover, many studies [6-8] associate the Frontal alpha asymmetry (FAA) EEG measure with approach and withdrawal motivational tendencies and individual differences in personality and also

© Springer International Publishing AG 2017

C. Frasson and G. Kostopoulos (Eds.): BFAL 2017, LNAI 10512, pp. 118–132, 2017

DOI: 10.1007/978-3-319-67615-9_11

other studies [9, 10] underscore the role of prefrontal cortex in emotion and motivation process.

During a game, players' motivation is also influenced by achievement need which is a social factor where the player is driven by the motivation to excel and make success in challenging situations. To maintain the player's flow [11] during the game, the challenges should be in the same level of player's competences. When the challenge surpasses the player's skills, he will feel very frustrated, but the lack of challenge induces boredom [12, 13], which leads to make the player unmotivated in both cases and may stop playing the game.

The goal orientations motivational theory takes consideration of both approach withdrawal behavior and mastery goal in assessing the motivation. Coming from educational psychology, this theory investigates the learner's motivation in four achievement goal orientations in educational settings [14-16]. Up to our knowledge, this is the first approach addressing the study of players' motivational goal orientations in video game settings. In addition, it is important that such environments can detect the player's motivation in game scene and provide help in the right time to keep him playing and evolve his experience during the gameplay.

Modeling of the player's motivation during a game is a difficult process due to the complexity that exists to identify the player achievement goals and behavior. In a different situation, the same cause or stimulus provoke different behaviors depending of important factors like goal, personality and preferences. In this context a cognitive approach proposed by Ortony, Clore and Collins (1988)[17] was used to represent the game scene goal defined by the designer. The OCC model evaluates a situation with descriptive variables (global, central and local variables), that the designer gives for each scene to represent his scene's goals.

The present paper aims to predicting motivational goal orientations in a game scene by using the scene OCC description and player's personality traits. We ask in this paper the two following research questions: how to assess the player mastery goal in playing a video game and characterize his approach related behavior within a game scene? If so, can we predict players' motivational goal orientations toward a new scene using machine learning model?

The organization of this paper is as follows: in the next section, we present an overview of the motivation theories and video games. In the third section, we explain our empirical approach in assessing players' motivational goal orientations. In the fourth section, we detail our experimental methodology. In the fifth section, we present the obtained results and discuss them. In the last section, we conclude with a discussion of the present research as well as future work.

2   Background in motivation and video games

2.1   Motivation and motives

Psychologists [18] define motivation as "*hypothetical construct used to describe the internal and / or external forces producing the initiation, direction, intensity and persistence of behavior*"; which gives an idea about the wide broad that covers the concept of motivation. Therefore researchers in their studies approach motivation by working on the narrower more precise concept of motive.

A motive is a need or desire that stimulates and directs behavior towards a goal that is expected to be satisfied. For example, going to the gym can have different motives: interest in workout, want to be in shape and to have healthy body, willingness to impress someone, desire to escape the anxiety associated to overweight, etc. It pushes you to take action to achieve your goal. Two people could produce exactly the same behavior with very different motives. Several theories have been proposed to explain the range of motives that push humans and animals to act. Some focus on physiological needs (Water, food, sleep ...), others on superior needs and social motives such as the need for success. The theory of the hierarchy of needs of Maslow (1943) [19] covers all these needs. This theory gives an overview of human motives, from the most elementary to the noblest.

Among contemporary motivation theories, the theory of self-determination [20], which is based on the existence of two types of motivation (intrinsic vs extrinsic), each leading to different behaviors.

Intrinsic motivation. Intrinsic motivation characterizes individuals who practice an activity for self-interest, pleasure and satisfaction [20]. Intrinsic motivation is characterized by an internal locus of control to meet individual needs for competence and self-determination. The motives for these behaviors have an internal origin. For example, you study because the subject interests you or you eat because you're hungry.

Extrinsic motivation. Extrinsic motivations are linked to the interests of an individual to an activity with external tending causal locus, largely directed by external factors (rewards, obligations, pressure, etc.) [20]. The feeling of self-determination then decreases according to whether the individual loses control over the regulation of his behavior. The motives here have an external origin. For example, you study to have good grade or to avoid having bad one.

2.2   Motivation theories

It's generally accepted in contemporary psychology that no instinct really motivates human behavior. In fact, most recognize that biological forces imply human motivation. Moreover, others identify social motives as additional drives that guide and direct human behavior. Unlike the primary drive, social motives are learned: they are acquired through experience and interaction with others, for example: achievement, affiliation, curiosity ...etc.

Biological approaches.

Drive reduction theory. Theory of motivation that proposes: a need generates a drive that the organism is motivated to reduce [21]. A *drive* is an internal state of activation or tension generated by an underlying need that the organism is motivated to satisfy. This theory is based on the concept of homeostasis, according to which the organism tends to maintain a state of internal equilibrium essential to its survival (body temperature, glucose level, oxygen level, blood pressure ...). For example, a need to drink or eat disturbs the internal equilibrium, which gives rise to a drive that forces the organism to act to reduce tension by satisfying this need and restoring the state of internal equilibrium.

Arousal theory. This theory claims that an organism is motivated to maintain an *optimal level of arousal*. If the arousal level goes down under an optimal level, we look for increasing it and if it goes over that level, we try to decrease the arousal. If the arousal level is very low, *stimulation motives* push us to increase the arousal level. Stimulation motives refer to processes like: curiosity, exploration desire, playing, and object manipulation. Term arousal level refers to the degree of activity of the organism in a continuum that ranges from sleep to stress through various degrees of awakening, alertness and alertness. Stimulus with high intensity (like high noise, flashing lights...), stimulants (like caffeine, nicotine, cocaine ...), emotions (like anger, joy, surprise ...) or biological needs increase the arousal level. According to law Yerkes Dodson [22-24], there is a relationship between the arousal level and performance by attention and concentration, but only up to a point. A task is accomplished more efficiently when the arousal level suites the degree of difficulty: simple and routine tasks requiring a relatively high arousal level (to increase motivation); the moderately difficult tasks ask an average level of arousal and difficult and complex task, ask a lower arousal level (to facilitate concentration).

Personality and social motives approaches.

Achievement Motivation theory. The achievement need is an important dimension of human motivation; it is a desire to accomplish something difficult, and to excel in it. This need is influenced by internal drive for action (intrinsic motivation), and the pressure exerted by the expectations of others (extrinsic motivation). According to Henry Murray (1938) [25], this need is particular since the more success is made, the more the person is motivated to make more achievements. According to researchers [26-28], achievement-motivated people set ambitious but nevertheless realistic and achievable goals.

For these people, easy-to-reach goals are irrelevant because the easily attained success is not a genuine achievement. On the other hand, they avoid setting unrealistic goals and taking risks too high, which would be a waste of time. According to other research [29], low achiever people take no risk since they are motivated by the fear of failure rather than by the success possibilities. Their goals are either very easy to make or very difficult so they are not embarrassed by the failure.

Goal orientation theory. According to the goal orientation theory, the motivation to succeed varies depending on whether the goal is one of mastery (goal defined according to self) or performance (goal defined by comparison with others), and according to whether it aims at Approach (get something nice) or avoidance (avoid something unpleasant). This theory distinguishes **four goal orientations**: (i) *mastery-approach* where individuals seek to achieve mastery or self-improvement, (ii) *master-avoidance* where individuals seek to avoid failing achievement of a task mastery, (iii) *perfor-mance-approach* where the main focus is for individuals to accomplish and outper-form others, and (iv) *performance-avoidance* where one seeks to avoid doing worse than others in given tasks [2, 16, 30].

2.3 Motivation and video games

Looking at how users are engaged in playing with intrinsically motivating games, Malone (1981) [31] has been interested in studying the theory behind intrinsically motivating learning, or learning to which the individual engages without Motivation (rewards or punishments). He describes the characteristics of environments that make them intrinsically motivating, with individual motivations such as challenge, fantasy, curiosity and control [32]. These characteristics can be considered as theories on how to make learning fun [33]. In more recent research [34, 35] Przybylski, Rigby and Ryan identified two other motivational factors associated with games, autonomy and competence, originating from self-determination theory [20]. Games with motivating experience can be explained by the concept of flow [36], a term invented by Csikszentmihalyi to describe a condition in which a person experiences a challenge that extends its competences without being too difficult nor too easy (engaging in an appropriate level of challenge depending on the player's skill) and have clear objec-tives and immediate feedback on progress [11]. In his book "A Theory of Fun for Game Design" [37], the game developer Ralph Koster stressed out the importance of integrating psychological theories in game design. Additional study [38] on MMORPG games, finds that factors addressed by extrinsic motivation theories (re-wards) and intrinsic motivation (exploration, social needs, competence and mastery) contribute to players game enjoy. These findings actually provide some evidence supporting that intrinsic and extrinsic motivations are a false dichotomy.

3   Experimental settings

3.1   Participants

This study involves 21 participants (12 males; 9 female), aged between 18 and 35 years from a North American university. We have discarded 2 participants due to technical problem while collecting data. The players were categorized according to hours of play per week (5 extreme players, 6 intermediates and 8 novices).

3.2   The game - Outlast

In this study, participants were asked to play the first level of a horror commercial game named *Outlast* (developed by Red Barrels Games). This first-person game takes the player in a horrifying hospital full of dead bodies and monsters. The player takes the role of an investigative reporter that gathers evidences against the *Murkoff Corpo-ration* who made horrible experiments on mental patients in the hospital. The only means of survival are to flee the enemies or to hide from them, the player cannot attack them. This genre of games stimulates the player's emotional reactions and his approach/avoidance motivation.

3.3 Experiment and equipment

The Experiment begins by receiving the participant in our laboratory; we introduce him to the testing room. To avoid interferences with the equipment, the participant was invited to turn off his phone. The participant signs a consent form to register his experiment agreement. After installing the EEG and EDA (Electro-dermal activity) sensors on the participant, the researcher checks the webcam recording the user's face and the eye-tracker calibration. The experiment Design was conducted in the platform iMotions that allows the multimodal synchronization of different sensors. By clicking the start button, iMotions platform launches the data recording and the game where the participant plays the first level.

3.4 Measures

Because of the complexity of the motivation concept and its components, it is difficult to measure motivation. Different studies have used several methods, subjective or objective, in order to evaluate the motivation.

Subjective measures. We have used questionnaires before and after the play session to get the users information and their game evaluations. We first gave pre-test questionnaires to collect socio-demographic data and the player's profile (school level, their preferred games and hours of play per week) and also the "Big Five" questionnaire [39] for the assessment of the participant's personality traits (openness, neuroticism, extraversion, agreeableness and conscientiousness). In the post-test, we used the immersion and flow questionnaire. The questionnaire was adapted from the GameFlow questionnaire [40, 41]. These questionnaires are composed of Likert-type items where the answer is expressed on a scale between 1-"disagree at all" and 7-"completely agree". In addition, participants were asked to answer a final questionnaire about their emotions felt during stages of the game. In fact, post-test questionnaires can serve as an indicator of player's motivation. Since, improved motivation may bring improved performance of the player.

Objective measures. We believe that monitoring and analyzing objective measures like ocular and physiological signals is the most appropriate methodology for emotional and cognitive states recognition in the gaming context. We have collected multimodal data from the player's body and face to analyze his affective and mental state. In this study, we are using among these measures: EEG data to compute the *Frontal Alpha Asymmetry* (FAA) and eye-tracking data to detect the scenes visualization time and duration.

Frontal Alpha Asymmetry. The frontal asymmetry (FAA) is an unfiltered and unbiased phenomenon associated with emotion and motivation. Brain scientists have consistently found that higher engagement of the left compared to the right frontal brain is related to positive feelings and higher engagement [42]. Due to the inverse relationship between alpha power (8-12 Hz) and cortical activity, decreased alpha power reflects increased engagement. The special effect of the asymmetry in frontal alpha power was initially detected in studies investigating biomarkers of personality [43].

While this "emotional" effect was found to be indicative of a personality trait (supposed to be very stable across the life span), recent evidence suggests that it also varies depending on emotional stimulation, reflecting whether or not someone is drawn towards or away from something or someone. In short, this "approach/avoidance effect" reflects someone's motivation [44].

Eye-tracking analysis. For each participant, we annotated his play-session by defining Areas of Interest (AOI). The AOIs refer to the game stages/scenes. Through the game, a participant may take different duration for the different game scene. We used the software iMotions to replay and annotate chronologically the participants' game session. The annotation allows the software to compute the gaze statistics by AOI. Using hit time and the time spent metrics, we identified the time and duration that the player spent for each scene.

4   Method

Thus, we performed a multimodal analysis using several sources of information to determine the level of affective reactions of the players. We used several sources of information such as: questionnaires, eye tracking and EEG physiological data. This require the use of statistical analyzes and AI techniques for the selection and extraction of characteristics and the construction of the player's motivational model.

The EEG headset consists of 14 data-collecting electrodes and 2 reference electrodes, located and labeled according to the international 10-20 system. The participant's EEG data was calibrated using his neutral state of mind when looking at gray screen for 6 seconds which is considered as our baseline period.

4.1   The FAA computation

The frontal asymmetry index was computed from raw frontal EEG data using electrodes F3/F7 and F4/F8 (see Fig.1). We calculated FAA by following the steps below:

- Preprocess the data to attenuate artifacts (eye blink and muscle artifacts) by applying an order 5 Butterworth filter between 0.5 and 50Hz.
- Epoch the baseline-corrected data. In this step, the continuous data was broken into smaller parts of 2 seconds epoch [45] (with 75% overlap). For each epoch, we compute the Alpha Power using the library PyEEG[1](a python module to extract

---

[1] http://pyeeg.sourceforge.net/

EEG features). Using Fourier frequency analysis, the original signal is split up in frequencies in order to remove specific frequencies, before transforming back the signal with only the frequencies of interest.

— Average the Alpha power across all of the artifact-free epochs of the baseline and game scenes signal.

— Compute the normalized *FAA* as the log of the difference between alpha power density of the right hemisphere and the left hemisphere divided by their sum.

$$FAA = \log(\frac{Alpha\ Power_{Right} - Alpha\ Power_{Left}}{Alpha\ Power_{Right} + Alpha\ Power_{Left}})$$

Higher scores on this asymmetry index indicate greater relative left hemisphere activation which means that the scenes' motivation is APPROACH oriented otherwise it is AVOIDANCE oriented.

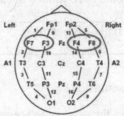

Fig. 1. Used EEG sensors in the FAA calculation

4.2 Player mastery goal assessment

To characterize the player category (Master or Performant), we identified the performance question in the 'Immersion-Game experience' survey (see Table 1). We categorized the player's achievement goal as Master if:

Average(Mastery) >= 1.5*Average(Performance).

We fixed the "1.5" threshold by checking information related to the preferred games, the play time per week and the GPA in the demographic self-report which is matching with the participants' report of 'immersion-Game experience' survey.

Table 1. Achievement goal related questions from the 'Immersion-Game experience' survey

Achievement goal	Questions
Mastery	I would have liked to succeed in the game.
Mastery	I wanted to replay the game despite the failures.
Mastery	I feel satisfied when I see that the game is progressing.
Performance	Winning or losing the game did not interest me. I was not interested in the outcome of the game (win or lose).
Mastery	At the end of the session, I regretted not being able to continue the game.

Performance	The level of the challenge of the game corresponded to my skills as a player.
Mastery	I try to play as best as I can to win the game.
Performance	Sometimes I wanted to give up because the level of difficulty was too high.
Performance	The actions to be performed were becoming more and more difficult as I progressed through the game.
Mastery	The game was easy to win.
Performance	I think I made some progress at the end of the session compared to the beginning.
Mastery	The more I progressed in the game, the more I got interesting rewards (number of fans, bonuses, new weapons, new abilities, medals ...).
Performance	Sometimes I would have wanted to change the keys used to better control the game.
Mastery	I would like to replay this game.

4.3 OCC game scene representation

To predict the player motivation for new game scenes, we need first to characterize the game scenes according to the designer perception and goals using variables from OCC model [17]. The OCC model evaluates a situation with descriptive variables (global, central and local variables). These cognitive variables characterize a person's interpretation of a situation as desirable or undesirable, expected or unexpected, etc. Global variables are included in all situations, whereas the central and local variables are specific to certain situations characterizing their informational content.

Table 2. Global, central and local variables and their associated values

Evaluation Variable	Global variables		Central variables			Local variables										
	Surprise	Sense of reality	Desirability	Approval	Attraction	Desirability by other	Esteem for other	Merit for other	Likelihood	Realization	Effort	Agent	Power of the link	Deviation	Disposition	Familiarity
Values	0 (False) or 1 (True)	0 (False) or 1 (True)	-1, -0.5, 0, 0.5, 1	-1, -0.5, 0, 0.5, 1	-1, -0.5, 0, 0.5, 1	-1, -0.5, 0, 0.5, 1	-1, -0.5, 0, 0.5, 1	-1, -0.5, 0, 0.5, 1	-1, -0.5, 0, 0.5, 1	-1, -0.5, 0, 0.5, 1	-1, -0.5, 0, 0.5, 1	0 (other) or 1 (self)	0, 0.5, 1	-1, -0.5, 0, 0.5, 1	0, 0.5, 1	-1, -0.5, 0, 0.5, 1

In the table above (see Table 2), we summarized the OCC variables and their possible values. Thus, we can formally represent a game scene with vector of 16 numerical values. Thanks to its generality, The OCC model representation of the scene remains applicable to game scenes for learning or entertainment purposes.

4.4   The Motivation Prediction

In this section we describe our approach to training and evaluating classifiers for the task of detecting the motivational state of mind of a person given the person's cognitive situation in game, personal and demographical data. We approach this problem as a 4-class classification problem.

Features extraction. We perform a feature selection over the feature vector by extracting features using Principal Component Analysis (PCA) and Univariate feature selection (Univariate feature selection examines each feature individually to determine the strength of the relationship of the feature with the response variable). Then we combine the results through a pipeline into a single transformer. The 10-fold Cross validation method allowed to train and validate our model with better generalization.

Training set construction. In order to train a scene's motivation predictive model, we used a training set containing scene descriptions, participant's sociodemographic information and personality traits and also the participant's mastery goal and his approach related behavior in the game scene (Performant/Master-Approach/Avoidance). That we determined through the combination of the FAA computation section above and the categorization of the players we present above. The model use 23-dimensions vector: 16 variables from the OCC model, 2 socio-demographic variables (gender, age), 5 personality trait values as **input** variables and the motivational goal orientations as the **output result**. The method has been developed with Python language and scikit-learn[2] library. We have trained and validated our model using the 10-fold Cross validation method. We are interested in inducing a classifier of the following form:

— MotivationClassifier(*Playerdata*)→[Performant-Approach, Performant-Avoidance, Master-Approach, Master-Avoidance]

Where "*Playerdata*" is the 23-dimension vector presented above [*Performant-Approach, Performant-Avoidance, Master-Approach, Master-Avoidance*] is the sets of motivational states to be discriminated. The dataset contains 245 examples distributed over the 4 classes as follow Performant-Avoidance: 66/245 – 26%, Performant-Approach: 52/245 – 21%, Master-Avoidance: 71/245 – 28%, Master-Approach: 55/245 – 22%. Thus if a classifier always predict the most present class which is Master-Avoidance it will get 28% of precision that will be considered as our baseline.

---

[2] http://scikit-learn.org/stable/

5   Results

In this approach, we evaluated classifier by performing the standard 10-fold cross validation in which 10% of the training set is held out in turn as test data while the remaining 90% is used as training data. The optimum parameters for the classifier were found with a grid search.

Table 3. the classifiers F-score and parameters

CLASSIFIER	F1-Score (parameters)
RFC	**81%** (PCA = 3, Univ=10, n_estim = 10)
SVM	**75%** (PCA=15, Univ=10, Kernel ='linear', C=1.0, gamma= 0.04)
KNN	**73%** (PCA=3, Univ=2, k=70)

Compared to KNN and SVM methods, Random Forest achieves the best performance with the average accuracy of 81% for all goal orientations classes, as illustrated in Table 3.

The confusion matrix of Random Forest is shown in Figure 2, which gives details of the strength and weakness of the generated model. Each row of the confusion matrix represents the target class and each column represents the predicted class. The element (i, j) is the percentage of samples in class i that is classified as class j. We can see that the goal orientations are generally recognized with very high accuracy of near ninety percent. The model differentiates between Mastery and Performance classes. But it makes some errors in recognizing whether it is Performance-Avoidance or Performance-Approach and also fewer errors between Mastery-Avoidance and Mastery-Approach.

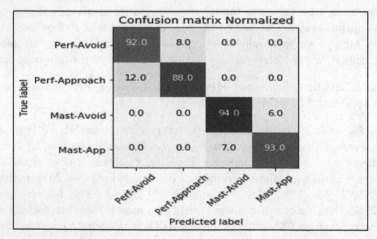

Fig. 2. Confusion matrix of the motivational goal orientations prediction with RFC

With these results, our motivation prediction approach provides a simple and reliable way to predict the motivational goal orientations of the learner/player that can be implemented in a distant game environment. The resulting model predicts the learner /player's goal orientations from only the game scene's OCC representation and the Big Five result without using invasive technique (physiological sensors, EEG, etc.).

Additionally, based on this assessment, we can make adaptations in the environment according to learner's motivation. In fact, Kaplan and Maehr [46] made comparison between aspects of educational environments (Task, Authority, Recognition, Grouping, Evaluation and Time) in mastery goals Vs performance goals emphasizing environments. For example, these environment aspects can be modified based on this assessment to foster learner's motivation. Moreover, based on the model of motivated action theory [47], Goal orientations describe a profile of structured hierarchies of goals that lead to the learner/player's specific action plan goals (Seek feedback, Manage impression, Allocate resources and Explore problem). Using this predicted player's actions, the adaptation strategies can modify the environment by providing hints, messages, feedbacks, rewards or changing the problem difficulty.

6   Conclusion

In this paper, we assessed players' motivational goal orientations in their interaction with the commercial game "Outlast" using game scene's design goals, player characteristics, EEG and eye-tracking data. We presented our method in categorizing the player as "Master" or "Performant" using the GameFlow questionnaire. We also assessed the Approach withdrawal behavior toward a visualized game scene using the Frontal Alpha Asymmetry (FAA) during time window calculated from eye tracking data. We have also built a machine learning model for predicting player's motivational goal orientation using game scene's design goal (defined by OCC variables) and the player's personality traits (using the Big Five questionnaire).

The obtained results are very promising for their future integration in a motivationally intelligent serious game. This integration would clearly contribute to learning since it combines the game scene's design objectives to the learner/player's motivation. Furthermore, a practical real-time non-invasive assessment of learners' motivation is now feasible, since we can rely on this assessment as a substitute for self-reports that can disturb a learning/gaming session. Moreover, the system can become more adaptive in terms of its response to learner's motivation within the game scenes. In further work, we will target the learner's reported emotions in the prediction which would contribute to more comprehensive models of learner/player affect.

Acknowledgments. We thank the Natural Sciences and Engineering Research Council of Canada NSERC and BMU Games for funding this research.

References

1.   Driver, M. *Coaching Positively: Lessons For Coaches From Positive Psychology: Lessons for Coaches from Positive Psychology*. McGraw-Hill Education (UK), 2011.

2.   Elliot, A. J. and Covington, M. V. Approach and avoidance motivation. *Educational Psychology Review*, 13, 2 2001), 73-92.

3.   Cosmides, L. and Tooby, J. Reasoning and natural selection. *Encyclopedia of human biology*, 61991), 493-503.

4.   Davidson, R. J. The neural circuitry of emotion and affective style: Prefrontal cortex and amygdala contributions. *Social Science Information*, 40, 1 2001), 11-37.

5.   Phan, K. L., Wager, T., Taylor, S. F. and Liberzon, I. Functional neuroanatomy of emotion: a meta-analysis of emotion activation studies in PET and fMRI. *Neuroimage*, 16, 2 2002), 331-348.

6.   Davidson, R. J. What does the prefrontal cortex "do" in affect: perspectives on frontal EEG asymmetry research. *Biological psychology*, 67, 1 2004), 219-234.

7.   Amodio, D. M., Master, S. L., Yee, C. M. and Taylor, S. E. Neurocognitive components of the behavioral inhibition and activation systems: Implications for theories of self-regulation. *Psychophysiology*, 45, 1 2008), 11-19.

8.   Horan, W. P., Wynn, J. K., Mathis, I., Miller, G. A. and Green, M. F. Approach and withdrawal motivation in schizophrenia: an examination of frontal brain asymmetric activity. *PLoS One*, 9, 10 2014), e110007.

9.   Derbali, L., Ghali, R. and Frasson, C. *Assessing Motivational Strategies in Serious Games Using Hidden Markov Models*. City, 2013.

10.   Derbali, L. and Frasson, C. *Prediction of players motivational states using electrophysiological measures during serious game play*. IEEE, City, 2010.

11.   Nakamura, J. and Csikszentmihalyi, M. The concept of flow. *Handbook of positive psychology*2002), 89-105.

12.   Jennett, C., Cox, A. L., Cairns, P., Dhoparee, S., Epps, A., Tijs, T. and Walton, A. Measuring and defining the experience of immersion in games. *International journal of human-computer studies*, 66, 9 2008), 641-661.

13.   Chanel, G., Rebetez, C., Bétrancourt, M. and Pun, T. *Boredom, engagement and anxiety as indicators for adaptation to difficulty in games*. ACM, City, 2008.

14.   Elliot, A. J. and Murayama, K. On the measurement of achievement goals: Critique, illustration, and application. *Journal of Educational Psychology*, 100, 3 2008), 613.

15.   Elliot, A. J., McGregor, H. A. and Gable, S. Achievement goals, study strategies, and exam performance: A mediational analysis. *Journal of educational psychology*, 91, 3 1999), 549.

16.   Wolters, C. A. Advancing Achievement Goal Theory: Using Goal Structures and Goal Orientations to Predict Students' Motivation, Cognition, and Achievement. *Journal of educational psychology*, 96, 2 2004), 236.

17.   Ortony, A., Clore, G. L. and Collins, A. *The cognitive structure of emotions*. Cambridge university press, 1990.

18.   Vallerand, R. J. and Thill, E. E. Introduction au concept de motivation. *Introduction à la psychologie de la motivation*1993), 3-39.

19.   Maslow, A. H. A theory of human motivation. *Psychological review*, 50, 4 1943), 370.

20.   Ryan, R. M. and Deci, E. L. Intrinsic and extrinsic motivations: Classic definitions and new directions. *Contemporary educational psychology*, 25, 1 2000), 54-67.

21.   Hull, C. L. The conflicting psychologies of learning—a way out. *Psychological Review*, 42, 6 1935), 491.

22. Diamond, D. M., Campbell, A. M., Park, C. R., Halonen, J. and Zoladz, P. R. The temporal dynamics model of emotional memory processing: a synthesis on the neurobiological basis of stress-induced amnesia, flashbulb and traumatic memories, and the Yerkes-Dodson law. *Neural plasticity*, 20072007).

23. Yerkes, R. M. and Dodson, J. D. The relation of strength of stimulus to rapidity of habit-formation. *Journal of comparative neurology and psychology*, 18, 5 1908), 459-482.

24. Teigen, K. H. Yerkes-Dodson: A law for all seasons. *Theory & Psychology*, 4, 4 1994), 525-547.

25. Murray, H. A. Explorations in personality1938).

26. McClelland, D. C., Atkinson, J. W., Clark, R. A. and Lowell, E. L. The achievement motive1976).

27. McClelland, D. C. *Motives, personality, and society: Selected papers*. Praeger Publishers, 1984.

28. Conroy, D. E. Progress in the development of a multidimensional measure of fear of failure: The Performance Failure Appraisal Inventory (PFAI). *Anxiety, Stress and Coping*, 14, 4 2001), 431-452.

29. Elliott, E. S. and Dweck, C. S. Goals: An approach to motivation and achievement. *Journal of personality and social psychology*, 54, 1 1988), 5.

30. Elliot, A. J. Approach and avoidance motivation and achievement goals. *Educational psychologist*, 34, 3 1999), 169-189.

31. Malone, T. W. Toward a theory of intrinsically motivating instruction*. *Cognitive science*, 5, 4 1981), 333-369.

32. Malone, T. W. and Lepper, M. R. Making learning fun: A taxonomy of intrinsic motivations for learning. *Aptitude, learning, and instruction*, 3, 1987 1987), 223-253.

33. Lepper, M. R. and Malone, T. W. Intrinsic motivation and instructional effectiveness in computer-based education. *Aptitude, learning, and instruction*, 31987), 255-286.

34. Przybylski, A. K., Rigby, C. S. and Ryan, R. M. A motivational model of video game engagement. *Review of general psychology*, 14, 2 2010), 154.

35. Ryan, R. M., Rigby, C. S. and Przybylski, A. The motivational pull of video games: A self-determination theory approach. *Motivation and emotion*, 30, 4 2006), 344-360.

36. Flow, C. The psychology of optimal experience. *Harper&Row, New York*1990).

37. Koster, R. *Theory of fun for game design.* " O'Reilly Media, Inc.", 2013.

38. Yee, N. Motivations for play in online games. *CyberPsychology & behavior*, 9, 6 2006), 772-775.

39. Goldberg, L. R. The development of markers for the Big-Five factor structure. *Psychological assessment*, 4, 1 1992), 26.

40. Sweetser, P., Johnson, D. M. and Wyeth, P. Revisiting the GameFlow model with detailed heuristics. *Journal: Creative Technologies*, 2012, 3 2012).

41. Sweetser, P. and Wyeth, P. GameFlow: a model for evaluating player enjoyment in games. *Computers in Entertainment (CIE)*, 3, 3 2005), 3-3.

42. Coan, J. A. and Allen, J. J. Frontal EEG asymmetry and the behavioral activation and inhibition systems. *Psychophysiology*, 40, 1 2003), 106-114.

43. Hagemann, D., Naumann, E., Thayer, J. F. and Bartussek, D. Does resting electroencephalograph asymmetry reflect a trait? an application of latent state-trait theory. *Journal of personality and social psychology*, 82, 4 2002), 619.

44.   Harmon-Jones, E., Gable, P. A. and Peterson, C. K. The role of asymmetric frontal cortical activity in emotion-related phenomena: A review and update. *Biological psychology*, 84, 3 2010), 451-462.

45.   Tomarken, A. J., Davidson, R. J. and Henriques, J. B. Resting frontal brain asymmetry predicts affective responses to films. *Journal of personality and social psychology*, 59, 4 1990), 791.

46.   Kaplan, A. and Maehr, M. L. The contributions and prospects of goal orientation theory. *Educational psychology review*, 19, 2 2007), 141-184.

47.   DeShon, R. P. and Gillespie, J. Z. A motivated action theory account of goal orientation. *Journal of Applied Psychology*, 90, 6 2005), 1096.

Real-time Brain Assessment for Adaptive Virtual Reality Game : a Neurofeedback Approach

Hamdi Ben Abdessalem and Claude Frasson

Département d'Informatique et de Recherche Opérationnelle
Université de Montréal, Montréal, Canada H3C 3J7
{benabdeh, frasson}@iro.umontreal.ca

Abstract. Humans' cognitive and affective states are constantly subject to regular and sudden changes. The origins of these changes are multiple and unpredictable. Virtual Reality (VR) game environments could represent an immersive unconstrained experimental context in which game designers could control a wide range of parameters that act on these states. In this paper, we propose to track and adapt to individuals' frustration and excitement levels in real time while interacting with a VR environment. We developed "AmbuRun", a VR game designed to modify the speed and the difficulty in real time. A neural agent was created to control these parameters within the game using an intervention strategy that was intended to induce appropriate modifications of the players 'excitement and frustration level. An experimental study involving 20 participants was conducted to evaluate our neurofeedback approach. Results showed that intelligent control through neurofeedback of speed and difficulty affected excitement and frustration before and after the agent action.

Keywords: Neurofeedback, Intelligent Agent, Virtual Reality, Adaptive Game, Emotional Intelligence.

1   Introduction

In recent years the field of virtual reality has attracted a growing amount of interest, due to its various applications in different fields like neuroscience [1], learning [2], psychology [3], etc. and its advantages compared to other interactive environments. In neuroscience domain, the VR is useful for neurosurgery and brain assessment [4]. Brain assessment is another interesting field, which aims to assess cognitive and affective states. In this field, researchers used electroencephalograms (EEG) in order to detect emotions resulting from facial expressions [5]. Some other researchers focused on detecting mental states like engagement and workload [6] in order to adapt applications to users' needs.

The players' performance when interacting with video games varies depending on their brain states. Brain assessment using EEG allows an enhanced understanding of the players' emotional reactions. These emotional reactions are caused by different changes in the game and analyzing these reactions in real-time is challenging. The main hypotheses of this paper are :

© Springer International Publishing AG 2017   133
C. Frasson and G. Kostopoulos (Eds.): BFAL 2017, LNAI 10512, pp. 133–143, 2017
DOI: 10.1007/978-3-319-67615-9_12

H1. It is possible to analyze and track in real time user brain activity during its interaction with a virtual environment.

H2. It is possible to intervene on a virtual environment in order to modify the emotions of the user.

The Goal of our research in this paper is to measure the emotional reactions of the user involved in a VR game, and to modify this game in order to change the emotional state of the user and assess the impact through a neurofeedback approach.

The rest of this paper is organized as follows. A brief overview of the related work is given in Section 2. In section 3 we present our measuring module. Section 4 presents the neural agent. Section 5 describes our VR game AmbuRun. In Section 6 we detail the experiment, which led to the results presented and discussed in Section7.

2 Related Work

2.1 Virtual Reality

Virtual reality environments allow researchers to manipulate multimodal stimulus inputs. These manipulations generate a sensorimotor illusion to the user which gives him a sense of presence in the virtual environment [4].

The advantage of virtual reality compared to other interactive environments is that the user is isolated from any external visual distraction. And by adding headphones, we eliminate the external distraction and the user becomes completely isolated from any distraction. The immersion of virtual reality can make the user believe that he is in a real world and promotes his learning ability and performance in games [2]. In the field of neuroscience, most applications of virtual reality focus on the influence and measurement of changes in brain activity. There are applications that establish a direct link between the user's nervous system and the properties of the virtual environment [7]. For example, we can control objects in virtual reality using EEG signals [8]. Meanwhile, in the field of psychology, virtual reality offers a means to control the user experience that approaches dosage control in psychiatric treatments, with a potentially high degree of realism to enhance the transfer of results to the real world. VR treatment has been applied to a range of disorders, including relief of fear [3], anxiety disorders [9] and brain damage [10].

2.2 Brain Assessment and Adaptation

Many researchers used diverse approaches for learners' adaptation that could be grouped into two categories: detection of learners' emotions and/or behaviors using physiological sensing approaches, and focusing on the system's feedback or learners' seek for help.

The first category generally uses the eye tracking or the electroencephalography EEG. D'Mello et al. [11] have used eye tracking data to detect emotions of boredom and disengagement. Whereas Chaouachi et al. [6] integrated two mental states indexes extracted from EEG (engagement and workload) in their system, Mentor. This system used some rules in order to maintain students in a positive mental state while learn-ing[12].

Moreover, other researchers focused on adapting games for players. Ramla et al. [13] changed assistance strategies in real-time according to players indexes of engagement and frustration in order to improve their intuitive reasoning in a physics VR game.

2.3   Neurofeedback

Neurofeedback is a type of biofeedback that measures brain waves to produce a signal that can be used as feedback. When measured activity is cerebral activity, biofeedback is called neurofeedback [14]. Neurofeedback can be used to enable people to learn to manage specific aspects of their neuronal activity and develop skills for self-regulation of brain activity, through a brain-computer interface [15, 16]. Neurofeedback is used also to treat Attention Deficit Disorder (ADHD) [17]. Indeed, it trains the brain using principles of operational conditioning based on the real-time measurement of brain ac-tivity [16]. In this paper, we use neurofeedback to track and change the emotional state of the user.

3   Measuring Module

Our first objective is to determine the ways of analyzing the cerebral state and the emo-tion of the user during his interaction with the virtual environment in order to follow his emotional state. To achieve this goal, we made a measuring module.

The role of the measuring module is to detect different emotions and mental states. It receives the different signals from different measuring tools, synchronizes, and ana-lyzes them, and then extracts the emotions and brain states values. The module sends these values to other modules or agents in the system through the network, and stores these data in a database in order to allow offline treatments.

3.1   Architecture of the Measuring Module.

Our measurement module contains five components: "Sensors", "Virtual Reality Envi-ronment", "Measurement", "Processing" and "Database". Figure 1 illustrates the archi-tecture of the measuring module.

Sensors. This component is composed of physiological sensors (EEG, EDA, Eye Tracker), which are connected to the user. Using these sensors, we can collect the phys-iological reactions of the user while he interacts with the VR environment.

VR Environment. It is able to produce sounds, music, effects, 3D models, etc. It could be a game, video, etc. This environment is what the user constantly sees in which many elements could change in real time.

Measurement. This component manages the communication and synchronization between the various physiological sensors. It collects different data from different sen-sors and transmits them to the processing component.

Processing. It analyzes and processes data coming from measuring component then converts the results into indexes of emotions and brain states. It also manages the communication between this module and the other modules or agents in our system.

Database. This component is used to store the various data of the measuring module. It stores the raw data of the various physiological sensors, the results of processed data and the information about the virtual environment.

This measuring module sends the emotional values to our neural agent, which we will describe in the next section.

Measuring Module

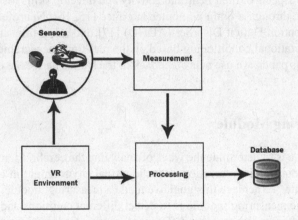

Fig. 1. Architecture of "Measuring Module"

4   Neural Agent

The neural agent is an intelligent agent that receives emotional states from the measuring module and information about the VR environment. This agent tracks the emotion of the user and intervenes on the VR environment in order to change his emotional state according to a rules base.

Giving the emotional state of the user, the agent chooses a rule from the rules base and intervenes on the VR environment. After each intervention, the agent observes the emotional reactions of the user to check whether it modifies his emotional state. After that, our agent analyzes all the parameters that have led to a failure or a success and intervenes again on the VR environment. The neural agent runs in real time to analyze evolution in the user's emotional state. The agent operates in a neurofeedback loop with the measuring module to improve the emotional state of the user. The emotional state of the user indirectly triggers a modification of the virtual environment, which in return will modify the emotional state of the user.

4.1   Architecture of the Neural Agent

The neural agent is composed of two modules: "Analysis, decision and action" and "Rules base Manager" and two databases "Decisions base" and "Rules base". This agent works independently and interacts with the real-time measurement module. Figure 2 illustrates the architecture of the neural agent and its interactions with the measuring module. This architecture allows real-time interaction with the user in a neurofeedback loop.

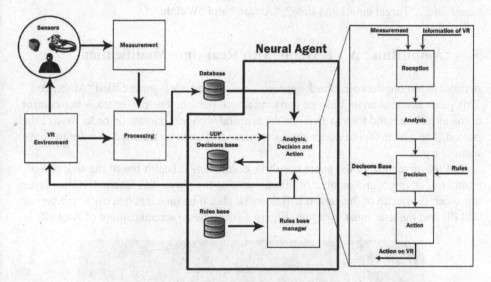

Fig. 2. Architecture of "Neural Agent"

Analysis, decision and actions. This module has four components "reception", "analysis", "decision" and "action". The first one handles the reception of the data received from the measurement module. These data are the emotional states of the user and the information about the virtual environment. The communication protocol must be the same as on the measuring module. It must also handle the synchronization of all the incoming data.

The analysis component receives the information from the reception component. It uses this information to recognize the user's emotional state and the state of the VR environment. Then it analyzes these states in order to identify the main emotion. After that, it detects whether these measures correspond to the measures expected in this environment or not.

The Decision component receives the user's emotional states, VR environment information, and results of analysis component. Subsequently, it consults the rules base to extract the rule that can be applied in this case.

The last component receives the decision from the previous one and the state of the VR environment. Then, it adapts the action requested by the rule to the type of the VR environment and sends an intervention action. The VR environment receives the intervention action and executes it instantly.

Decisions base. The decision base is a database containing the history of decisions taken by the module presented previously. Each decision is stored with the system time, the emotion of the user, and the chosen rule.

Rules base manager. This module allows the management of the intervention rules. The three main functionalities are adding, modifying, and deleting of an intervention rule.

Rules base. The rules base is the base that contains all the rules of intervention. An intervention rule is composed of a unique "Id", "Name", "Description", "Initial emotional sate", "Target emotional state", "Action" and "Weight".

5   AmbuRun : A VR Game with Real-time Modification

In order to test our neurofeedback approach, we created a VR game called "AmbuRun". This game is about an ambulance carrying a sick person. The player takes the control of the ambulance and tries to arrive at the hospital with less damage in order to save the person. The player should dodge the cars, buses and track on the road in order to arrive without harm.

The user interface of the game has three components: health bar of the sick person, number of attempts and number of kilometers that the player has reached. If the player hits a car, the health of the person will decrease, but if he hit a bus or a truck, the person will die and the user must try again. Figure 3 illustrates a screen capture of AmbuRun.

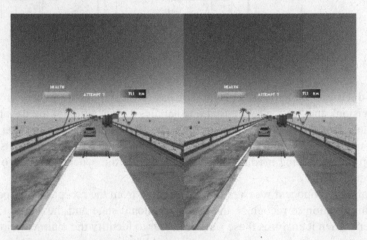

Fig. 3. Screen capture of AmbuRun

In order to create this game, we used Unity3D, which contains a built-in physics engine able to simulate collisions. AmbuRun was optimized in order to run and react quickly in Fove headset. Fove is the first VR headset that contains integrated eye tracking module. The player can control the game with a wireless gamepad on which the player moves the left joystick to translate the ambulance on the left and on the right, and with the rotation of his head, he can see the VR environment in 360 degrees. In this way, the player is immersed and can react quickly into the game. We designed the game in a way that we can modify the speed and the difficulty of the game dynamically in real time and remotely from another application. The modification of the speed, affects directly the ambulance speed, from slow to fast or the reverse. The modification of the difficulty affects the frequency of the cars, trucks and buses by increasing their number in order to increase difficulty or decreasing their number to decrease the difficulty. So, the difficulty changes from easy to hard and the inverse.

6 Experiment

In order to study the effectiveness of our neurofeedback approach, we built the game "AmbuRun" described in the previous section. We experimented our approach on 20 participants (10 females and 10 males, mean age = 31.05, SD age = 4.9619).

For this experiment, we test our approach with two emotional states from the measurement module, which are *excitement* and *frustration*. Our strategy is to vary the speed of the game in order to affect excitement, and the difficulty of the game to induce frustration. Therefore, we added four rules to the rules base of the neural agent. In the first one, we suppose that the excitement of the participant will increase if we increase the speed. In the second one, we suppose that the excitement of the participant will decrease if we decrease the speed of the ambulance. The third rule supposes that the frustration will increase if we increase the difficulty. Finally, the fourth one supposes that the frustration will decrease if we decrease the difficulty of the game.

In the first step of experiments (see figure 4), the participant signs an ethic form that explains the study and mentions its advantages and disadvantages. In the second step, the participant is equipped with the Emotiv EPOC headset.

In the third step, we install the Fove headset on the participant and we give him a wireless gamepad to control the game. The participant also uses earphones connected to the computer in order to be more immersed in the game. After these steps, the agent starts and shows a gray background for the participant in order to calculate his baseline of frustration and excitement. Then, during the experiment, every 20 seconds, the agent calculates the means of frustration and excitement and compares it to the baseline to extract the main emotion. Finally, the agent chooses the appropriate intervention rule, and sends the action to the game.

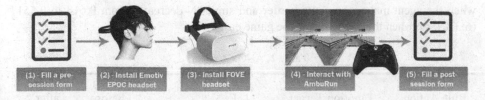

Fig. 4. The experimental process

This neurofeedback loop (AmbuRun → Measurement of emotions → choose appropriate intervention rule → AmbuRun) targets to adapt the game according to the frustration and excitement of the participant.

In another way, the intervention in the game changes the frustration and the excitement of the participant.

7   Results and Discussions

To confirm the effectiveness of our approach and to study the emotional state effect resulting after the appliance of each intervention rule, a paired-samples t-test was conducted to compare excitement and frustration before and after the intervention of the agent. We note that the rule that makes the ambulance faster was executed 225 times, 186 for the rule that makes the ambulance slower, 210 times for the rule that makes the game harder, and finally 173 times for the rule that makes the game easier.

As described in table 1, we see that when the rule action **Fast** is applied $t(225)=3.908$ and $p=0.000* < 0.01\%$. Also when the rule action **Slow** is applied, $t(186)=-4.008$ and $p=0.000*< 0.01\%$. Moreover, when the action is **Hard**, $t(210)=4.626$ and $p=0.000*< 0.01\%$. Finally, when the neural agent send the action **Easy** to the VR game, $t(173)=-4.125$ and $p=0.000*<0.01\%$. These results are significant and show the difference between the level of frustration and excitement before and after each action.

Table 1. T-test results

Rule Action	Mean (after action - before action)	SD	t	p
Fast	0.052	0.199	3.908	0.000*
Slow	-0.060	0.206	-4.008	0.000*
Hard	0.069	0.216	4.626	0.000*
Easy	-0.063	0.200	-4.125	0.000*

We also conducted an analysis of variance ANOVA to see if the frustration and excitement before and after the interventions are statistically different. As described in table 2, the results are significant and show that frustration and excitement before and after the intervention on the game are different. We notice that the mean excitement increases from 0.437 to 0.489 (5.2% more) when the action is to make the ambulance faster, and decreases from 0.548 to 0.488 (6% less) when the action is to make the ambulance slower. In addition, the level of frustration increases from 0.531 to 0.600 (6.9% more) when the agent makes the game harder and similarly decreases from 0.614 to 0.551 (6.3% less) when the agent makes the game easier.

Table 2. ANOVA results

Rule Action	Emotion Target	F	P	Mean before action	Mean after action
Fast	Increase Excitement	6.96497	0.009*	0.437	0.4888
Slow	Decrease Excitement	7.8645	0.005*	0.5485	0.4881
Hard	Increase Frustration	13.602	0.000*	0.5312	0.6002
Easy	Decrease Frustration	9.46848	0.002*	0.6144	0.5517

Figure 5 shows the reaction of one participant after each intervention for 280 seconds. We note that after every intervention, we consider the result after 20 seconds to see the impact. The values of frustration and excitement are the mean values for each 20 seconds. When the agent applied the rule supposing that if we make the game harder, the frustration will increase, for example in sec 80 and in sec 160, we notice that the frustration has increased from 0.46 to 0.65 and from 0.36 to 0.43 respectively. In addition, when the neural agent applied the rule, which supposes that if we make the game easy the frustration will decrease, in sec 20 and in sec 140 for example, we notice that the frustration has decreased from 0.53 to 0.45 and from 0.56 to 0.36, respectively. Another example, when the agent applied the rule supposing that if we make the ambulance slower, the excitement will decrease, in sec 60 and in sec 220 for example, we notice that the excitement has decreased from 0.30 to 0.16 and from 0.35 to 0.20, respectively. Finally, when the applied rule supposes that when we make the ambulance faster, the excitement will increase, in sec 40 and in sec200 for example, we notice that the frustration has increased from 0.26 to 0.3 and 0.25 to 0.35, respectively. However, we note that when this rule was applied in sec 260, the excitement has decreased from 0.65 to 0.55.

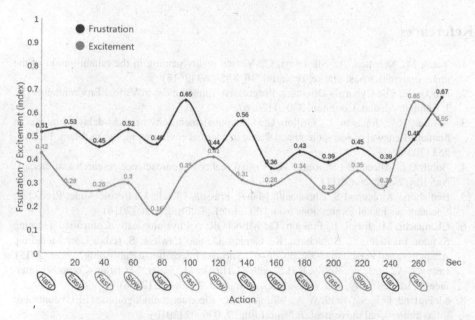

Fig. 5. Example of one-participant reactions

We can explain this result by noticing the big increase of the excitement in the previous action when the game become hard. Hence, in this case, the excitement was already too high. Therefore, we conclude that the change of speed could not only affect excitement and the change of difficulty could not only affect frustration.

8   Conclusion

In this paper, we presented a neurofeedback approach to adapt a VR game through real-time brain assessment. We presented a measuring module, a neural agent and the VR game AmbuRun. We conducted experiments, and tests. Results showed that when the agent adapts the game for the participant by changing speed and difficulty according to his excitement and frustration, it affects the level of his excitement and frustration in the right way. In addition, the intervention of the agent does not affect only the target emotion but could affect other emotions. Further work will aim to analyze the effect of each intervention with machine learning techniques in order to define all the emotional effect of each intervention. Moreover, we would like to experiment more rules that could affect other emotions.

Acknowledgments

We acknowledge NSERC-CRD and BMU for funding this work.

References

1. Yates, M., Kelemen, A., Sik Lanyi, C.: Virtual reality gaming in the rehabilitation of the upper extremities post-stroke. Brain Inj. 30, 855–863 (2016).
2. Biocca, F.: The Cyborg's Dilemma: Progressive Embodiment in Virtual Environments [1]. J. Comput.-Mediat. Commun. 3, 0–0 (2006).
3. Alvarez, R.P., Johnson, L., Grillon, C.: Contextual-specificity of short-delay extinction in humans: Renewal of fear-potentiated startle in a virtual environment. Learn. Mem. 14, 247–253 (2007).
4. Bohil, C.J., Alicea, B., Biocca, F.A.: Virtual reality in neuroscience research and therapy. Nat. Rev. Neurosci. (2011).
5. Benlamine, Mohamed S, Chaouachi, Maher, Frasson, Claude, Dufresne, Aude: Predicting Spontaneous Facial Expressions from EEG. Intell. Tutoring Syst. (2016).
6. Chaouachi, M., Jraidi, I., Frasson, C.: MENTOR: A Physiologically Controlled Tutoring System. In: Ricci, F., Bontcheva, K., Conlan, O., and Lawless, S. (eds.) User Modeling, Adaptation and Personalization. pp. 56–67. Springer International Publishing, Cham (2015).
7. Lecuyer, A., Lotte, F., Reilly, R.B., Leeb, R., Hirose, M., Slater, M.: Brain-Computer Interfaces, Virtual Reality, and Videogames. Computer. 41, 66–72 (2008).
8. McFarland, D.J., Sarnacki, W.A., Wolpaw, J.R.: Electroencephalographic (EEG) control of three-dimensional movement. J. Neural Eng. 7, 036007 (2010).
9. Gorini, A., Riva, G.: Virtual reality in anxiety disorders: the past and the future. Expert Rev. Neurother. 8, 215–233 (2008).
10. Rose, F.D., Brooks, B.M., Rizzo, A.A.: Virtual Reality in Brain Damage Rehabilitation: Review. Cyberpsychol. Behav. 8, 241–262 (2005).
11. D'Mello, S., Olney, A., Williams, C., Hays, P.: Gaze tutor: A gaze-reactive intelligent tutoring system. Int. J. Hum.-Comput. Stud. 70, 377–398 (2012).
12. Chaouachi, M., Jraidi, I., Frasson, C.: Adapting to Learners' Mental States Using a Physiological Computing Approach. FLAIRS 2015 Twenty-Eighth Int. Flairs Conf. (2015).

13. Ghali Ramla, Ben Abdessalem Hamdi, Frasson Claude: Improving Intuitive Reasoning Through Assistance Strategies in a Virtual Reality Game, (2017).
14. Sherlin, L.H., Arns, M., Lubar, J., Heinrich, H., Kerson, C., Strehl, U., Sterman, M.B.: Neurofeedback and Basic Learning Theory: Implications for Research and Practice. J. Neurother. 15, 292–304 (2011).
15. Van Doren, J., Heinrich, H., Bezold, M., Reuter, N., Kratz, O., Horndasch, S., Berking, M., Ros, T., Gevensleben, H., Moll, G.H., Studer, P.: Theta/beta neurofeedback in children with ADHD: Feasibility of a short-term setting and plasticity effects. Int. J. Psychophysiol. 112, 80–88 (2017).
16. Heinrich, H., Gevensleben, H., Strehl, U.: Annotation: Neurofeedback ? train your brain to train behaviour. J. Child Psychol. Psychiatry. 48, 3–16 (2007).
17. Duric, N.S., Elgen, I., Assmus, J.: Self-reported efficacy of neurofeedback treatment in a clinical randomized controlled study of ADHD children and adolescents. Neuropsychiatr. Dis. Treat. 1645 (2014).

Event-Related Brain Potentials from Pictures Relevant to Disaster Education

Angeliki Tsiara[1*], Tassos A. Mikropoulos[1], Dimitris Mavridis[1], and Julien Mercier[2]

[1] Educational Approaches to Virtual Reality Technologies (EARTH lab), Department of Primary Education, University of Ioannina, Greece
[2] Département d'éducation et formation spécialisées, Université du Québec à Montréal (UQAM), Canada
atsiara@cc.uoi.gr, amikrop@uoi.gr, dmavridi@cc.uoi.gr, mercier.julien@uqam.ca

Abstract. Decision-making can be regarded as a cognitive process integrated in our interaction with the environment. This interaction comprises of a plethora of sensory or mental stimuli. Among them, visual awareness and semantic recognition during decision-making tasks are of main importance. Nowadays, disaster education becomes a part of the curricula to foster a more resilient population, and relevant research emerges. The purpose of this exploratory study was to investigate visual awareness and semantic recognition during a visual decision-making task concerning earthquakes, by measuring brain activity and especially event-related potentials. The task consisted of digital images, representing useful and non-useful items constituting a survival kit in case of an earthquake. The subjects, seven adult males, had to distinguish between those useful and non-useful items. A late positive component (P300) and an early posterior negativity (N200) were studied since they are the most prominent components for categorization tasks. Our results suggested that participants distinguished the useful items in a series of non-useful stimuli based on their semantic content. These preliminary results indicate that these stimuli could be integrated in an educational digital environment concerning disaster preparedness.

Keywords: Visual Processing, Event-related Potentials, P300, N200, Disaster Education.

1 Introduction

1.1 Visual Processing

Visual processing examines the way we perceive and process a visual stimulus (i.e. a digital image with scientific content) from its display time up to making a decision depending on its semantic content. The time course and speed of visual processing of specific stimuli categories have been studied as a function of behavioral and neural responses in relevant brain areas [44, 45]. In general, these studies examine images belonging to two (or more) categories according to selected physical features or higher-

© Springer International Publishing AG 2017
C. Frasson and G. Kostopoulos (Eds.): BFAL 2017, LNAI 10512, pp. 144–158, 2017
DOI: 10.1007/978-3-319-67615-9_13

order stimulus categories using one of them as the target category and the other (or the rest) as the non-target (standard) category. Thorpe et al. [44] argue that the time needed to perform a visual categorization task is about 150ms from stimulus onset. In more detail, according to [45], the visual categorization process is divided into two distinct stages regarding stimuli differentiation. The first is completed around 75-80ms and the second one around 150ms after the stimulus presentation. The first stage is driven by low-level sensory properties while the second corresponds to high-level characteristics (semantic categories). This latter stage is very important for decision-making tasks as it appears even during comparing objects of the same category with or without the presence of the behavioral response.

Event-Related Potentials (ERP) enable the recording and analysis of neural responses to specific visual events with millisecond temporal resolution, within the temporal scale of the previous operations in visual categorization. The ERP component under study depends on factors such as the experimental method, the type and properties of the stimuli, effects such as familiarity, semantic priming, etc. Several ERP components have been associated with the processing of target compared to non-target (standard) stimuli in decision-making tasks. The P300 and N200 signals are the two most prominent components for categorization tasks of this type in an oddball paradigm experimental design. On the one hand, the P300 wave is an event-related potential component with a parieto-central scalp distribution elicited in the processes of stimulus evaluation and decision-making [8]. Gray et al. [13] argue that the P300 latency is an indicator of the duration of the stimulus categorization. On the other hand, the N200 wave is considered to reflect processes involved mainly in the detection of novelty or mismatch [12].

Tasks related to face recognition [24, 36, 46], categorization and decision-making comparing facial stimuli with objects in natural scenes such as means of transport, animals, food, etc. [33, 34], words [2, 37, 43] or different representations of facial images - schematic, Mooney, photographs [19] have been broadly studied. The multitude of studies on facial recognition is well justified by its importance in social interaction. Nelson [24] supports the notion of face-sensitivity in the human brain as the neural mechanisms involved in face recognition differ from non-facial stimuli. Rossion and Caharel [33] show that two event-related components, specifically P1 (P100) and N1 (N170), are associated with face recognition. The N170 appears to reflect a stage of visual processing at which objects are recognized, being generally larger and peaking earlier in response to human faces than other non-face stimuli [34]. Moreover, effects of the stimulus structure, familiarity [4, 13, 15, 20, 29, 42], semantic priming and congruency affect the attentional resources devoted to categorization tasks for further processing [7, 30-32, 38]. According to Marzi and Viggiano [20], ERPs recorded at around 250ms after the stimulus presentation in frontal scalp locations differ between famous and non-famous faces. The P250 component is thought to reflect the access to semantic memory and the necessity of retrieving a stored representation. Tacikowski et al. [42] argue that P300 amplitude increases by the successive presentations of stimuli mostly over centro-parietal sites within 320-900ms after the stimulus onset.

The Information and Communication Technologies (ICT)-supported learning process involves discrimination tasks that require skills such as visual perception, decision making, rational thinking and executive behavior that are not only exclusively connected to school-relevant subjects, but also concern everyday life skills. The corresponding literature on visual processing reveals a lack of studies on visual stimuli with specific semantic content of a certain subject matter. The stimuli used in the literature are based either on their semantic content i.e. faces, means of transport, furniture, food, etc., or on object's properties such as affect, familiarity, etc., and not within a specific context. Studies of such topics are therefore necessary to examine the way the human brain processes stimuli in order to categorize them based on their contextual information.

1.2   Disaster Education

Disaster education, concerning natural disasters such as earthquakes and extreme weather conditions, relates with students' education about how to protect themselves in case of a disaster [39]. According to Briere and Elliott [5], the term "disaster" is used to describe all the large-scale environmental events that adversely affect a significant number of people. Natural disasters include all the negative effects that are produced as a result of the expression of a natural phenomenon such as earthquakes, hurricanes, floods, etc. More specifically, in order to be classified as a disaster, a phenomenon should cause widespread social or economic losses. Therefore, research on disasters aims both on the prevention of the disaster and the mitigation of the disaster effects.

An efficacious way to disaster prevention is education [40]. However, educational competencies should be aligned with the design and implementation of disaster research in order to be effective [1]. Studies on disaster education are mainly focusing on professionals, such as nurses, who have a key role in processes of recovering after a disaster and dealing with mass casualty events. These studies are conducted in order to define, firstly, the necessary competencies of healthcare professionals in the frame of disaster preparedness, and secondly the instructional methods to deliver the appropriate educational content [9, 17]. Today, it is commonly accepted that formal and non-formal education targeting disaster preparedness should be extended throughout the society in the context of the regular curriculum in order to foster a more resilient population.

1.3   ICT and Disaster Education

The advent of ICT is a key factor that may allow significant improvements in disaster research and education. Simulations and virtual environments, serious games and other innovative technological agents may facilitate disaster preparedness as they have the potential to enhance user's participation, sense of presence, etc. and to provide situated learning in authentic environments. However, the basic principle for implementing an effective digital learning environment is to design the sensory representations in order to be compatible with the visual, auditory and tactile perception of the user. For example, a serious game which provides an engaging virtual environment for training on disaster communication and decision-making processes is presented by Haferkamp, Kraemer, Linehan and Schembri [14]. Based on the concept of problem-based learning, the players develop communication and group decision-making skills. Mitsuhara et al. [22] have designed another digital tool; they propose a web-based system for designing game-based evacuation. The players can learn about disaster prevention measures by viewing the materials and real-world scenery and making appropriate decisions during a virtual evacuation. Natsis et al. [23], compared students' views on three different web-based learning tools, an educational game, a dynamic simulation and a digital concept map. These three learning tools were used for educational purposes aiming at natural disaster readiness. The results showed that students remained highly-engaged while using all three learning objects. These examples suggest that educational material that is embedded in digital environments for disaster risk reduction should be designed and implemented in order to capitalize on the interactivity and the high sense of presence to promote the development of skills, such as critical thinking and problem-solving that users would carry in a real world situation.

The main research objective of the present study was to examine the visual decision-making in constituting an earthquake survival kit from images of useful items and non-useful items. Because the timeline of constituent processing steps in visual decision-making is below the earliest response time for a motor response (around 700ms), the study hinges on measuring the electrical brain activity. Activity, that is related to visual processing in terms of visual awareness and semantic recognition during the identification of ten different images depicting useful items and non-useful items that they have to bring with them in their earthquake survival kit, in case of an earthquake.

1.4 Research Objectives

The research objectives of the present study were to investigate the:
1. Visual awareness of useful images in a sequence of non-useful images.
2. Semantic recognition (i.e. conscious categorization) of useful and non-useful images.
3. Assessment of semantic recognition time.
4. Brain areas that are involved in semantic recognition.

2 Method

2.1 Participants

The sample consisted of seven (7) young adults, all male volunteers of ages 28 to 31 years. The participants were only men in order to avoid possible gender differences in brain activity. All participants had normal vision, were right–handed native Greek speakers, without certain diagnosed learning difficulties or mental disease. None of the participants received any medication or substances that affected the operation of the nervous system and they had not consumed caffeine or alcohol in the last 24 hours before the experiment. The alpha rhythm of all the participants was checked and found to be normal (8–12Hz, 10Hz peak).

2.2 Stimuli

Ten different images depicting the content of an earthquake survival kit (useful items, UI) as well as the non-useful items (NUI) were presented to each subject (Fig.1.). The five useful items were a cereal bar, a flashlight, a pocketknife, a bottle of water and a whistle, whereas the non-useful items were an ice cream stick, a hamburger, a laptop, a bottle of milk and a toolkit.

Fig. 1. The useful (up) and non-useful (down) objects

2.3   Procedure

Each participant was comfortably seated at eye level and 100cm away from α 17" TFT monitor, passively observing the displayed images. In the beginning of the experiment, each participant had a few minutes to adapt to the specific conditions, to relax and reduce the movements of their eyes. Before the EEG recording the researchers gave a briefing to each participant about earthquakes and the relevant precaution measures. Each participant was familiarized with the useful and non-useful objects.

The experiment consisted of one session including 300 trials of which 15% were UI (target stimuli) and 85% were NUI (non-target stimuli). The images under study from both stimulus categories were randomly displayed. Each stimulus was presented centrally in the screen for 2000ms. A central fixation cross was presented during the inter-stimulus interval of 1000ms. The schematic representation of the experimental procedure is given in Fig. 2. The participants were instructed to observe the displayed images and respond mentally only to target stimuli representing objects that they have to bring in their earthquake survival kit. By mental response we refer to the almost immediate response that is elicited when the brain perceives a stimulus. This mental response can then lead to behavioral responses (i.e. pushing a button, etc). For each participant the whole procedure lasted on average about 30-40min, starting from the placement of the cap on participant's head until the completion of the session.

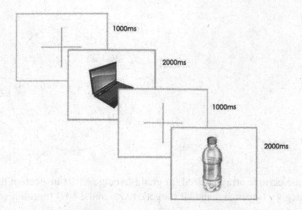

Fig. 2. Schematic view of experimental procedure

2.4   Data Collection and Analysis

EEG was recorded using a g.tec 36-channel amplifier with a sampling rate of 256Hz. The digital EEG data acquisition system had a 1–48Hz band pass filter. EEG activity was monitored from 19 Ag/AgCl electrodes using an electrode cap with a standard 10-20 International Electrode Placement System layout. Raw EEG data was recorded from Fp1, Fp2, F7, F3, Fz, F4, F8, T3, C3, Cz, C4, T4, T5, P3, Pz, P4, T6, O1 and O2 electrode positions. The rest of the electrodes that are available by the amplifier were not used since the scalp locations that were pertinent to examine, based on the literature review, were covered by the above-mentioned electrode locations. All leads were referenced to linked ear lobes and a ground electrode was applied to the forehead. Horizontal and vertical eye movements were recorded simultaneously using four electrodes round the eyes. The electrodes' impedance was kept below 5KΩ.

In the process of the offline signal analysis, eye movement and other artefacts were first removed by visual inspection, and then individual subject EEG data were filtered with a 30Hz low-pass digital filter and divided into epochs. Each epoch began 100ms prior to stimulus onset and continued for 600ms thereafter. Single trials were then averaged per UI and NUI and subject using a 100ms pre-stimulus baseline. Finally, the grand mean for each group of objects across all subjects was calculated. Event-related potentials were studied within frontal (F7, F3, Fz, F4, F8), fronto-parietal (Fp1, Fp2), central (C3, Cz, C4), parietal (P3, Pz, P4), temporal (T3, T4, T5, T6) and occipital (O1, O2) areas. The processing and analysis of the signals were performed using the gBSanalyze and Matlab software packages.

Single and grand average ERP waveforms were calculated for target and non-target stimuli on all 19 scalp locations. Based on the inspection of grand average ERP waveforms (Fig. 3.) and prior studies [2, 13, 25], P300 was defined as the most positive point between 250ms–600ms in the grand average ERP waveforms.

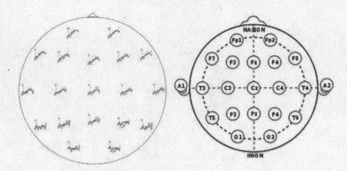

Fig. 3. Layout of electrode array utilized for grand-average ERPs inspection for each stimulus category (green signals: UI (target), red signals: NUI (non-target))

3   Results

Table 1 shows the descriptive statistics (average, standard deviation, minimum value, maximum value) of P300 values over all brain areas, separately for useful (target) stimuli and non-useful (non-target) stimuli. Median and interquartile ranges are presented because the amplitude seems to have a skewed distribution, although the asymmetry is not extreme as can be seen in Fig. 4.

Table 1. Descriptive statistics for the P300 amplitude (in µV) elicited by target (T) and non-target (NT) stimuli

Brain area	average		std. deviation		minimum		maximum	
	T	NT	T	NT	T	NT	T	NT
frontal	62.47	59.32	25.41	40.61	7.64	8.11	127.97	171.69
parietal	38.85	22.02	19.88	14.32	-6.50	-5.48	73.31	51.07
central	51.32	32.15	16.77	17.34	21.77	4.52	73.51	65.54
occipital	21.34	7.89	21.19	8.48	-13.48	-6.43	57.62	19.81
temporal	33.92	21.46	21.72	14.23	3.29	1.02	98.51	53.10

Figure 4 shows the amplitude boxplots for each one of the five brain areas and object type. It seems that there are no differences in the distribution of the amplitude between useful and non-useful items in the frontal area, but the amplitude appears to assume larger values for non-useful items in the other four zones. It is also notable that the variance of amplitude is much larger in the frontal area compared to the other areas. Although the distribution of the amplitude is non-symmetric in most sub-populations, the asymmetry is not extreme.

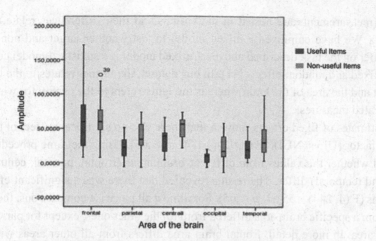

Fig. 4. Boxplot for target and non-target stimuli (μV)

Figure 5 shows that targets (UI) appear to elicit both a negative (N200) component between 200ms and 250ms after the stimulus onset and a positive P300 component between 500ms and 600ms. Non-targets (NUI) elicited neither N200 nor P300 component. Our results showed that the P300 component is most prominent at parieto-central scalp locations such as Cz and Pz. P300 latency for both Cz and Pz locations appears prolonged with the mean P300 latency for targets to be about 550ms. The P300 amplitudes at Cz and Pz are about 40μV and 30μV respectively.

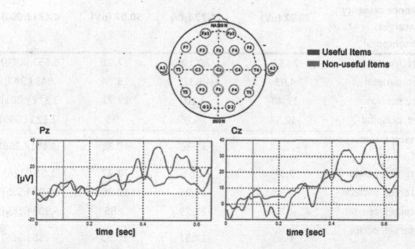

Fig. 5. Grand-average ERP waveforms recorded at Pz and Cz for each stimulus category. Time 0 corresponds to stimulus onset (green signals: UI (target, red signals: NUI (non-target)

Each participant contributes multiple measurements in the data and those measurements are correlated. To obtain a valid inference, we should take into account the hierarchy in the data (measurements are nested in individuals and their differences relate to that hierarchy). We have employed a mixed model to test whether target and non-target values differ on the task described above. A mixed model is a statistical model containing both fixed and random effects [11]. In our dataset, the former relates to the type of the object and the area of the brain whereas the latter refers to the person for which we have repeated measures.

The estimates of fixed effects showed that there was no significant effect of the object type factor (UI vs. NUI), (F (1, 12) = 1.70, p > .05). Using the same procedure we examined whether the values from different brain areas (frontal, parietal, central, occipital, and temporal) differ. The results revealed that there was a significant effect of brain areas (F (4, 244) = 55.51, $p < .05$). For almost all pairwise comparisons, the mean values from a specific brain area differed from all the other ones, except for parietal vs. temporal area. In more detail, frontal brain area differs from all other areas with a p-value equal to .00. Central and occipital brain areas also differ from each other and with the rest of the brain areas with a p-value less than .05.

Table 2. Estimates of fixed effects

| | Effect size (µV) | 95% Confidence interval | | t (Sig.) |
		Lower bound	Upper bound	
Intercept Reference category item=target, area=temporal	33.92 (µV)	17.77 (µV)	50.07 (µV)	4.433 (.000)
target, frontal	28.55	20.10	37.01	6.652 (.000)
target, parietal	4.93	-5.37	15.24	.943 (.347)
target, central	17.40	7.10	27.71	3.327 (.001)
target, occipital	-12.58	-24.26	-.90	-2.121 (.035)
non-target, temporal	-12.46	-35.30	10.38	-1.151 (.266)
non-target, frontal	9.31	-2.65	21.27	1.53 (.126)
non-target, parietal	-4.38	-18.95	10.20	-.592 (.555)
non-target, central	-6.72	-21.29	7.85	-.908 (.365)
non-target, occipital	-0.99	-17.51	15.53	-.118 (.906)

Table 2 summarizes the results from the mixed model. The reference value was calculated for target item and temporal brain area and the estimated amplitude for this combination is 33.92µV. All other coefficients show the change in amplitude if we move to a different combination of type of object and brain area. 95% confidence intervals and p-values are also indicated. The results reveal that parietal is the only area that has no statistical difference with temporal area for target stimuli (p = .35). The occipital area

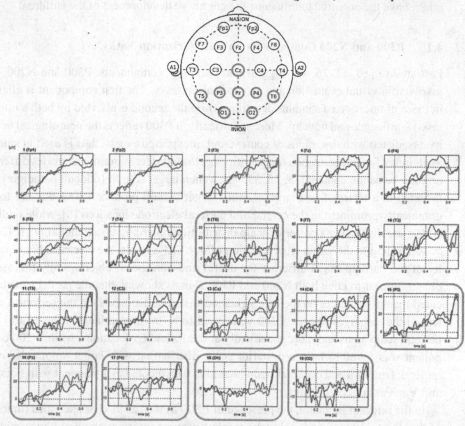

Fig. 6. N200 component with posterior scalp distribution

for both stimulus categories give almost the same estimate which probably means that participants show the same level of visual awareness for target and non-target items.

Figure 6 shows that the N200 component has a posterior scalp distribution with larger amplitudes over parietal, temporal and occipital scalp locations (i.e. Pz, P3, P4, T5, T6, O1, O2 and Cz).

4   Discussion

This study presented neurophysiological results of young male adults while observing pictures of different content coming from a digital learning environment concerning earthquake precaution measures. Despite the individual differences at the scalp-recorded brain potential, the general understanding of how the brain network is structured and how it could be altered by experience could lead to educational interventions that might have the potential to influence the cognitive development of the children.

4.1 P300 and N200 Components on Categorization Tasks

Past studies [10, 12, 26, 41] suggest that two ERP components, P300 and N200, are involved in visual evaluation and categorization tasks. The first component is elicited in cases of unexpected stimulus detection while the second is affected by both stimulus task-significance and novelty. More specifically, a P300 reflects the neurological activity associated with deviations of context and unexpected events, thus is used in studies as an index for categorization tasks, with target/non-target stimulus categories differing on their semantic content [13, 25, 35, 42]. When target stimuli (oddball paradigm) are detected in a series of non-target stimuli, target stimuli produce P300s that are topographically prominent in the central and parietal electrode locations [8], while oddball N200s are displaying a posterior scalp distribution regarding visual modality [12].

According to the visual representation of our ERP signals, the electrical brain activity of the participants is different for useful and non-useful objects. Only the useful objects appear to elicit both N200 and P300 signals showing that the participants allocated mental resources on the categorization task and distinguished the semantic content of the displayed images. P300 was found to be most prominent at the central and parietal scalp areas and more specifically at the Pz and Cz locations, while N200 component was found to have a posterior scalp distribution with larger amplitudes over parietal, temporal and occipital scalp locations which come in agreement with Folstein and Van Petten's [12] results.

In the relevant literature, the presence of P300 as well as its characteristics (in terms of amplitude, latency and scalp topography) provide information about the stimuli as they are influenced by factors such as the task-relevance of the stimulus, the motivational significance of the task, the arousal level/valence of the stimulus, the difficulty of the categorization task and the mental resources (such as attention) allocated on the task. The amplitude of the P300 is suggested to be an indication about the attentional resources engaged in processing a given stimulus [16] and the amount of cognitive processing needed to complete the task [2]. In our study, the P300 amplitude at Cz and Pz were about 40μV and 30μV respectively. In general, the P300 amplitude varies with the improbability of targets and is about 10-20μV visual event-related potentials [26, 27], although amplitudes of up to 40μV have also been documented [6].

As a P300 component is elicited only after a stimulus has been evaluated and categorized, P300 latency is suggested to be an index of the stimulus evaluation time [8, 18]. In our results, latency of the P300 component appeared prolonged with the mean

P300 latency for targets to be about 550ms. The P300 latency is related to task-processing demands and participant's cognitive performance [21, 28]. Since the difficulty of the categorization task was not high, the mental fatigue caused to the participants due to the long duration of the experimental procedure (30min-45min) should have affected the P300 latency. Some participants after the experiment reported that they felt tired due to the several repetitions of images and frequent switching, which is something that may affected their level of attention and consequently the latency of the P300 component.

4.2 Public Awareness through Education for Disaster Risk Reduction – Implications for the Future

Nowadays it is widely accepted that education has a key role in hazard exposure and vulnerability reduction to natural disasters. Educational technology is a promising tool that has the power to increase preparedness for the correct response in dangerous conditions through highly interactive and engaging digital environments such as virtual environments, serious games, etc. These technological agents comprise of a plethora of multimedia elements that are perceived by the users as sensory stimuli. For implementing an effective learning environment, all sensory representations should be designed in order to be compatible with the visual, auditory and tactile perception of the user. Electrophysiological measurements such as EEG provide information about the low-level, fast cognitive response of the human to specific stimulus, thus it can be regarded as an appropriate method for assessing the appropriateness of the stimuli.

This exploratory study is the only one that examines visual stimuli with a certain semantic content that may be integrated in an educational digital environment with a specific subject content related to disaster preparedness. In this direction, future research could be conducted using a larger sample and also gender differences could be examined.

References

1. Alkire, S. A Conceptual Framework for Human Security, http://www3.qeh.ox.ac.uk/pdf/crisewps/workingpaper2.pdf last accessed 2016/09/13.

2. Azizian, A., Freitas, A.L., Watson, T.D., Squires N.K.: Electrophysiological correlates of categorization: P300 amplitude as index of target similarity. Biological Psychology (71), 278–288 (2006).

3. Azizian, A., Watson, T.D., Parvaz, M.A., Squires, N.K.: Time Course of Processes Underlying Picture and Word Evaluation: An Event-Related Potential Approach. Brain Topography 18 (3), 213-222 (2006).

4. Bar, M., Neta, M.: Humans prefer curved visual objects. Psychological Science 17(8), 645-648 (2006).

5.   Briere, J., Elliott, D.: Prevalence, Characteristics, and Long-Term Sequelae of Natural Dis-
     aster Exposure in the General Population. Journal of Traumatic Stress 13 (4), 661-679
     (2000).

6.   Coles, M., Smid, H., Scheffers, M., Otten, L.J.: Mental chronometry and the study of human
     information processing. In: Rugg, M., Coles, M. (eds). Electrophysiology of the Mind, pp.
     94-95. Oxford University Press, New York (1995).

7.   Demiral, Ş.B., Malcolm, G.L., Henderson, J.M.: ERP correlates of spatially incongruent
     object identification during scene viewing: Contextual expectancy versus simultaneous pro-
     cessing. Neuropsychologia 50 (7), 1271-1285 (2012).

8.   Duncan-Johnson, C.C. Donchin, E.: On Quantifying Surprise: The Variation of Event-Re-
     lated Potentials With Subjective Probability. Psychophysiology 14, 456–467 (1977).

9.   Farra, S.L., Miller, E.T., Hodgson, E.: Virtual reality disaster training: Translation to prac-
     tice, Nurse Education in Practice 15 (1), 53-57 (2015).

10. Ferrari, V., Bradley, M.M., Codispoti, M., Lang, P.J.: Detecting Novelty and Significance.
     Journal of Cognitive Neuroscience 22(2), 404–411 (2010).

11. Fitzmaurice, G.M., Laird, N.M., Ware, J.H.: Applied Longitudinal Analysis. John Wiley &
     Sons, Inc., 326-328 (2004).

12. Folstein, J.R., Van Petten, C.: Influence of cognitive control and mismatch on the N2 com-
     ponent of the ERP: A review. Psychophysiology 45(1), 152–170 (2008).

13. Gray, H.M., Ambady, N., Lowenthal, W.T., Deldin, P.: P300 as an index of attention to self-
     relevant stimuli. Journal of Experimental Social Psychology 40, 216–224 (2004).

14. Haferkamp, N., Kraemer, N.C., Linehan, C., Schembri, M. Training disaster communication
     by means of serious games in virtual environments. Entertainment Computing 2(2), 81-88
     (2011).

15. Hazenberg, S.J., van Lier, R. Disentangling effects of structure and knowledge in perceiving
     partly occluded shapes: An ERP study. Vision Research (2015).

16. Johnson, R.: The amplitude of the p300 component of the event-related potential: review
     and synthesis. In: Ackles, P.K., Jennings, J.R., Coles, M.G.H. (eds). Advances in Psycho-
     physiology 3, 69-138 (1988).

17. Jose, M.M., Dufrene, C.: Educational competencies and technologies for disaster prepared-
     ness in undergraduate nursing education: An integrative review. Nurse Education Today 34
     (4), 543-551 (2014).

18. Kutas, M., McCarthy, G., Donchin, E.: Augmenting mental chronometry: the P300 as a
     measure of stimulus evaluation time. Science 197 (4305), 792-795 (1977).

19. Latinus, M., Taylor, M.J. Face processing stages: Impact of difficulty and the separation of
     effects. Brain Research 1123 (1), 179-187 (2006).

20. Marzi, T., Viggiano, M.P.: Interplay between familiarity and orientation in face processing:
     An ERP study. International Journal of Psychophysiology 65 (3), 182-192 (2007).

21. McCarthy, G., Donchin, E.: A metric for thought: a comparison of P300 latency and re-
     sponse time. Science 211, 77-80 (1981).

22. Mitsuhara, H., Inoue, T., Yamaguchi, K., Takechi, Y., Morimoto, M., Iwaka, K., Kozuki, Y., Shishibori, M.: Web-based System for Designing Game-based Evacuation Drills. Procedia Computer Science 72, 277-284 (2015).

23. Natsis, A., Hormova, H., Mikropoulos, T.A.: Students' views on different learning objects. In L. Gómez Chova, A. López Martínez, I. Candel Torres (eds.), INTED 2014 Proceedings, 8th International Technology, Education and Development Conference, pp. 2363-2372, Valencia: IATED Academy (2014).

24. Nelson, C.A.: The development and neural bases of face recognition. Infant and Child Development, 10, 3-18 (2001).

25. Olofsson, J.K., Nordin, S., Sequeira, H., Polich, J.: Affective picture processing: An integrative review of ERP findings. Biological Psychology 77(3), 247–265 (2008).

26. Patel, S.H., Azzam, P.N.: Characterization of N200 and P300: Selected Studies of the Event-Related Potential. International Journal of Medical Sciences 2 (4), 147–154 (2005).

27. Picton, T.W.: The P300 wave of the human event-related potential. Journal of Clinical Neurophysiology, 9(4), 456-79 (1992).

28. Polich, J.: Updating P300: An Integrative Theory of P3a and P3b. Clinical Neurophysiology: Official Journal of the International Federation of Clinical Neurophysiology 118 (10), 2128–2148 (2007).

29. Postman, L., Bruner, J.S., McGinnies, E.: Personal Values as Selective Factors in Perception. The Journal of Abnormal and Social Psychology 43 (2), 142-154 (1948).

30. Proverbio, A.M., Riva, F.: RP and N400 ERP components reflect semantic violations in visual processing of human actions. Neuroscience Letters 459 (3), 142-146 (2009).

31. Proverbio, A.M., Gabaro, V., Orlandi, A., Zani, A.: Semantic brain areas are involved in gesture comprehension: An electrical neuroimaging study. Brain and Language 147, 30-40 (2015).

32. Räling, R., Schröder, A., Wartenburger, I.: The origins of age of acquisition and typicality effects: Semantic processing in aphasia and the ageing brain. Neuropsychologia 86, 80-92 (2016).

33. Rossion, B., Caharel, S.: ERP evidence for the speed of face categorization in the human brain: Disentangling the contribution of low-level visual cues from face perception. Vision Research 51 (12), 1297-1311 (2011).

34. Rousselet, G.A, Macé, M. JM, Fabre-Thorpe, M.: Spatiotemporal analyses of the N170 for human faces, animal faces and objects in natural scenes. Neuroreport 15 (17), 2607-2611 (2004).

35. Rozenkrants, B., Olofsson, J.K., Polich, J.: Affective visual event-related potentials: arousal, valence and repetition effects for normal and distorted pictures. International Journal of Psychophysiology 67(2), 114-23 (2008).

36. Sagiv, N., Bentin, S.: Structural encoding of human and schematic faces: holistic and part-based processes. Journal of Cognitive Neuroscience 13 (7), 937-51 (2001).

37. Schacht, A., Sommer, W.: Emotions in word and face processing: Early and late cortical responses. Brain and Cognition 69 (3), 538-550 (2009).

38. Schupp, H.T., Flaisch, T., Stockburger, J., Junghöfer, M.: Emotion and attention: event-related brain potential studies. Progress in Brain Research 156, 31–51 (2006).

39. Shaw, R., Shiwaku, K., Takeuchi, Y.: Disaster Education. Emerald Bingley, UK (2011).

40. Shaw, R., Kobayashi, M.: Role of Schools in Creating Earthquake-Safer Environment. OECD Workshop, http://www.preventionweb.net/files/5342_SesiRoleSchoolsE-QSafety.pdf, last accessed 2016/06/09.

41. Squires, K.C, Donchin, E., Herning, R.I, McCarthy, G.: On the influence of task relevance and stimulus probability on event-related-potential components. Electroencephalography and Clinical Neurophysiology 42 (1), 1-14 (1977).

42. Tacikowski, P., Jednoróg, K., Marchewka, A., Nowicka, A.: How multiple repetitions influence the processing of self-, famous and unknown names and faces: An ERP study. International Journal of Psychophysiology 79 (2), 219-230 (2011).

43. Theios, J., Amrhein, P.C.: Theoretical analysis of the cognitive processing of lexical and pictorial stimuli: Reading, naming, and visual and conceptual comparisons. Psychological Review 96 (1), 5-24 (1989).

44. Thorpe, S., Fize, D., Marlot, C. Speed of processing in the human visual system. Nature 381 (6582), 520-522 (1996).

45. Vanrullen, R., Thorpe, S.J.: The time course of visual processing: from early perception to decision-making. Journal of cognitive neuroscience 13 (4), 454-461 (2001).

46. Yang, Y., Qiu, Y., Schouten, A.C.: Dynamic Functional Brain Connectivity for Face Perception. Frontiers in Human Neuroscience 9, 662 (2015).

Real-time Spindles Detection for Acoustic Neurofeedback

Stella Zotou[1], George K. Kostopoulos[2] and Theodore A. Antonakopoulos[1]

[1] Department of Electrical and Computers Engineering, School of Engineering, University of Patras, Rion Achaias, Greece, email: <stzotou, antonako>@upatras.gr

[2] Department of Physiology, Medical School, University of Patras, Rion Achaias, Greece, email: gkkostop@upatras.gr

Abstract. Real-time neurofeedback plays an increasing role in today's clinical and basic neuroscience research. In this work, we present a real-time sleep EEG spindles detection algorithm fast enough to be used for real time acoustic feedback stimulation. We further highlight the architecture of a system that implements the algorithm and its experimental evaluation. This system can handle EEG data acquired by various means (i.e. conventional EEG systems, wireless sensors) and a response time of a few msecs has been achieved. The presented algorithm is dynamically adaptive and has accuracy similar to other well-known non real-time algorithms. Comparison and evaluation was performed using EEG data from an open database.

1 Introduction

Following the discovery that sleep has extremely important involvement in our physiology and many disease mechanisms, the electroencephalographic (EEG) study of sleep's macro- and microstructure has evolved into one of the fastest advancing research frontiers. A prominent microstructural EEG feature characterizing the second stage of non-Rapid-Eye-Movements sleep is spindles [1; 2]. They emerge on the EEG as brief bursts of activity in the sigma frequency range (~11Hz- 16Hz) with varying amplitude, but mostly below 50uV peak-to-peak in an adult. These EEG bursts consisting of mostly negative waves of waxing-and-waning amplitude last for 0.5 msecs up to 2secs grouped in sequences that recur with a refractory period of about 4 secs [3]. Magnetoencephalographic studies have recently described the spatiotemporal characteristics of the emergence of spindles after sleep onset [4].

Spindles have been shown to play pivotal roles in sleep maintenance (gating/hypnagogic role) [5], in potentiation of synaptic strengths leading to memory consolidation [6; 7] and in sensory-motor development [8]. Their density and other parameters have been found to vary with the cognitive abilities as well as with the severity of several neuropsychiatric disorders [9; 10] for example increased spindles density has been associated with more effective learning, while marked deficits in sleep spindles have been established in schizophrenia. Furthermore, the thalamocortical mechanisms underlying spindles generation have been implicated in the genesis of some disorders including generalized epilepsy [11]. It therefore became tempting to suggest a putative therapeutic prospect of effective manipulation of the emergence of spindles in some diseases [12].

© Springer International Publishing AG 2017
C. Frasson and G. Kostopoulos (Eds.): BFAL 2017, LNAI 10512, pp. 159–168, 2017
DOI: 10.1007/978-3-319-67615-9_14

Manipulation of specific forms of brain activity via closed loop stimulation is a rapidly developing neuro-engineering project [13]. It demands fast detection of sporadically emerging EEG graphoelements to be hooked to controlled stimulation (electrical, sensory etc.). This appears as a promising tool in the study of a wide variety of biological functions, including pain relief, control of seizures and some psychiatric disorders and cognitive processing during sleep.

It has recently been suggested that enhancing spindles through closed loop acoustic stimulation during sleep may increase our ability for memory consolidation [14]. Developing such a tool would allow neuroscientists to experiment and better understand the mechanisms underlying the role of spindles in learning, with obvious gains for both engineers striving to develop intelligent machines and educators interested in advancing their methods based on how brain learns [15; 16].

Since the manual scoring of sleep spindles is time-consuming, subjective and inaccurate, there has been great interest in developing automated methods for spindle detection. In recent works, various spindle detection algorithms have been proposed including fuzzy logic, neural network, bandpass filtering, Fourier transform, wavelet transform and matching pursuit [17]. Unfortunately most of these algorithms are not suitable for implementation in a neurofeedback system that has a response time of a few msecs. This paper reports the progress we made in overcoming the challenges of developing a system for closed loop auditory stimulation, with the intension to use it is sleep studies of brain plasticity and sleep functions in general in health and disease. Auditory evoked potentials in sleep has been a traditional tool in evaluating brain excitability and plasticity [18] the timing and phase-locking of stimulation to detected spindles will reveal the effect spindles may have on these brain properties.

2   Spindle Detector with Adaptive Thresholding

To further understand the mechanisms and roles of spindles, it would be very instrumental to detect spindles and impose a feedback on their appearance. For this purpose, we considered that it was necessary to develop an automatic sleep spindle detection algorithm (ASDA) that can be applied in real-time and to be used in a system that can provide user-defined acoustic feedback. Most of the algorithms that have been presented in the literature so far, process the EEG signal offline and usually require long-lasting epochs to make a credible decision.

The proposed ASDA is based on dynamic level detection in respect of local max and mean power and adaptive threshold as well. During a preprocessing stage, the DC component is removed from the raw EEG signal and then bandpass filtering is applied, with passband at 11-15Hz. ASDA calculates continuously the signal's power for the $P(x_n)$ and the mean power for the last k samples, where k is selected so that corresponds approximately to user defined window. In case $P(x_n)$ is greater than the mean power multiplied by a threshold K_1, we consider this as the event of a possible spindle and proceed with calculating the adaptive threshold K_2. In order to do that, we find the local max power in the specific time interval and multiply it by constant factor (0.35 obtained after validating various EEG data streams). Finally, we make a positive or negative decision depending on whether the signal power is greater than the K_2 threshold or not, respectively. The ASDA algorithm is shown in Fig. 1 and the algorithm is also highlighted in the following pseudo-code.

```
Input:  xᵢ
Output: Spindle_detection
  1. Compute yᵢ = xᵢ - xᵢ₋₁ + pyᵢ₋₁ - yᵢ₋₂
  2. Compute wᵢ = Σⱼ hⱼ yᵢ₋ⱼ₊₁
  3. Compute P(wᵢ)
  4. Compute Pmean = Σₖ P(wₖ)/k , k=i-N,...,i
  5. if     P(wᵢ)< k₁.Pmean    theni++; go to 1;
  6. Calculate adaptive threshold k₂
  7. if     P(wᵢ)< k₂ (1)      theni++; go to 1;
  8. if  (1) is true for the next 500ms then Spindle
     _detection=TRUE
        else i++; go to 1;
```

Fig. 2 shows the how the ASDA algorithm is applied to an EEG signal and the generated acoustic signal. The EEG raw signal is initially sampled (a) and then signal is filtered by a sharp bandpass filter, out of band noise is removed and a signal with high SNR (signal to noise ratio) is generated (b). The in-band power is calculated (c) and when it exceeds a dynamically determined threshold a possible spindle is marked. That system does not initiate the acoustic feedback immediately but validates the signal's power for a user-specified duration and if the signal's power remains above that threshold then the acoustic feedback is activated. The acoustic signal remains active either for a user specified period of time or until the signal's power becomes less than a user specified power threshold and duration.

In Fig. 2d the duration of the acoustic signal was prespecified to be 0.5 secs and its frequency is 1 kHz. The acoustic signal can either be a single tone of a specific amplitude, a chirp signal or one of a prestored set of acoustic patterns. Its amplitude can also be constant or variable according to a user specified pattern. All these parameters can also be determined on-the-fly, using a set of cognitive rules, and be applied after an adequate period of training.

3   Neurofeedback System Architecture

Fig.3 showsthe general block diagram of a prototype of acoustic neurofeedback system, while in Fig.4 details of the experimental prototype for ASDA are shown. The core element of ASDA prototype system supports software and hardware utilization where all main operations, control, setup, data acquisition, preprocessing and processing, as well as the audio are implemented.

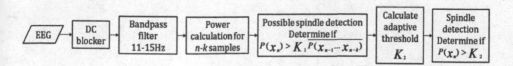

Fig. 1.Block diagram of the ASDA algorithm.

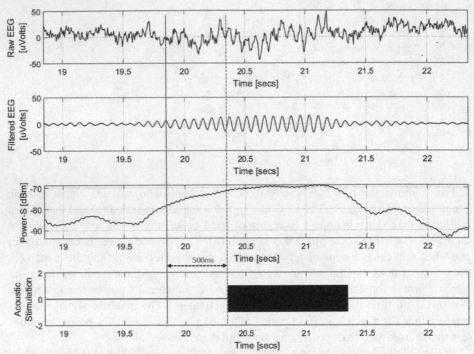

Fig. 2.Sleep spindle detection using ASDA and its acoustic stimulation. a) EEG raw signal sampled at 200Hz. b) EEG signal filtered at 11-15Hz. c) Calculated signal power and spindle detection using adaptive power threshold. d) Acoustic stimulation with 1 msec delay. Start of spindle is marked with the solid line, while with the dashed line is marked the start of the acoustic stimulation. This delay corresponds to the minimum spindle duration.

Although three different input interfaces can be used, that provide greater flexibility with respect to the EEG signal source, the experimental results presented in this work (Fig. 6) are based on two of these interfaces. The system may process data either from conventional EEG systems (using either directly the raw analog signal or digital values using a network interface) or from wireless EEG systems (using protocols like Bluetooth or 802.11). The acoustic feedback can be provided by single or multiple acoustic sources with user-selectable predetermined patterns. The system has been implemented in a single board, using a Zynq FPGA(Field Programmable Gate Array) and various peripherals.

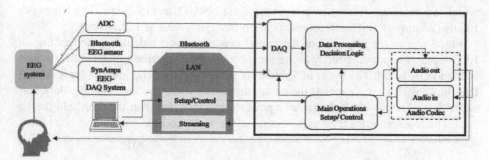

Fig. 3. Block diagram of an acoustic neurofeedback system.

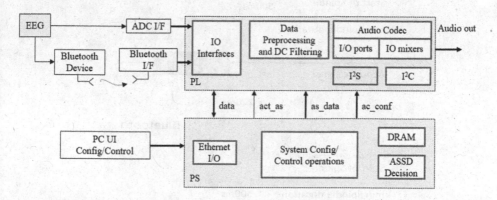

Fig. 4. The architecture of the acoustic neurofeedback setup based on ASDA. Depending on the used configuration, the EEG data are either provided directly to the A/D converter or transmitted wirelessly using a pair of Bluetooth devices.

4 Prototype Setup and Experimental Results

The core element of the experimental setup was the development kit ZedBoard using the Zynq-7020 All Programmable SoC (AP SoC) which couples a Dual-core ARM Cortex-A9 Processing System (PS) and an Artix-7 Programmable Logic (PL). The board contains the low-power stereo audio codec ADAU1761chip that is connected in the PL and can be configured through I^2C and I^2S buses for control and data transmission respectively. The codec was used for the generation of the acoustic stimulation, with the stereo digital-to-analog converter programmed at 44.1kHz and 16-bit data resolution for each channel.

EEG data were acquired through two different interfaces (I/F), an analog-to-digital converter (ADC) and a Bluetooth sensor. The ADC I/F uses the low-power, successive approximation AD7476A chip with 12-bit conversion and a 2-pole Salen key anti-alias filter. The Bluetooth sensor contains an MSP430 microprocessor with integrated 12-bit ADC and a Roving Networks RN-42 Class 2 Bluetooth module for communication via an integrated 2.4GHz antenna with range more than 10 meters which is connected with the microprocessor via USART at 115.2kbps. The Bluetooth I/F also employs RN-42 and communication through UART at 115.2kbps.

Fig. 5 shows the response of the experimental prototype demonstrated in Fig. 4. EEG signal is captured directly at the source while the rest three signals at the outputs of the FPGA board. The 'Start of Spindle' is generated when the internal logic detects that the signal's power exceeds the power threshold, while the 'min Spindle duration' signal is generated only if the signal's power remains higher than the threshold for 0.5 secs. The 'Acoustic signal' is at the output of the audio codecs.

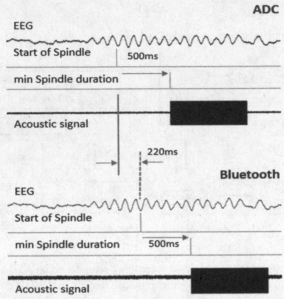

Fig. 5. Experimental data using the two modes of interfacing the EEG signal. The latency introduced when Bluetooth is employed can be compensated by decreasing the required minimum spindle duration. In this case the activated acoustic signal can be seized after a few msecs when the criterion of minimum spindle duration is not finally satisfied.

5   Validation

In order to validate the ASDA algorithm and to test its reliability, we used two methods: In the first case, we used the raw data provided by the DREAMS online database[1].As input signal, we used four out of six online excerpts (2, 4 ,5 ,6) with sampling frequency of 200Hz and duration of 30 mins each. At first, we compared the results of the ASDA to the visual scorings of the experts (Vs1, Vs2) and then to the DREAMS algorithm. The corresponding results are reported in Table 1 and Table 2.

---

[1]The DREAMS database is available at:
        http://www.tcts.fpms.ac.be/~devuyst/Databases/DatabaseSpindles/

Table 1. Number of spindles detected on the 4 excerpts

excerpt	Vs1	Vs2	ASDA	DREAMS
2	60	81	94	94
4	44	25	41	52
5	56	86	97	84
6	72	87	100	100

Table2. Results of ASDA based on the 4 excerpts

Metrics	Vs1	Vs2	Vs1∪Vs2	Vs1∩Vs2
#TP (True Positive)	20	62	158	76
#FP (False Positive)	62	20	171	253
#FN (False Negative)	89	65	154	46
#TN (True Negative)	9946	10045	9211	9464
Agreement rate (%)	98.51	99.17	96.65	96.6
Sensitivity (TPrate) (%)	18.35	48.82	50.64	62.3
FP proportion (%)	56.88	15.75	54.81	207.38

In the second case of validation, we used an artificial signal with spindles of known starting position, known duration and frequency content. The initial signal was also corrupted with colored noise having the same characteristics as a typical EEG signal. In order to generate the proper noise signal, we analyzed the frequency content of a set of raw EEG signals and then we designed a digital filter having the same frequency response. Fig. 6 shows the experimental data of the EEG signal and the respective filter response. The frequent content in the range 10 – 15 Hz is due to the spindles of the original EEG signals, while at 50 Hz we observe the noise introduced by the powerline sources. The proper EEG noise was generated by using a source of White Gaussian Noise and its output was filtered the EEG Noise filter. Then the signal to be processed was generated by using the original signal plus the colored noise at various noise levels in order to test the signal during different SNR scenarios.

Since the locations of the real spindles were known, we were able to calculate accurately the number of properly detected spindles and the number of false spindles, and thus to calculate the normalized TP and FP metrics for various signal-to noise ratios for the ASDA algorithm. These results are shown in Fig 7. Based on experimental results, in a typical EEG signal the mean SNR is in the range of 7 to 9 dB, while during a spindle it increases to 18 up to 22 dB.

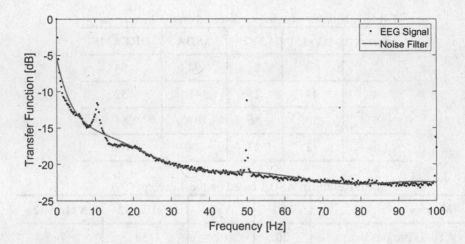

Fig. 6. Experimental characterization of noise in EEG signals. The red solid-line indicates the filter's response used for noise shaping.

In EEG signals with decent quality, ASDA demonstrates high spindle detection accuracy. Depending on the maximum TP and minimum FP specs, the whole set-up should guarantee a minimum SNR value.

6   Conclusions

In this work an automatic spindle detection algorithm is presented as well as a prototype of the neurofeedback system with acoustic stimulation, that can be used online to give real time results. Although several reliable algorithms have been presented in the bibliography, the advantage of the particular one lies in its reduced complexity and fast computation, so it can be used in real-time applications.

References

1. Lüthi A. Sleep Spindles: Where They Come From, What They Do. Neuroscientist. 2014 Jun;20(3):243-56. doi: 10.1177/1073858413500854. Epub 2013 Aug 27. Review. PubMed PMID: 23981852.
2. De Gennaro L, Ferrara M. Sleep spindles: an overview. Sleep Med Rev. 2003 Oct;7(5):423-40. Review. PubMed PMID: 14573378.
3. Koupparis AM, Kokkinos V, Kostopoulos GK. Spindle power is not affected after spontaneous K-complexes during human NREM sleep. PLoS One. 2013;8(1):e54343. doi: 10.1371/journal.pone.0054343. Epub 2013 Jan 10. PubMed PMID: 23326604; PubMed Central PMCID: PMC3542283.
4. Ioannides, Andreas & Liu, Lichan & Poghosyan, Vahe & K. Kostopoulos, George. (2017). Using MEG to Understand the Progression of Light Sleep and the Emergence and Func-

tional Roles of Spindles and K-Complexes. Frontiers in Human Neuroscience. 11. . 10.3389/fnhum.2017.00313.

5. McCormick DA, Bal T. Sensory gating mechanisms of the thalamus. Curr Opin Neurobiol. 1994 Aug;4(4):550-6. Review. PubMed PMID: 7812144.

6. Rosanova, M., and Ulrich, D. (2005). Pattern-specific associative long-term potentiation induced by a sleep spindle-related spike train. J. Neurosci. 25, 9398–9405. doi: 10.1523/JNEUROSCI.2149-05.2005.

7. Ulrich D. Sleep Spindles as Facilitators of Memory Formation and Learning. Neural Plast. 2016;2016:1796715. doi: 10.1155/2016/1796715. Epub 2016 Mar 28. Review. PubMed PMID: 27119026; PubMed Central PMCID: PMC4826925.

8. Khazipov, R., Sirota, A., Leinekugel, X., Holmes, G. L., Ben-Ari, Y., and Buzsáki, G. (2004). Early motor activity drives spindle bursts in the developing somatosensory cortex. Nature 432, 758–761. doi: 10.1038/nature03132.

9. Weiner OM, Dang-Vu TT. Spindle Oscillations in Sleep Disorders: A Systematic Review. Neural Plast. 2016;2016:7328725. doi: 10.1155/2016/7328725. Epub 2016 Mar 10. Review. PubMed PMID: 27034850; PubMed Central PMCID: PMC4806273.

10. Castelnovo A, D'Agostino A, Casetta C, Sarasso S, Ferrarelli F. Sleep Spindle Deficit in Schizophrenia: Contextualization of Recent Findings. Curr Psychiatry Rep. 2016 Aug;18(8):72. doi: 10.1007/s11920-016-0713-2. Review. PubMed PMID: 27299655.

11. Kostopoulos, George. (2000). Spike-and-wave discharges of absence seizures as a transformation of sleep spindles: The continuing development of a hypothesis. Clinical neurophysiology : official journal of the International Federation of Clinical Neurophysiology. 111 Suppl 2. S27-38. 10.1016/S1388-2457(00)00399-0.

12. Astori S, Wimmer RD, Lüthi A. Manipulating sleep spindles--expanding views on sleep, memory, and disease. Trends Neurosci. 2013 Dec;36(12):738-48. doi: 10.1016/j.tins.2013.10.001. Epub 2013 Nov 6. Review. Erratum in: Trends Neurosci. 2014 Apr;37(4):243. PubMed PMID: 24210901.

13. Sitaram R, Ros T, Stoeckel L, Haller S, Scharnowski F, Lewis-Peacock J, Weiskopf N, Blefari ML, Rana M, Oblak E, Birbaumer N, Sulzer J. Closed-loop brain training: the science of neurofeedback. Nat Rev Neurosci. 2017 Feb;18(2):86-100. doi: 10.1038/nrn.2016.164. Epub 2016 Dec 22. Review. PubMed PMID: 28003656.

14. Antony JW, Paller KA. Using Oscillating Sounds to Manipulate Sleep Spindles. Sleep. 2017 Mar 1;40(3). doi: 10.1093/sleep/zsw068. PubMed PMID: 28364415.

15. Leminen MM, Virkkala J, Saure E, Paajanen T, Zee PC, Santostasi G, Hublin C, Müller K, Porkka-Heiskanen T, Huotilainen M, Paunio T. Enhanced Memory Consolidation Via Automatic Sound Stimulation During Non-REM Sleep. Sleep. 2017 Mar 1;40(3). doi: 10.1093/sleep/zsx003. PubMed PMID: 28364428.

16. Nelly A. Papalambros, Giovanni Santostasi, Roneil G. Malkani, Rosemary Braun, Sandra Weintraub, Ken A. Paller, Phyllis C. Zee. Acoustic Enhancement of Sleep Slow Oscillations and Concomitant Memory Improvement in Older Adults. *Frontiers in Human Neuroscience*, 2017; 11 DOI: 10.3389/fnhum.2017.00109

17. Nonclercq A. et al.,Sleep spindle detection through amplitude–frequency normal modelling," JournIMPORTANTal of Neuroscience Methods 214 192– 203, 2013.

18. Santostasi G, Malkani R, Riedner B, Bellesi M, Tononi G, Paller KA, Zee PC. Phase-locked loop for precisely timed acoustic stimulation during sleep. J Neurosci Methods. 2016 Feb 1;259:101-14. doi: 10.1016/j.jneumeth.2015.11.007. Epub 2015 Nov 28. PubMed PMID: 26617321; PubMed Central PMCID: PMC5169172.

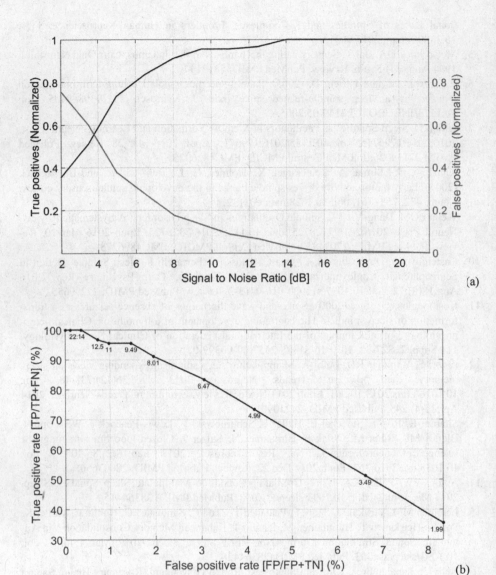

Fig. 7. Normalized TP and FP metrics for various signal-to noise ratios for the ASDA algorithm. Based on experimental results, in a typical EEG signal the mean SNR is in the range of 7 to 9 dB, while during a spindle it increases to 18 up to 22 dB. In EEG signals with decent quality, ASDA demonstrates high spindle detection accuracy. The values indicated in (b) are the respective SNR values. Depending on the maximum TP and minimum FP specs, the whole set-up should guarantee a minimum SNR value.

Examining the Efficiency of Feedback Types in a Virtual Reality Educational Environment for Learning Search Algorithms

Foteini Grivokostopoulou[1,2], Isidoros Perikos[1,2] and Ioannis Hatzilygeroudis[1]

[1] Department of Computer Engineering and Informatics, University of Patras, Greece
[2] Technological Educational Institute of Western Greece, Greece
{grivokwst,perikos,ihatz}@ceid.upatras.gr

Abstract. Feedback constitutes a fundamental aspect of educational systems that has a substantial impact on students learning and can shape their mental models. The delivery of appropriate feedback in terms of time and content is crucial for facilitating students' knowledge construction and comprehension. In this paper, we examine the complex nature and the efficiency of feedback in the context of a virtual reality educational environment. More specifically, we study the effect that different types of feedback such as feedback with visualized animations of procedures, can have on students learning and knowledge construction in a virtual reality educational environment for learning blind and heuristic search algorithms. An experimental study was designed where participating students were engaged with learning activities and solved exercises in different feedback conditions. Results from the study indicate that visual types of feedback can have a substantial impact on students' learning, assisting them in better understanding the functionality of the process studied with respect to performance and mistakes.

Keywords: Feedback Efficiency, 3D Virtual World, Learning Analytics, Search Algorithms

1   Introduction

Learning is a very complex mental process which is scaffolded and affected by a wide spectrum of factors. A factor that has a substantial impact on the efficiency of learning procedures and the construction of learners' mental models is the type of feedback offered to them [18]. Indeed, feedback is one of the most powerful factors to enhance learning and via feedback the behavior and the mental models of students can be enhanced and properly shaped. In this context, feedback can serve on mental level as reinforcement that shapes behaviors and supports learning [12] [17].

In educational environments the delivery of the appropriate feedback to learners which will assist the construction of their mental model and their understanding is highly desirable [5][19]. Various studies have examined the functionality and the effectiveness of types of feedback in tutoring systems [10] [15] [16] and research

© Springer International Publishing AG 2017
C. Frasson and G. Kostopoulos (Eds.): BFAL 2017, LNAI 10512, pp. 169–175, 2017
DOI: 10.1007/978-3-319-67615-9_15

findings point out that different types of feedback can have effect on a different level and degree to the learning processes of students [1] [2] [11].

Over the last decade, educational environments that are based on virtual reality have the potential to offer innovative learning activities and training procedures to learners. The 3D virtual reality environments naturally allow more complex interactions and increase interactivity and also scaffold more constructive models of learning [3] [4]. Although intelligent educational systems have been used for a long time and the effects of feedback have been widely studied, the delivery of appropriate feedback in virtual environments and the examination of their efficiency and impact on students learning are yet to be explored.

In this work, we examine the efficiency and the effect that different types of feedback have on comprehension and knowledge construction of students in a virtual reality educational system for learning search algorithms. More specifically, we analyze students learning actions and performance with respect to the feedback type they received by the system. In this context, to do this, participating students were engaged with learning activities and solved problems in different feedback conditions and after that they were assessed in their ability to transfer their knowledge and understanding to different problems and exercises that had the same underlying structure. The main finding indicates that the delivery of visualized feedback to learners can have a substantial impact on their learning and assisted them in understanding and connecting abstract concepts such as heuristics and backtracking to concrete examples.

The reminder of the paper is structured as follows: Section 2 presents the virtual reality educational environment, describes its capabilities and illustrates the types of feedback offered to learners. In Section 3, the experimental study designed and conducted with the aim to assess the efficiency of the feedback types is presented and the main findings of the study are examined. Finally, Section 4 concludes the paper and provides directions for future work.

2   The 3D Virtual World Environment for Teaching Search Algorithms

2.1   Learning activities in the virtual world educational environment

The 3D virtual world environment offers immersive learning processes to the students and gives them various opportunities to explore how algorithms operate via a wide range of learning activities [7]. Students in the virtual world can participate in learning activities and solve exercises that necessitate them to correctly apply algorithms. In this context, students can solve predetermined mazes in the virtual world under different conditions and in a specific amount of time. The various learning activities are designed in the spirit to necessitate students to apply a specific search algorithm and properly move in a maze by simulating the way that the algorithm functions in order to accomplish the level's requirements. The mazes require in general from the learner to reach a specific point in the maze by moving according to a specific algorithm. In this approach, students are requested, starting from a random position in a maze, to reach the goal (e.g. exit, specific item etc.) by moving based on the specific search algorithm that the maze specifies.

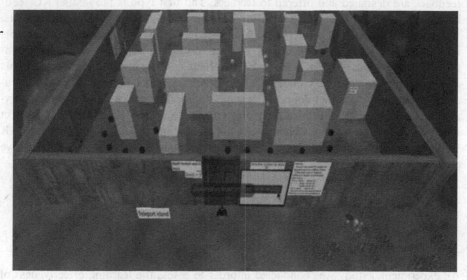

Fig. 1. An example learning activity in a maze

The learning activities and the mazes are designed based on the principle of active learning that maintains that the more the users directly manipulate and act upon the learning material, the higher the mental efforts and psychological involvement and therefore the better the learning outcome [13]. Also, learning activities have been designed in a way that supports students forming appropriate mental models of involved concepts, by visualizing them and allowing interactions with the virtual phenomena and processes.

2.2   Feedback in the Virtual Reality Educational Environment.

Various types of feedback have been designed and offered to learners. In general, feedback during the learning activities comes as messages that appear in a text area in the users' interface. These messages that are delivered to the user can vary in the information that they contain and also in the way they are presented. For example a message can inform the user about the correctness of an action that he/she made, present the corresponding theory involved in the learning activity or even present a visualization of the algorithm's functionality.

More specifically, the types of feedback offered to students in virtual reality educational environment are Knowledge of Result (KR), Knowledge about Concepts (KC) and Knowledge of Correct Response (KCR). Knowledge of Result is offered to student to inform whether the selection/action/move based on the learning activity is correct or not. Knowledge about Concepts provides students with appropriate hints and explanations on the terms and the processes involved in the learning activity. The content of Knowledge about Concepts feedback can vary based on the characteristics of the learning activity and the search algorithm involved. Indeed, two types of KC feedback are designed and offered to learners. The first type is the textual KC feedback where textual messages of the corresponding concepts are delivered to students. The second type is the visual KC feedbacks, where the involved aspects and concepts in the learning activity are delivered to students via proper visualized animated examples. The aim of the visual KC feedback is to help students connect abstract concepts and procedures to concrete experiences and examples. Indeed, it can be hard for students to learn new abstract concepts, without appropriate connection to concrete examples [14]. Finally, the third type of feedback examined Knowledge of Correct Response is used to provide students with the correct answer or a part of it. The KCR feedback type can be provided to a student after a request for help or after consecutive errors on an exercise.

3   Experimental Study

3.1   Method

An experimental study was conducted in order to assess the learning effectiveness of the feedback types offered in the virtual reality educational environment and the degree to which they affect student's learning. The participants were 65 students that were in the 4th year of their study. The participants were randomly divided into two groups, named GroupA and GroupB respectively. GroupA consisted of 32 students, where 15 were female and 17 were male and GroupB consisted of 33 students where 16 were female and 17 were male.

To assess the learning effectiveness and the effect of feedback on students learning a pre-test and post-test study design was followed. The experimental study consisted of three main phases which are the pre-test, the learning phase and the post-test. The overall structure of the evaluation study is illustrated in Figure 2. Initially, all the participants were given a pre-test on search algorithms. In the pretest, the students' were asked to apply blind and heuristic search algorithm on various problems and cases and the duration of the test was 60 minutes. The pretest was used to ensure the two groups had equivalent prior knowledge on AI search algorithms.

After the pretest, the learning phase took place. The duration of the learning phase was three weeks and the students of the two groups were given access to the 3D virtual world educational environment where they participated in the same learning activities and solved the same sets of exercises under different feedback conditions. More specifically, the students of GroupA interacted with the virtual world in a concept were the Knowledge about concepts type of feedback was provided to them via proper textual messages. On the other hand, the students of GroupB interacted with the virtual world and studied in a context were the Knowledge about concepts type of feedback provided them with appropriate visualizations with respect to the algorithm studied in the learning activity.

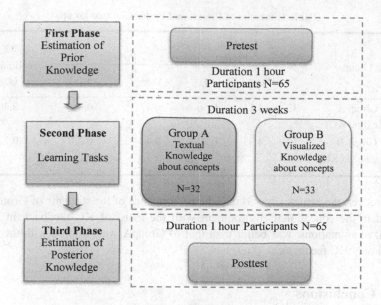

Fig. 2. The phases of the experimental evaluation study

Finally, the students of the two groups took the posttest and were assessed in their ability to transfer their knowledge and understanding to different problems and exercises. The duration of the posttest was 60 minutes and it consisted of exercises and activities that were of the same difficulty level and complexity compared to the pretest [8][9]. All the students' answers were assessed automatically in a consisted manner by automated assessment mechanisms [6].

3.2 Results

A preliminary analysis of the pre-test was performed using one-way analysis of variance (ANOVA) to investigate that here was no significant difference between two groups on the pre-test performance. The participants of GroupA had a mean pre-test score of 4.11 (SD=0.50) and those of GroupB a mean pre-test score of 4.31 (SD=0.71). The results show that there were no significant initial differences between the pretest group means (F=1.87>1, p=0.176 > 0.05).

In addition, an Analysis of Covariance (ANCOVA) was conducted to extract the difference between the groups using the pre-test scores as the covariate and the post-test scores as dependent variables. The ANCOVA results indicate that the differences in post test scores are statistically and significantly different between the two groups (F(1, 62)=125.6, p=0.000 <0.01). The effect size (Cohen's d) is 0.818, which is a significant enhancement. Table 1 summarizes the results of the pretest and post-test where the mean of posttest scores were 6.47 for GroupA and 8.44 for GroupB respectively.

Table 1. Results of Pretest and Posttest for two groups

Group	N	Pretest		Posttest		Normalized Gain
		Mean	SD	Mean	SD	
Group A (Textual KC)	32	4.11	0.50	6.47	0.65	0.40
Group B (Visualized KC)	33	4.31	0.71	8.44	0.73	0.72

Moreover, the results showed that the performance of the students of GroupB, who studied in the educational environment with the assist of KC feedback in terms of visualized animations, was better than that of GroupA who studied with the assist of textual only KC feedback.

4   Conclusions

Feedback is acknowledged to be a fundamental aspect of learning and the design and provision of appropriate feedback type in terms of content and presentation is crucial for the learning capabilities of educational systems. In this work we examined the efficiency of feedback in a virtual reality environment for learning search algorithms. Specifically, we examined the effect that knowledge about concepts feedback provided in visualized and in textual form have on students learning. The main findings of the experimental study indicate that the delivery of visualized feedback can have a greater impact on learners understanding and their knowledge construction compared to textual form.

There are various directions that future work will examine. Firstly, a bigger scale evaluation study could be designed to provide a more analytical understanding of the efficiency of additional feedback types. In addition, learning analytics methods could be examined with the aim to analyze learners' behavior after the delivery of each type of feedback in terms of mistakes and also shed light on learners' metacognitive behavior. Finally, additional types of formative feedback based on the analysis of the types of the errors made by the student will be designed and integrated into the educational system with the aim to enhance the learning capability of the system.

References

1. Attali, Y., & van der Kleij, F. (2017). Effects of feedback elaboration and feedback timing during computer-based practice in mathematics problem solving. *Computers & Education*, *110*, 154-169.
2. Butler, A. C., Godbole, N., & Marsh, E. J. (2013). Explanation feedback is better than correct answer feedback for promoting transfer of learning. *Journal of Educational Psychology*, *105*(2), 290.

3. Christopoulos, A., Conrad, M., & Shukla, M. (2016). How Do Students 'Really' Interact with Virtual Worlds? - The Influence of Proper Induction for Virtual Interactions. In *CSEDU (1)* (pp. 43-54).

4. De Freitas, S., Rebolledo-Mendez, G., Liarokapis, F., Magoulas, G., & Poulovassilis, A. (2010). Learning as immersive experiences: Using the four-dimensional framework for designing and evaluating immersive learning experiences in a virtual world. *British Journal of Educational Technology, 41*(1), 69-85.

5. Goldin, I. M., Koedinger, K. R., & Aleven, V. (2013). Hints: You Can't Have Just One. In EDM (pp. 232-235).

6. Grivokostopoulou, F., Perikos, I., & Hatzilygeroudis, I. (2017). An educational system for learning search algorithms and automatically assessing student performance. *International Journal of Artificial Intelligence in Education, 27*(1), 207-240.

7. Grivokostopoulou, F., Perikos, I., & Hatzilygeroudis, I. (2016). An innovative educational environment based on virtual reality and gamification for learning search algorithms. In Technology for Education (T4E), 2016 IEEE Eighth International Conference on (pp. 110-115). IEEE.

8. Grivokostopoulou, F., Perikos, I., & Hatzilygeroudis, I. (2017). Difficulty Estimation of Exercises on Tree-Based Search Algorithms Using Neuro-Fuzzy and Neuro-Symbolic Approaches. In *Advances in Combining Intelligent Methods* (pp. 75-91). Springer International Publishing.

9. Grivokostopoulou, F., Perikos, I., & Hatzilygeroudis, I. (2015, November). Estimating the Difficulty of Exercises on Search Algorithms Using a Neuro-fuzzy Approach. In *Tools with Artificial Intelligence (ICTAI), 2015 IEEE 27th International Conference on* (pp. 866-872). IEEE.

10. Hattie, J., & Timperley, H. (2007). The power of feedback. *Review of educational research, 77*(1), 81-112.

11. Koedinger, K. R., & Aleven, V. (2007). Exploring the assistance dilemma in experiments with cognitive tutors. *Educational Psychology Review, 19*(3), 239-264.

12. Le, N. T. (2016). A classification of adaptive feedback in educational systems for programming. *Systems, 4*(2), 22.

13. Lee, M. H., & Rößling, G. (2010). Integrating categories of algorithm learning objective into algorithm visualization design: a proposal. In Proceedings of the fifteenth annual conference on Innovation and technology in computer science education (pp. 289-293). ACM

14. Ma, T., Xiao, X., Wee, W., Han, C. Y., & Zhou, X. (2014). A 3D Virtual Learning System for STEM Education. In Virtual, Augmented and Mixed Reality. Applications of Virtual and Augmented Reality (pp. 63-72). Springer International Publishing.

15. Mory, E. H. (2004). Feedback research revisited. Handbook of research on educational communications and technology, 2, 745-783.

16. Narciss, S., Sosnovsky, S., Schnaubert, L., Andrès, E., Eichelmann, A., Goguadze, G., & Melis, E. (2014). Exploring feedback and student characteristics relevant for personalizing feedback strategies. *Computers & Education, 71*, 56-76.

17. Perikos, I., Grivokostopoulou, F., & Hatzilygeroudis, I. (2017). Assistance and feedback mechanism in an intelligent tutoring system for teaching conversion of natural language into logic. *International Journal of Artificial Intelligence in Education, 27(3)*, 475-517.

18. Shute, V. J. (2008). Focus on formative feedback. *Review of educational research, 78*(1), 153-189.

19. Woolf, B. P. (2010). Building intelligent interactive tutors: Student-centered strategies for revolutionizing e-learning. Morgan Kaufmann.

Virtual Sophrologist: A Virtual Reality Neurofeedback Relaxation Training System

Guoxin Gu and Claude Frasson

University of Montreal, Montreal QC H3T 1N8, Canada
{guguoxin, frasson}@iro.umontreal.ca

Abstract. Relaxation techniques can relieve us from stress, anxiety, pain and maladies. Many researchers succeed in relaxing subjects by various methods. However, few concerned about the ability of relaxation. Hence, the main goal of this study is to help people relax faster. We developed a virtual reality neurofeedback relaxation training system, called Virtual Sophrologist, which 1) immerses users in fantastic environments by a Virtual Reality headset, 2) guides users to follow the Sophrology instructions by a female voice, and 3) displays feedback in real time, which are translated from the Meditation Score collected by EEG. To evaluate this system, we recruited 6 subjects to participate in our 8-session relaxation training and collected their subjective data (by self-report) and objective data (by EEG) to measure from psychological level and to calculate the Time Interval to Relaxation that they took to reach the maximum Meditation Score. The results show 1) decreases in Anxiety and Depression Score from the psychological level, 2) a decrease in Time Interval to Relaxation and 3) an increase in the maximum Meditation Score. Therefore, our system will be useful as a training tool for users who need or want to relax fast and deep whenever they need.

Keywords: Sophrology, Autogenic Training, Virtual Reality, Neurofeedback, EEG, EEG Biofeedback.

1   Introduction

Life is the progress of change. Any change contains the demand that we need to adapt to it. And how we manage to adapt to it depends on how we perceive the change. Hence, the effects of stress depend on whether we perceive the situation as being positive or negative [1]. We will embrace the change if the perception is positive. However, if the perception is negative, our bodies will automatically respond to this perceived threat. For instance, the heart rate and the blood pressure will increase, the perspiration will increase, and hands and feet will get cold, sometimes our hearing and vision will be acute. For a long time, stress will bring harmful biochemical effects, anxiety or depression [2].

Since stress, as a response to a threat, is predictable [3] but inevitable, we can take a better reaction (to relax) to the stress instead of being anxiety, which also is the goal of many studies [4]. For example, a group of Simon Fraser University designed a neurofeedback virtual environment (by a screen) to help people reduce the stress [5].

© Springer International Publishing AG 2017
C. Frasson and G. Kostopoulos (Eds.): BFAL 2017, LNAI 10512, pp. 176–185, 2017
DOI: 10.1007/978-3-319-67615-9_16

Perhakaran et al. proved that the meditation effectiveness by employing an upgraded Head Mounted Display (HMD), according to Virtual Reality Therapy (VRT), is better than that by using the imaginary technique [6]. Then a neurofeedback virtual reality meditation system provided a better result than a system of the screen, moreover, showed that neurofeedback can improve the feeling of presence [7].

However, most researchers focused on relaxing subjects rather than the subject's ability of relaxation such as the Time Interval to Relaxation (TItR), i.e. how long did it take the subject to reach a given level of relaxation. As we know, more time to practice a relaxation technique, better effect we can acquire [4]. Therefore, our motivation is to develop a system, Virtual Sophrologist, for helping people relax faster. We 1) combined the advantages of previous studies, such as Virtual Reality (VR) and neurofeedback, 2) chose a popular and convincing relaxation technique (Sophrology), 3) followed subjects for 8 sessions in one month (twice per week), 4) collected their subjective data (by self-report) and objective data (by EEG) to calculate Anxiety Score, Depression Score and TItR for evaluating the effectiveness of this system. The results demonstrate that our system, Virtual Sophrologist, can help users' effort to relieve stress, anxiety, even pain and maladies.

2   Related Work

2.1   Autogenic Training and Sophrology

As early as 1932, the German psychiatrist Johann Heinrich Schultz proposed Autogenic Training (AT), a relaxation technique based on autohypnosis and yoga [8]. He presumed that the link mind-body is nonconscious but controllable and combined with some medical principles of his time, for instance 1) the *heavier* is related to a tendency to elongate of our extensor muscles and 2) the *warmth* results from a greater flow of blood. Both *heavier* and *warmth* are key components in AT.

Influenced by AT, Sophrology was introduced by Alfonso Caycedo in 1964 [9]. He named Sophrology from ancient Greek roots: "SOS" (safety, tranquility, security, serenity, harmony), "Phren" (mind, consciousness) and "Logos" (treatise, study). Thus Sophrology is a study of consciousness in harmony, unlike nonconscious mind-body in AT. Since then, Sophrology has been used widely in business, sport, schools, universities, relationships, hospitals and even childbirth. For example, in reducing perinatal stress, Sophrology works better than epidural anesthesia [10]. By repeating Sophrology Instructions, people generally experience more restful sleep, improved concentration, fewer worries, increased self-confidence [11] and a feeling of inner happiness, as Caycedo said: "Sophrology is learning to live" [12].

2.2   Virtual Reality

Since the introduction of VR in the 1960s, the dream of cyberspace is to give people the sensory experiences of a virtual space or environment. This dream has been vigorously pursued by the pioneers in the field and it is slowly but steadily realized. Although Ivan Sunderland built the first HMD system in 1968, VR became popular from 1989, in which year the term *virtual reality* was coined by Jaron Lanier. Then it took about three decades to bring affordable and portable VR headsets from the lab to the home, such as Samsung Gear, HTC Vive and Oculus Rift. Thanks to the advancement of the technology, the improvement of immersion yields a better sense of presence for users [13]. And both *immersion* and *presence* are two key concepts for the VR experience.

VR displays first met Medicine in 1993 by treating mental health disorders. Then VR was soon accepted widely by the medical community, because VR 1) enhances exposure therapy to treat clinical anxiety disorders, phobias, Post-Traumatic Stress Disorder, eating disorders and obesity, smoking and others, 2) enhances distraction therapy to reduce the pain of dental procedures, of chemotherapy-related side effects, of severe burns, in childbirth and so on, and 3) becomes a tool for diagnosing, medicine, physical and cognitive rehabilitation, surgical planning and performance, prevention of physical and emotional illness. In particular, in VR, we can simulate many situations that it is difficult to control in our real life without excessive cost, and treat patients in a manipulable way within a safe environment. Under these conditions, VR is considered as a promising tool which worth exploring numerous valuable healthcare applications for medical therapy, preventive medicine, surgical procedures, rehabilitation, medical education and training, and so forth [14].

2.3   EEG and Neurofeedback

In 1924, Hans Berger recorded the electric field of human brains and named it Electroencephalography (EEG). EEG measures spontaneous activities on the scalp or on the surface of the brain. Most EEG is noninvasive, placing the electrodes on the scalp by the internationally standardized 10-20 system. When measured on the scalp, the amplitude of EEG is about 100 μV, while 1-2 mV on the surface of the brain [15]. The actual bandwidth of EEG is very wide extending from infralow frequencies of a fraction of an mHz to many many hundreds of Hz. The measurements for the very low and very high frequencies are difficult and often contaminated with noise, so in most routine EEG applications the emphasis is placed on the more easily accessible range of 1 (or a few) to 48 Hz. Within this range different bands are believed to relate to specific mental operations with delta waves (0.5-4 Hz) encountered mainly in sleep and pathology, theta waves (4-8 Hz) associated with meditation and arousal, alpha waves (8-13 Hz) enhanced when a person is awake with eyes closed, beta waves (13-30 Hz) related to concentration, high alert and anxiety and finally, gamma waves (>30 Hz) related to cognition. During the past nine decades, EEG has been widely used in medical and research fields [16].

EEG has been used in a biofeedback system from the 1960s, namely EEG Biofeedback or Neurofeedback. A biofeedback loop includes 1) a precise instrument to measure physiological activity, 2) a processor to translate from physiological changes into feedback, and 3) a user to receive that information. Neurofeedback mostly uses EEG as the instrument and displays the feedback using video or sound. And Neurofeedback has been proved its successful effectiveness in various cases, such as a treatment for Attention Deficit Hyperactivity Disorder (ADHD) [17], an improvement of learners' outcomes in an Intelligent Tutoring Systems (ITS) [18], etc.

3 Experiment

3.1 Virtual Sophrologist System

In order to help people to relax faster and deeper, we developed a new virtual reality neurofeedback relaxation training system, called Virtual Sophrologist, which consists of three key components: **VR environments, Sophrology instructions** and **EEG feedback**. Figure 1 shows how Virtual Sophrologist works: firstly, VR provides one of our three relaxing and comfortable environments to immerse the user. Then Sophrology instructions are displayed and spoken sentence by sentence in VR, meanwhile, according to the biofeedback loop, 1) EEG measures the brain activities of the user, 2) a processor translates the Meditation Score into a sentence following the decision rules, and 3) the user gets this feedback displayed in VR.

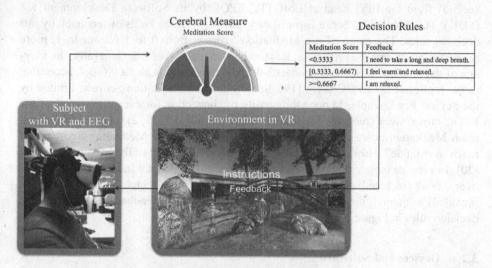

Fig. 1. Virtual Sophrologist System

VR Environments. There are three environments in Virtual Sophrologist for users to choose, including Seaside, Japanese Garden and Waterfall, see Figure 2. All environments are complete and allow users to turn heads for a favorite view. There is the sun in the sky of all environments because it is related to the *warmth* in Sophrology. Moreover, among three environments, there is a background sound (river sound) in the environment Japanese Garden, while no background sound in the other two environments, for more choices to users.

Sophrology Instructions. There are 93 Sophrology instructions in total in Virtual Sophrology, including 84 instructions to relax users and 9 instructions to wake users up slowly to complete the whole relaxation procedure. All instructions are displayed and spoken sentence by sentence every 10 seconds. Thus each session lasts about 15 minutes. Each instruction keeps short and in the first person, associated with the practice of the heaviness, the warmth, the heart beat, the breathing or the forehead, etc. For instance, "*I feel supremely calm*", "*My right arm is getting limp and heavy*".

Fig. 2. Three environments in Virtual Sophrologist

EEG Feedback. The Meditation Score is computed every 16.7 milliseconds (0.0167 second) from the EEG headset EMOTIV EPOC by its Software Development Kit (SDK). This Meditation Score is translated into one of three kinds of feedback by our decision rules. The range of the Meditation Score is from 0 to 1 (closer to 1, more relaxed subjects are). Nevertheless, it is too hard to reach over 0.8. Generally, the average of the Meditation Score is about 0.3-0.4, the maximum is about 0.6-0.7, according to the replies of the EPOC users [19]. Sometimes, the Meditation Score is limited by the device. For example, 1) once the quality of connection for even one sensor of the EPOC turned weak (red), the Meditation Score stays at 0.3333, 2) 0.6667 is the maximum Meditation Score of some devices, in other words, the Meditation Score never reach over 0.6667. However, this cannot stop the employment of the Meditation Score [20]. In view of these situations, we consider under 0.3333 (not included) as nervous, over 0.6667 (included) as relaxed, and between them (0.3333 included but 0.6667 not included) as natural, then give each state its corresponding feedback as shown in the decision rules in Figure 1.

3.2   Devices and Software

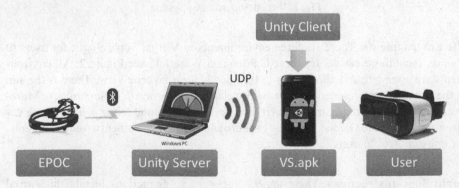

Fig. 3. Devices and software needed in Virtual Sophrologist System

We chose 1) the EMOTIV EPOC, which is a 14-channel EEG headset and employs the 10-20 system, as the cerebral measuring instrument, 2) a Windows computer to run a project Unity Server, which collects data from the EPOC, translates into the feedback as a processor, and sends the feedback 60 times per second by User Datagram Protocol (UDP) to the VR application, Virtual Sophrologist, built by the project Unity Client, 3) a Samsung Galaxy S6 and 4) a Samsung Gear VR to run Virtual Sophrologist, as shown in Figure 3.

3.3   Subject Criteria and Protocol

Six subjects (2 females, 4 males) were recruited to participate in our 8-session relaxation training and allowed to select only a favorite environment to enter during the whole 8 sessions. All of them met: 1) 18-40 years old (Mean = 29.67, SD = 4.84, range from 25 to 37), 2) do not have attention deficit disorder, dyslexia, dyspraxia and so on, 3) have normal hearing, 4) never suffered a cranial trauma, 5) not taking any medications acting on the nervous system, 6) able to understand English (due to Virtual Sophrologist only support English up to now), and 7) willing to stay on and complete the 8-session, training twice a week for one month.

Thanks to their insistence, we obtained all 48 files of data, including the Meditation Score and all data from the 14 channels of EPOC (AF3, F7, F3, FC5, T7, P7, O1, O2, P8, T8, FC6, F4, F8, and AF42). In addition to these objective data, in order to collect the subjective data, 6 subjects were asked to fill a psychological questionnaire three times: before the first session, after the fourth session, and after the last/eighth session.

3.4   Evaluation

In order to measure the effectiveness of Virtual Sophrologist, we employed TItR and HADS Scores as metrics.

Time Interval to Relaxation. TItR is extracted from the log of the Meditation Score for each session of the subject. It is the total time in seconds when the subject reached relaxed (0.6667 of the Meditation Score, as I explained in Section 3.1) during one session. However, everyone has his own baseline. If the subject never reached 0.6667 of the Meditation Score, TItR is considered as the total time of reaching his maximum Meditation Score. The maximum TItR is 936 seconds. Because it takes 5 seconds to wait to enter the selected environment and 93 Sophrology instructions take 930 seconds, we count to 936 seconds. Accordingly, a decrease of the TItR in 8 sessions can indicate that Virtual Sophrologist helps subjects relax faster.

HADS Scores. The Hospital Anxiety and Depression Scale (HADS) is a fourteen-item questionnaire devised by Zigmond and Snaith in 1983 [21]. It is so popular that it is cited by 25,551 papers in Google Scholar by April 2017. Some clinical research used it to evaluate until 2015 [22]. The simplicity and ease of use are the beauty of HADS. Seven of its fourteen items are related to anxiety, and the other seven related to depression. Each item is scored on a scale of 0-3, 3 indicates higher symptom frequencies.

Both score for anxiety and score for depression range from 0 to 21 with scores categorized as follows: normal 0-7, mild 8-10, moderate 11-14, and severe 15-21. In this study, as I mentioned in Section 3.3, we collected three times for the HADS Anxiety Score (HADS-A) and the Depression Score (HADS-D) of subjects: before the training, at the 4th session, and at the final session respectively. Thus, the changes of HADS-A and HADS-D will indicate whether Virtual Sophrologist works from the psychological level.

4   Results and Discussion

Our results proved the positive effectiveness of Virtual Sophrologist on both the speed and the deepness of the relaxation with 1) a decrease of the TItR in the group that subjects can reach 0.6667 of the Meditation Score, 2) an increase of the maximum Meditation Score, and 3) the decreases of both HADS-A and HADS-D.

4.1   Time Interval to Relaxation

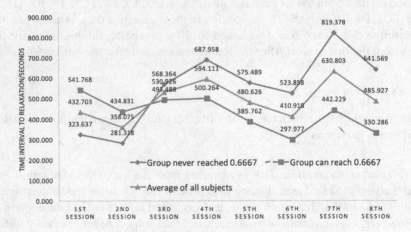

Fig. 4. TItR in 8 sessions

In Figure 4, although the tendency of the average TItR of all subjects is not clear, even negative, we found the positive result by dividing subjects into two groups. Because as I described in Section 3.4, we have two ways to calculate the TItR, which depends on whether the subject reached 0.6667 of Meditation Score. For three of our subjects, they reached 0.6667 in three sessions, six sessions, and all eight sessions respectively, named 'Group can reach 0.6667', and got a decrease of TItR from 541.768s (range from 227.274s to 913.595s) to 330.286s (range from 100.615s to 780.165s). While the other three, named 'Group never reached 0.6667', got an increase of TItR. We found one of the reasons for this "negative effectiveness" in the logs of Meditation Score: The TItR increased with an increase of the maximum Meditation Score. Another reason is the problem of the EEG headset: once one sensor's connection quality turned weak, the

Meditation Score goes 0.3333, which will make us miss the real maximum Meditation Score and result in the low TItR, like that in the first and the second sessions in Figure 4.

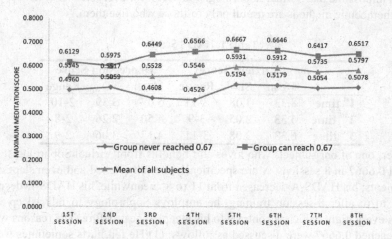

Fig. 5. Maximum Meditation Score in 8 sessions

Figure 5 indicates the positive tendency for the changes of the maximum Meditation Score, which is a little but reasonable, because as we know, the evident effect of any relaxation technique generally shows up with a long-term practice, at least three months by the suggestion [23].

4.2   HADS Scores

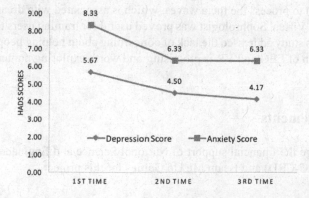

Fig. 6. The changes of HADS Scores

From the psychological view, the effectiveness is also proved positive. Both HADS-A and HADS-D decreased, as shown in Figure 6.

4.3   Discussion

Noticing at the range of HADS-A and HADS-D in Table 1, we need to admit one fact that it is impossible that Virtual Sophrologist is useful for everyone. As said in [8], "All psychotherapeutic methods are useful only to those who like them."

Table 1. HADS Scores

	Anxiety Score			Depression Score		
	Mean	SD	Range	Mean	SD	Range
1st time	8.33	3.08	3-11	5.67	3.39	2-10
2nd time	6.33	2.05	3-9	4.50	2.26	2-8
3rd time	6.33	3.08	3-11	4.17	3.06	2-9

However, one of our subjects who loves and benefits from Virtual Sophrologist never reached 0.6667 in 8 sessions. More specifically, he felt relaxed and even slept during experiments; his HADS-A decreased from 11 to 8, meanwhile, his HADS-D decreased from 9 to 6; after 8-session training, he employs Sophrology to fall asleep in 2-3 minutes every night, which is contrary to his sleeplessness before. The reasons why he never reached 0.6667 were discussed as follows: (1) He felt hurts sometimes wearing the EPOC and Samsung Gear VR at the same time; (2) Any little movement of his head every time when he was napping during experiments affects the Meditation Score; (3) Sometimes the movement of the head due to the breathing also affects the Meditation Score; (4) The unstable connection quality of the sensors on the EPOC makes the Meditation Score go 0.3333; (5) He was trying to translate the Sophrology instructions from English into his language; (6) He was thinking; (7) He was dreaming. Accordingly, to improve our system, we need (1) a new headset combining the EEG and VR; (2, 3) a filter to allow a little movement of the head; (4) to keep the connection quality stable; (5) to provide more choices in languages; (6) to record his concentration to remind him by feedback; (7) to process the theta waves, which is associated with dream sleep.

To conclude, Virtual Sophrologist was proved useful for training users to relax faster and deeper. This study addressed the lack of concerning about helping people relax fast. The combination of EEG and VR is promising and worth exploring numerous applications.

Acknowledgements

We acknowledge the financial support of National Science and Engineering Research Council (NSERC-CRD) and Beam Me Up Games for this project.

References

1. Selye, H.: The stress of life. (1956).
2. McEwen, B.S., Eiland, L., Hunter, R.G., Miller, M.M.: Stress and anxiety: structural plasticity and epigenetic regulation as a consequence of stress. Neuropharmacology 62(1), 3-12 (2012).

3. Jraidi, I., Heraz, A., Chaouachi, M., Frasson, C.: New architecture of a multi agent system which measures the learner brainwaves to predict his stress level variation. In: Proceedings of the World Conference on 2009, pp. 2726-2733

4. Manzoni, G.M., Pagnini, F., Castelnuovo, G., Molinari, E.: Relaxation training for anxiety: a ten-years systematic review with meta-analysis. BMC psychiatry 8(1), 41 (2008).

5. Prpa, M., Cochrane, K., Riecke, B.E.: Hacking Alternatives in 21st Century: Designing a Bio-Responsive Virtual Environment for Stress Reduction. In: International Symposium on Pervasive Computing Paradigms for Mental Health 2015, pp. 34-39. Springer

6. Perhakaran, G., Yusof, A.M., Rusli, M.E., Yusoff, M.Z.M., Mahalil, I., Zainuddin, A.R.R.: A Study of Meditation Effectiveness for Virtual Reality Based Stress Therapy Using EEG Measurement and Questionnaire Approaches. In: Innovation in Medicine and Healthcare 2015. pp. 365-373. Springer, (2016)

7. Kosunen, I., Salminen, M., Järvelä, S., Ruonala, A., Ravaja, N., Jacucci, G.: RelaWorld: Neuroadaptive and Immersive Virtual Reality Meditation System. In: Proceedings of the 21st International Conference on Intelligent User Interfaces 2016, pp. 208-217. ACM

8. Heller, M.C.: Body psychotherapy: History, concepts, and methods. WW Norton & Company, (2012)

9. Caycedo, A.: Sophrology and psychosomatic medicine. American Journal of Clinical Hypnosis 7(2), 103-106 (1964).

10. Suzuki, M., Isonishi, S., Morimoto, O., Ogawa, M., Ochiai, K.: Effect of sophrology on perinatal stress monitored by biopyrrin. (2012).

11. Dyé, A.: Sophrology. (2015).

12. Sophrology. https://en.wikipedia.org/wiki/Sophrology. Accessed 2017/05/07

13. Oh, S.Y., Bailenson, J.: Virtual and Augmented Reality. The International Encyclopedia of Media Effects (2017).

14. Wiederhold, B.K.: The potential for virtual reality to improve health care. The Virtual Reality Medical Center (2006).

15. Malmivuo, J., Plonsey, R.: Bioelectromagnetism. MEDICAL AND BIOLOGICAL ENGINEERING AND COMPUTING 34, 9-12 (1996).

16. EEG. https://en.wikipedia.org/wiki/Electroencephalography. Accessed 2017/05/09

17. Lubar, J.F., Swartwood, M.O., Swartwood, J.N., O'Donnell, P.H.: Evaluation of the effectiveness of EEG neurofeedback training for ADHD in a clinical setting as measured by changes in TOVA scores, behavioral ratings, and WISC-R performance. Applied Psychophysiology and Biofeedback 20(1), 83-99 (1995).

18. Chaouachi, M., Jraidi, I., Frasson, C.: MENTOR: A Physiologically Controlled Tutoring System. In: International Conference on User Modeling, Adaptation, and Personalization 2015, pp. 56-67. Springer

19. Emotiv Forum: Meditation Score. https://www.emotiv.com/forums/topic/Meditation_Score/. Accessed 2017/01/20

20. Roo, J.S., Gervais, R., Hachet, M.: Inner garden: An augmented sandbox designed for self-reflection. In: Proceedings of the TEI'16: Tenth International Conference on Tangible, Embedded, and Embodied Interaction 2016, pp. 570-576. ACM

21. Zigmond, A.S., Snaith, R.P.: The hospital anxiety and depression scale. Acta psychiatrica scandinavica 67(6), 361-370 (1983).

22. Golding, K., Kneebone, I., Fife-Schaw, C.: Self-help relaxation for post-stroke anxiety: A randomised, controlled pilot study. Clinical Rehabilitation 1, 7 (2015).

23. Autogenics Training. http://www.guidetopsychology.com/autogen.htm. Accessed 2016/09/16

Different Frequency-Dependent Properties between Dorsal and Ventral Hippocampal Synapses.

Costas Papatheodoropoulos[1]

[1] University of Patras, Rion, Greece.
cepapath@upatras.gr

Abstract. The hippocampus is a brain region crucially involved in various cognitive functions including learning and memory processes. The hippocampal functions are performed by specific computations of its intrinsic neural circuitry in combination with interaction of the hippocampus with other brain regions. Therefore, the hippocampus has been conceived as a key network to studying and understanding the fundamental neural computations that supports higher brain functions. The hippocampus-involving functions are segregated along the longitudinal axis of the hippocampus. Importantly, it has been recently revealed that the local hippocampal circuit presents significant specializations between the two opposite poles or segments of the structure, namely between the dorsal and the ventral hippocampus suggesting that distinct neural processing may support the different functions performed by the hippocampus segments. The signal processing by neural networks crucially involves synaptic computations. In this study, we examined the synaptic dynamics of the dorsal and ventral synapses under conditions of different activation frequencies. We found that under consecutive activation the dorsal synapses display strong facilitation at a wide range of frequencies (1-40 Hz) while in ventral synapses the facilitation is restricted only to low activation frequency (1 Hz) and it lasted very shortly during activation. Thus, ventral synapses are mostly depressing. This evidence suggests that the dorsal hippocampal synaptic circuit presents wide-band filtering characteristics while the ventral are depressing low-pass synapses. The differing synaptic properties of the dorsal and the ventral hippocampus may underlie the higher ability for long-term plasticity of the dorsal hippocampus and the initiation of basic endogenous network oscillation in the ventral hippocampus.

Keywords: Hippocampus, Synaptic computation, Short-term plasticity, Activity frequency, Information processing, Neural network, Septotemporal, Dorsoventral, *In vitro*.

1   Introduction

The hippocampus is an elongated brain structure crucially involved in several cognitive functions including processes of learning and memory, spatial navigation and emotionality [1, 2]. The hippocampal neuronal circuitry has been therefore recognized as a model to studying how local brain networks compute and process information supporting cognitive functions [3, 4]. It has been established that the different consec-

© Springer International Publishing AG 2017
C. Frasson and G. Kostopoulos (Eds.): BFAL 2017, LNAI 10512, pp. 186–191, 2017
DOI: 10.1007/978-3-319-67615-9_17

utive segments along the long axis (called also septotemporal or dorsoventral axis) of the hippocampus are distinctly involved in the various functions. A general idea is that the dorsal hippocampus plays a dominant role in spatial information processing while the ventral hippocampus is more importantly involved in emotionality [2]. The functional diversification of the hippocampus along its long axis can be significantly supported by a corresponding segregation of extrinsic anatomical connections [5]. The internal hippocampal organization is based on the repetition of a basic trisynaptic circuitry, which is transversally oriented to the longitudinal hippocampal axis and can function as a semi-autonomous module [6]. Information from the cortex enters in this circuit through the dentate gyrus, flows through the CA3 field and exits from the hippocampus via the circuit of the CA1 field. Although this pattern of organization point to the idea of internal homogeneity along the long hippocampal axis several lines of evidence recently revealed important specializations in the local neural circuitry along the hippocampus; for a review see [7].

The information processing in the hippocampus importantly involves synaptic plasticity [8]. The hippocampus show an exceptionally large variety of synaptic plasticity phenomena, from the short-living facilitation that lasts several tens or a few hundreds of milliseconds to very long-term potentiation that can lasts at least several weeks [9]. Understanding the computational processes operated by the local hippocampal circuitry is of fundamental importance of knowing how hippocampus achieves its diverse functions. While long-term changes in synaptic efficacy have been vigorously implicated in the memory function of the hippocampus [10], evidence regarding the particular functional implications of short-term plastic changes is still largely lacking. However, the high potentionality of hippocampal synapses for short-term synaptic plasticity suggests that it most probably plays significant roles in signal processing. Indeed, the various phenomena of short-term plasticity endow synapses with paramount computational abilities [11]. Motivated by the fact that the frequency of activation is a fundamental parameter that determines the direction and the amount of plastic synaptic changes [12] we examined the synaptic responses in the dorsal and the ventral hippocampus following stimulation trains applied at different frequencies ranging from 0.1 to 100 Hz. We observed striking dorsoventral differences.

2   Methods

Transverse slices 500 μm thick were prepared from the dorsal (n=4) and the ventral (n=4) hippocampus of adult Wistar male rats. The slices were maintained in an interface type chamber perfused with artificial cerebrospinal fluid containing (in mM): 124 NaCl; 4 KCl; 2 $MgSO_4$; 2 $CaCl_2$; 1.25 NaH_2PO_4; 26 $NaHCO_3$; 10 glucose; at pH 7.4, equilibrated with 95% O_2 and 5% CO_2 and at a temperature of 31±0.5 °C. Recordings of fEPSP were made from the stratum radiatum of CA1 field following stimulation of Schaffer collaterals. Frequency stimulation consisted of trains of ten consecutive pulses delivered at varying frequencies (0.1-100 Hz). The stimulation current strength was set at a value that elicited a subthreshold fEPSP. The fEPSP was measured by the slope of its rising phase. The change of fEPSP during the train was calculated as the percent change of each successive fEPSP with respect to the first fEPSP.

3   Results

The dorsal and ventral synapses responded to frequency stimulation with remarkably different mode. Dorsal hippocampal synapses showed facilitation at the frequency range of 1-40 Hz through the entire train (Fig. 1A). The facilitation was maximum at frequencies 3-20 Hz. No change was observed at any fEPSP elicited by the stimulation frequency of 50 Hz. At the stimulation frequency of 50 Hz no considerable change in fEPSPs was observed. With increasing frequency and number of fEPSP in the train the dorsal synapses depressed. Thus, at 75-100 Hz all fEPSPs were depressed but the second fEPSP was facilitated; in general, the second fEPSP displayed wideband frequency facilitation. Also, regardless the stimulation frequency, facilitation or depression in the dorsal synapses reached a steady state from the 6th to 7th pulses thereafter (Fig. 1A). Finally, the very low frequency of 0.1 Hz did not produce any change in either the dorsal or the ventral synapses at any fEPSP in the train.

The ventral hippocampal synapses showed facilitation only at the frequency of 1 Hz and during the envelope of the stimulation train. Also, facilitation of the fEPSP elicited by the second stimulus was observed at frequencies from 1 to 50 Hz (Fig. 1B). At frequencies greater than 10 Hz, however, ventral synapses virtually showed only depression, which increased with increasing frequency and successive stimulation pulses (Fig. 1B).

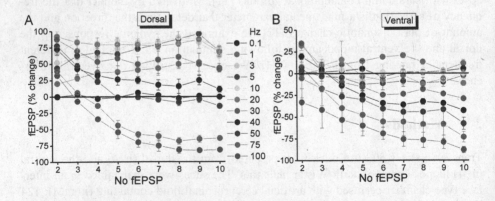

Fig. 1. Change of fEPSP induced by a train of ten pulses delivered at various frequencies in dorsal (A) and ventral hippocampus (B).

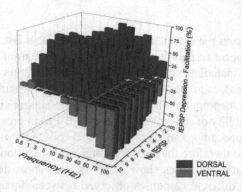

DORSAL
VENTRAL

Fig. 2. Facilitation or depression of fEPSP in dorsal and ventral hippocampus in relation with frequency and the number of fEPSP.

Both dorsal and ventral synapses depressed similarly at high frequencies (75-100 Hz) (Fig. 1 & Fig. 2). However, the facilitation displayed by the dorsal hippocampal synapses was several folds higher than that observed in the ventral hippocampal synapses. When the change of fEPSP was considered regardless the frequency of stimulation dorsal synapses showed only facilitation while in the ventral synapses all fEPSPs in the train were depressed but the second one was slightly facilitated (Fig. 3A). Similalry, when the average change of all fEPSPs was calculated for individual frequencies, dorsal synapses showed facilitation for frequencies up to 50 Hz while ventral synapses virtually displayed only depression (Fig. 3B). Notably, at high frequencies (75-100 Hz) the average changes during the whole train both dorsal and ventral synapses were depressed similarly (Fig. 3B).

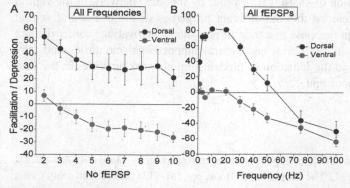

Fig. 3. Average change of each fEPSP in the ten-pulses train regardless the stimulation frequency (A) and average change of all fEPSPs at each frequency (B). The differences between the dorsal and the ventral hippocampus were significant at all fEPSP and for all frequencies between 1 and 50 Hz (Mann-Whitney U test, $P<0.01$).

4   Discussion

Activity-dependent synaptic plasticity is the change in synaptic efficacy that lasts over short or long periods of time and appear to play important roles in information processing by neural networks [11-13] including synaptic filtering of information [14, 15]. The excitatory hippocampal synapses in the "output" CA1 field show remarkable heterogeneity in terms of facilitation/depression during consecutive activation significantly depending on the basal probability of transmitter release (TRP) from presynaptic terminals [16]. In the dorsal hippocampus most of the excitatory CA1 synapses release with low probability [17] and therefore they show substantial facilitation [16]. Typically, during frequency stimulation synapses show either facilitation or depression [11]. Accordingly, the striking different responses observed between dorsal and ventral synapses point to important dorsoventral differences in signal processing. The fact that dorsal synapses show robust frequency facilitation along a wide range of frequencies (1-40 Hz) suggests that they have characteristics of band-pass filters [11, 18]. Because facilitation is inversely related with TRP [16] and TRP is inversely related with long-term synaptic potentiation (LTP) [14], dorsal synapses may be more reliable for LTP, as it actually happens [19]. The ventral synapses, on the other hand, are prominently depressing displaying therefore features of low-pass filters [11, 18]. Importantly, depressing synapses considerably increase the sensitivity of a neuron to small changes in the input firing rate [11, 15]. This may facilitate the synchronization of the local neuronal population and the initiation of network activity and thus the flow of information through the whole (i.e. longitudinal) hippocampus circuit. One of the basic population activities of the hippocampus is the complex activity of sharp wave-ripples, which is crucially involved in the process of memory consolidation [20]. The generation of sharp wave-ripples requires subtle increases in the excitability of the local network [21]. Therefore, an increased sensitivity of the depressing ventral hippocampal synapses to subtle changes in input activity may importantly contribute to the favourable initiation of sharp wave-ripples by the local network of the ventral hippocampus. It is concluded that the different properties of the dorsal and ventral hippocampal synapses in response to a train of presynaptic activations confer distinct computational abilities to the dorsal and ventral hippocampal circuitries and may significantly contribute to the initiation of fundamental network activities in the ventral segment of the hippocampus.

References

1. Morris, R.G.: Theories of Hippocampal Function. In: Andersen, P., Morris, R., Amaral, D., Bliss, T., O'Keefe, J. (ed.) The Hippocampus Book, pp. 581-713. Oxford University Oress, Oxford (2007)
2. Strange, B.A., Witter, M.P., Lein, E.S., Moser, E.I.: Functional organization of the hippocampal longitudinal axis. Nat Rev Neurosci 15, 655-669 (2014)
3. Marr, D.: Simple memory: a theory for archicortex. Philos Trans R Soc Lond B Biol Sci 262, 23-81 (1971)

4. Burgess, N.: Computational models of the spatial and mnemonic functions of the hippocampus. In: Andersen, P., Morris, R., Amaral, D., Bliss, T., O'Keefe, J. (eds.) The Hippocampus Book, pp. 715-749. Oxford University Press, Oxford (2007)

5. Risold, P.Y., Swanson, L.W.: Structural evidence for functional domains in the rat hippocampus. Science 272, 1484-1486 (1996)

6. Andersen, P., Soleng, A.F., Raastad, M.: The hippocampal lamella hypothesis revisited. Brain research 886, 165-171 (2000)

7. Papatheodoropoulos, C.: Electrophysiological evidence for long-axis intrinsic diversification of the hippocampus. Frontiers in Bioscience (Landmark Ed.). 23, 109-145. (2018)

8. Eichenbaum, H., Amaral, D.G., Buffalo, E.A., Buzsaki, G., Cohen, N., Davachi, L., Frank, L., Heckers, S., Morris, R.G., Moser, E.I., Nadel, L., O'Keefe, J., Preston, A., Ranganath, C., Silva, A., Witter, M.: Hippocampus at 25. Hippocampus 26, 1238-1249 (2016)

9. Bliss, T.V., Collingridge, G.L., Morris, R.: Synaptic Plasticity in the Hippocampus. In: Andersen, P., Morris, R., Amaral, D., Bliss, T., O'Keefe, J. (eds.) The Hippocampus Book, pp. 343-474 (2007)

10. Morris, R.G.: Long-term potentiation and memory. Philos Trans R Soc Lond B Biol Sci 358, 643-647 (2003)

11. Abbott, L.F., Regehr, W.G.: Synaptic computation. Nature 431, 796-803 (2004)

12. Regehr, W.G.: Short-term presynaptic plasticity. Cold Spring Harbor perspectives in biology 4, a005702 (2012)

13. Lindner, B., Gangloff, D., Longtin, A., Lewis, J.E.: Broadband coding with dynamic synapses. The Journal of neuroscience : the official journal of the Society for Neuroscience 29, 2076-2088 (2009)

14. Lisman, J.E.: Bursts as a unit of neural information: making unreliable synapses reliable. Trends in neurosciences 20, 38-43 (1997)

15. Abbott, L.F., Varela, J.A., Sen, K., Nelson, S.B.: Synaptic depression and cortical gain control. Science 275, 220-224 (1997)

16. Dobrunz, L.E., Stevens, C.F.: Heterogeneity of release probability, facilitation, and depletion at central synapses. Neuron 18, 995-1008 (1997)

17. Raastad, M., Storm, J.F., Andersen, P.: Putative Single Quantum and Single Fibre Excitatory Postsynaptic Currents Show Similar Amplitude Range and Variability in Rat Hippocampal Slices. The European journal of neuroscience 4, 113-117 (1992)

18. Rosenbaum, R., Rubin, J., Doiron, B.: Short term synaptic depression imposes a frequency dependent filter on synaptic information transfer. PLoS computational biology 8, e1002557 (2012)

19. Papatheodoropoulos, C., Kostopoulos, G.: Decreased ability of rat temporal hippocampal CA1 region to produce long-term potentiation. Neuroscience letters 279, 177-180 (2000)

20. Buzsaki, G.: Hippocampal sharp wave-ripple: A cognitive biomarker for episodic memory and planning. Hippocampus 25, 1073-1188 (2015)

21. Mizunuma, M., Norimoto, H., Tao, K., Egawa, T., Hanaoka, K., Sakaguchi, T., Hioki, H., Kaneko, T., Yamaguchi, S., Nagano, T., Matsuki, N., Ikegaya, Y.: Unbalanced excitability underlies offline reactivation of behaviorally activated neurons. Nature neuroscience 17, 503-505 (2014)

Using Electroencephalograms to Interpret and Monitor the Emotions

Amin Shahab and Claude Frasson

Département d'Informatique et de Recherche Opérationnelle
Université de Montréal, Montréal, Canada H3C 3J7
{shahabam, frasson}@iro.umontreal.ca

Abstract. Detecting the real-time human emotions became recently one important issue in Artificial Intelligent (AI). Numbers of research on emotional facial expressions, the effect of emotion on heart rate, eye movement and the evolution of emotions with the time show the interest of this topic. This paper presents a method for observing the human's emotional evolutions (sequence of emotions) based on brain activities in its different parts. The Emotiv EPOC headset collects the data of Electroencephalograms (EEG) of the participant to calculate the arousal and valence. After training the system with headset output data, the noise and brain's data other than emotional information will be cut out according to two levels of filtering. Finally, mapping the result (arousal and valence) with two dimensions circumplex space model presents the real-time emotional evolutions of the participant. Real-time emotional evolutions show all the picks of positive and negative feelings, moreover, analyzing the EEG data will allow recognizing the general emotions, which are the strongest routine senses of the participant. Comparing the unexpected reaction, the time taken by general emotion and feelings in picks, give us a tool to observe the health situation of the people and on the other hand, is an instrument to measure the mood of the people against a video game, news and advertising.

Keywords: Artificial Intelligence, Emotion, Sentiment Analysis, Virtual Reality, Arousal, Valence, Opinion Mining.

1   Introduction

Every day we see the quick changes in lifestyle which are the result of the advanced facilities, ease in life and new medical solutions, for humanity. However, this development leads people to a new and modern lifestyle, among noises and air pollutions [1], that could make a mental problem. Emotions and resulting from emotions are unobservable parts of human being, and it makes this kind of research more complicated. Recently, the number of investigation on sentiments analysis and also named opinion mining that are methods based on detect real-time emotions and feeling of human, in both aspect of academic and commercial is growing [2,3]. The researchers used different applications to identify emotions, such as facial expression [4-6], heart rate variation, skin conductivity and respiration [7,8], although these

© Springer International Publishing AG 2017
C. Frasson and G. Kostopoulos (Eds.): BFAL 2017, LNAI 10512, pp. 192–202, 2017
DOI: 10.1007/978-3-319-67615-9_18

methods are not reliable, because of lots of reason. For example, when facial expression system is detecting person's emotion using his/her face with natural frown eyebrows, or a person who smiles whenever is nervous, or when we use a heart rate variation system to detecting person's emotion who has blood pressure problem, cannot work precisely. For these reasons, researchers are progressively interested in using EEG as a reliable source to identify the emotional situation of human [4,9]. EEG-based system was designed to be used by disabled people [9] but reliability and excitement of controlling the environment just by the power of thinking, is going to make it the next generation of wearable computer in a variety of applications, such as

— A better choice than controller or Kinect in VR and gaming [10,11].
— Designing software and problem-solving system [10,12].
— Marketing, transport, and health [13,14]

In this paper, we analyze the emotion of participants when they are watching 360 degrees movies, an image or a text as well as when they are listening to the music in a virtual reality (VR) environment. Emotiv EPOC extracts the brain participant EEG data. Mapping the arousal and valence, calculated by the value of the brain waves of EEG data, on the two dimensions circumplex space model, return one feeling. By comparing the time series of emotions of participants when they are under the effect of an emotional factor and compare the time series of emotions of one participant. During the experiment, we tried to (1) find the evolution of emotions, (2) compare the formulas, (3) find the general emotion of participant. This paper is structured as following: section 2 explains the emotional evolutions, section 3 explains the experiment and the method used to interpret the data, and in section 4 the results obtained will be discussed.

2   Emotional Evolutions

The most complex and unreachable part of human being is the mind, and fortunately, very soon, researchers find out that there is a close interrelationship between brain waves and the psychological state of the person [3,15,16] and it became a way to catch people's emotion. Reading emotion of individuals is crucial, and it could help lots of people to live a better life. The first task of psychologists is understanding the mental situation of a patient; the patient should talk until the doctor analyzes him/her, and this would be facilitated if the patient could explain how does he/she feel. For another example, if the system could analyze the emotional state of the person facing critical jobs related to human lives, like a pilot or a surgeon, whenever his/her mind is not enough ready and focused, the person and his/her colleagues could be alarmed. Usually, the team trusts their leaders, and they could hesitate to interrupt him/her until it is unfortunately too late.

The goal of this research is to detect the emotional state of a participant in different emotional situations, then to show their emotional evolutions on two dimensions circumplex space model. Emotional evolution is the sequence of emotional changes of a human. We create a software called Emotimap to interpret the EEG to show the human's emotional state and evolution of the emotions. In this paper, we will talk about

1. The effect of emotional factors on participants (monitored by Emotimap).
2. The methods of calculating the arousal and valence and comparing them.
3. General emotions in the evolution of emotions (interpreted by Emotimap).

3   Experiment

The objective of this experiment is to put the participant in a sequence of emotional states and detect their emotions using their brain activities. The emotional states are produced by four kinds of emotional factors (360 degrees film, image, text, and music) in a virtual reality environment.

3.1   Subjects

The subjects are 20 and include 10 males and 10 females in the age range between 22 – 39 (mean = 30.95 and SD = 5.01) all resident of Montreal with four different origins.

3.2   Experimental Procedure

The subjects participated in the experiment individually; every experiment takes almost 40 minutes include filling the pre-experiment and post-experiment forms. The experiment is divided into four steps illustrated in figure 1.

Fill the pre-experiment form   Participate in experiment   Fill the post experiment form   Talk about their emotions

Fig. 1. The steps of experiments

In step one, every participant is assigned to one unique key, and he/she fills up the big five personality test which is a test that categorizes the people by their characters [17]. Step two is the main part when the subject participates in the experiment, we will detail it in following. In step three, the participant fills up the form about his/her feeling and positive or negative effect of every emotional factor. The goal of this form is to find out if there is a logical reason when a subject has a different emotion from the feels that emotional factor should normally create. In the last step, we discuss with the participant about their feelings. In the middle of the experiment, we observed what a participant sees, hears and their emotional evolution in Emotimap, and we look at their face and body reaction. In all the experiments, we observed a strange and unexpected feedback from the participant.

Software. The experiment uses two software. The first one is the virtual reality mobile base software, and the other one is a windows desktop that connects to the mobile based software and controls it, at the same time, logs into the Emotiv headset to collect the EEG data, also calculates the emotions and keeps the data in a data base. Figure 2 illustrates the procedure of experiment.

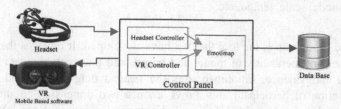

Fig. 2. Experiment software relation

Headset. In this experiment, we use Emotiv EPOC headset which is a fourteen-channel EEG headset. This headset can return the value of α, β_{low}, β_{High}, γ and θ of any single sensor.

VR. The participant uses Google Cardboard VR, which is not expensive, easy to use and supports different models of cell phone. Whenever the control panel (the Windows desktop software) sends a command to the mobile base VR software, the VR reads the command and follows the orders to display images, 360 degrees films, messages and play music.

Control panel. Control panel is the core of the system which (1) connects to the Emotiv to collect the EEG data, (2) interprets the result and (3) control what VR is showing and playing. After the beginning of every experiment, the control panel shows a 360 degrees film for 97 seconds to pre-train the participant individually, then it shows 7 seconds rest. The rest displays quiet black surroundings; we chose a black color because in the VR the sharp light bothers the eyes. Then in a loop to the end of the emotional factors, the system shows one negative emotional factor which makes the participant feeling negative (7 seconds). Then in continue one of the positive emotional factors include an image (15 seconds), text message (20 seconds), 360 degrees film (50 seconds) and music (50 seconds).

Emotional factor. Emotional factors are the elements we used to effect on the emotion of the participants. We needed an emotional factor to trigger negative emotions and positive ones. For negative emotional factor, we used images from IAPS (International Affective Picture System) [18] which is a standard database of images used in studies about emotions. For positive emotional factor, we have four categories.

— Images (positive): we used IAPS, with some added images.
— Text: we used the quote of scientist, philosophers, and politicians. Every quote in three languages (English, French, Farsi). The participants talk at least, one of these languages natively or in advanced and they just pay attention to the concept.

— 360 degrees film: we used YouTube to find 360 degrees film with different parameters such as color, ambiance, etc.
— Music: we selected instrumental music with one primary instrument to avoid the
effect of the different instrument sound (the feeling that sound of the violin makes
is different than the sound of the saxophone) when the music track follows the variety in mode, scale, tempo, etc.

Emotimap. Emotimap is the tool that we have developed. It receives the data of the
EEG headset, independently of model and brand, and interprets the data to calculate
the arousal and valence. Emotimap uses the nearest neighbor method to find the
current emotion of participant and shows it on a two dimension circumplex space
model (arousal and valence) [2]. Figure 3 shows the Emotimap in the left part of the
control panel. Emotimap shows the evolution of emotions from the beginning of the
experiment and currently detected emotion is showed on top of Emotimap. The
diagram of Emotimap (two-dimensions circumplex space) is taken from Georgios
Paltoglou et al. [2]. List of the emotional factors that control panel sends to VR is
shown in the middle. In the right side, we can see what the participant see or hear.

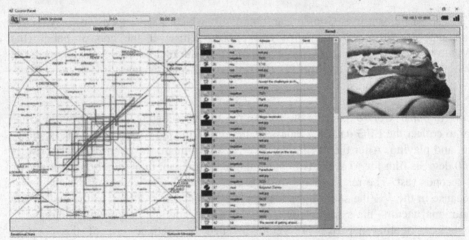

Fig. 3. Control panel, send the emotional factor to the VR and let the examiner see the emotional state of a participant in Emotimap at left and what he/she see and hear at right.

Arousal indicates the value of emotion varying from unpleasant to pleasant, and valence demonstrates the amount of quantitative activation varying from calm to excited
[19]. Arousal and valence are the results of comparing the brain activity of human in
different parts of the brain. We use the formulas (explained in the following part) to
calculate the arousal and valence. Brain manages all the internal organs such as heart,
lung, glands and their hormones while the human is thinking, watching, remembering
and saving the memories. To extract the pure data of emotions we use two level of
filtering (explain in following).

Formulas. Based on the ratio of activation of α and β waves in different parts of brain there are formulas that calculate the arousal and valence [20], in the experiment we kept the values of all of them to compare. We have three categories of formulas with two EEG sensors (2s: F_3, F_4), four EEG sensors (4s: F_3, F_4, AF_3, AF_4) and twelves EEG sensors (12s: $F_3, F_4, AF_3, AF_4, F_7, F_8, T_7, T_8, P_7\ P_8, O_1, O_2$), based on international EEG positions [5,21], and when it is mentioned low or high, that means the formula uses β_{low} or β_{high}. Formulas (1) and (2) in order are the arousal and valence with 12-sensors, to calculate other formulas, remove the sensors which are not in its category.

$$Arousal = \frac{\beta F_3 + \beta F_4 + \beta AF_3 + \beta AF_4 + \beta F_7 + \beta F_8 + \beta T_7 + \beta T_8 + \beta P_7 + \beta P_8 + \beta O_1 + \beta O_2}{\alpha F_3 + \alpha F_4 + \alpha AF_3 + \alpha AF_4 + \alpha F_7 + \alpha F_8 + \alpha T_7 + \alpha T_8 + \alpha P_7 + \alpha P_8 + \alpha O_1 + \alpha O_2} \tag{1}$$

$$Valence = \frac{\beta AF_4 + \beta F_4 + \beta F_8 + \beta T_8 + \beta P_8 + \beta O_2}{\alpha AF_4 + \alpha F_4 + \alpha F_8 + \alpha T_8 + \alpha P_8 + \alpha O_2} - \frac{\beta AF_3 + \beta F_3 + \beta F_7 + \beta T_7 + \beta P_7 + \beta O_1}{\alpha AF_3 + \alpha F_3 + \alpha F_7 + \alpha T_7 + \alpha P_7 + \alpha O_1} \tag{2}$$

Filters. We have access to data of the brain cortex. The brain is governing all areas of the body all the time. Human being emotions are complicated which means that one person in a short period of the time has more than one feeling and some of them are stronger than the others. For example, when a person sees a celebrity, he/she is happy, excited, shocked and sometimes nervous. Then Emotimap reduces the small changes in emotional evolutions time series and attention to keep the stronger feels, using two filters.

-   Smoother: ignores small shift to avoid the unnecessary movement. The position of the arousal and valence on Emotimap, are always shaking, when this movement is in a small area, and detected emotion does not change too much, so to avoid the complexity and to increase readability, Emotimap ignore this shaking.
-   Jump-remover: reduces the small changes, by avoiding sharp variation when is not stable, that means we do not keep the feelings which pass very fast.

4   Results

In the experiment, we look at participants and observe their face and body reactions to the emotional factor and the feeling that Emotimap recognizes. After that, we had talked to them and ask them to explain how they felt while they saw or heard the emotional factor when they had an unexpected reflex; the most exciting part was that participants felt exactly like what Emotimap showed, and they had a reason to feel like that. For example, when one of the participants watched a breathtaking green landscape, Emotimap detected sadness; participant explained that it is a lovely and beautiful image, but she had bad memories in a similar place. In every experiment, we saw examples like that, or sometimes the whole of the experiment was under the effect of some emotions, explained in general emotion section. The reason is that nobody has a white empty mind that reflects the emotion of a scene or music as a mirror, everyone has unique memories and life story which strongly affect on his/her emotional state (figure 4).

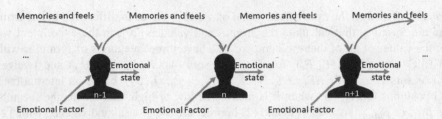

Fig. 4. The emotional state of people depends on the emotional factors around them, and their memories, effect of memory is much stronger than the emotional factors.

4.1   Typical Effect of the Emotional Factor

Effect of Emotions. We calculate the error rate of what participants feel the emotion that emotional factor creates. To find the emotions of one emotional factor, we take the percentage of the accumulative sum of the descending sort of count of emotions of all the participants when they were under effect of emotional factor. Then we take all the emotions with accumulative sum under 70% or if there were no emotion, we took first emotion. (figure 5)

Fig. 5. Error rate of the emotions of emotional factors and what the participant feels

B series (Blue bar) represents the percentage of the number of emotions of an emotional factor which is not in participant's emotion, plus the contrariwise, divided by total numbers of the emotions on both sides. O series (Orange bar) shows the percentage of the numbers of participant emotions which is not in emotional factors divided by the total of the feelings of participant's emotions. G series (Green bar) illuminate O series, but just count the accumulative sum of percentage less than 70% of participant emotions and if there were no item, count the first emotion. According to Table 1, B series display almost 50% failure, although in O series, failure average drops to 19.93%, but it is not reliable rate. G series with 6.32% average of error is stable. The fourth column shows the metric average of distance.

Table 1. Error rate of the Blue, Orange and Green Series and metric distance

Failure	B series	O series	G Serie	Metric dist.
Average	46.49 %	19.93 %	6.32 %	8.63 %
SD	17.01 %	13.55 %	**6.41 %**	8.11 %
No failure	0.64 %	13.35 %	**37.73 %**	1.55 %

The last row mentions the percentage of times with no error. G series shows 37.73, and if we notice that every emotional factor creates many emotions, it is an excellent mark.

The Relation Between Emotional Reaction and Characteristics. Before the experiment, all the participants fill a Big five form. Figure 6 shows the similarities of characteristics of participants when the emotional reaction to the emotional factor was similar. As much as the participant id is closer, their reaction is more similar. According to the diagram, there is no relation between personal character and emotional reflex.

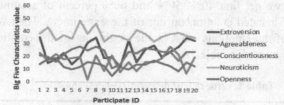

Fig. 6. Relation between characteristics and emotional reactions

4.2 Formula Comparing

Researchers use different formulas to calculate the arousal and valence. As explained in section formulas, we use three categories of them to compare. We tried to find the similar formula, based on the detected emotions, illustrated in figure 7. The most similar formulas are the formulas in the same category when they use β and β_{low}, brain waves which are less than 45 percent.

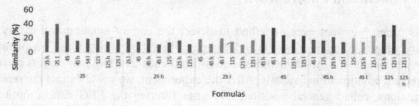

Fig. 7. Similarity (%) of the formulas based on the emotions they detect

We compared the reaction of formulas according to the time. Figure 8 shows that formulas that use frontal sensors are more reliable and between the formulas in the same category, the formula with β_{high} are stronger in picks.

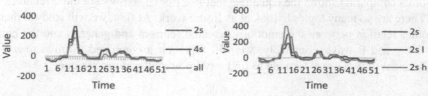

Fig. 8. Compare the formulas, based on their reaction on emotion picks

4.3   General Emotions

In the middle of the experiment, whenever the participant did not engage with the emotional factor, Emotimap showed some emotions, unique for everybody. After experiment when we asked them why they felt like that, they were surprised that we detected their emotions and confirmed the Emotimap result, we called that, general emotion. General emotion could help the humanity to diagnose, to measure the ability to take responsibilities for a critical task, etc.

Usually, general emotions are powerful when the person is not on the emotional pick. At the beginning of emotional cut when the participant is not yet engaged. To detect the general emotion in real time, we get the most repetitive emotion of all the test. To validate it, we get first 40%, 50% and 60% percent of accumulative of the percentage count of irritated emotion during of the experiment. Then we count how many percentages of the emotions exist at the beginning of the emotional cut. The error rate result is presented in table 2.

Table 2. Error rate of detecting general emotion

	40%	50%	60%
Average	5.00	3.50	7.31
SD	22.36	11.82	10.99
No failure	**95%**	90%	65%

The result shows we can detect the general emotion for 95% which is a great note when we get 40% of most repeated emotion as the general emotions.

5   Conclusion Future work

In this paper, we went over a method to detect the current emotion and a way to identify general emotion of people and compare the different formulas. We planned one experiment to verify our methods used in Emotimap as a tool that detects current and general emotion of individuals. After the experiment, we could extract the repeated emotions, called general emotion, and after filtering the EEG data, Emotimap could recognize the current feeling. The result shows the importance of the background memories on the current feelings. Also, we could detect the current emotion with 6.41 % of error with the average of 8.11 % of the metric distance that means, even in error case, Emotimap noticed an emotion close to the real one. Also, Emotimap could detect correctly 95% of the general emotion. Finally, the outcome of the formula comparing shows the equations that use frontal sensors are more reliable.

There are so many topics to look at as future work. At first, we will study if there is another relation between the emotions detected (current and general) and the pattern of the γ and θ waves. Secondly, we will work on a combined formula to use the different ability of every formula to find more powerful and precise one.

Acknowledgement

We thank the NSERC-CRD and BMU for funding this research.

References

1. Turner, J., Kelly, B.: Emotional dimensions of chronic disease. Western Journal of Medicine **172**(2), 124 (2000).
2. Paltoglou, G., Thelwall, M.: Seeing stars of valence and arousal in blog posts. IEEE Transactions on Affective Computing **4**(1), 116-123 (2013).
3. Bobrov, P., Frolov, A., Cantor, C., Bakhnyan, M., Zhavoronkov, A.: Brain-computer interface based on generation of visual images. PloS one **6**(6), e20674 (2011).
4. Nie, D., Wang, X.-W., Shi, L.-C., Lu, B.-L.: EEG-based emotion recognition during watching movies. In: Neural Engineering (NER), 2011 5th International IEEE/EMBS Conference on 2011, pp. 667-670. IEEE
5. Benlamine, S., Chaouachi, M., Villata, S., Cabrio, E., Frasson, C., Gandon, F.: Emotions in argumentation: an empirical evaluation. In: International Joint Conference on Artificial Intelligence, IJCAI 2015 2015, pp. 156-163
6. Benlamine, M.S., Chaouachi, M., Frasson, C., Dufresne, A.: Physiology-based recognition of Facial micro-expressions using EEG and identification of the relevant sensors by emotion.
7. Picard, R.W., Vyzas, E., Healey, J.: Toward machine emotional intelligence: Analysis of affective physiological state. IEEE transactions on pattern analysis and machine intelligence **23**(10), 1175-1191 (2001).
8. Derbali, L., Ghali, R., Frasson, C.: Assessing Motivational Strategies in Serious Games Using Hidden Markov Models. In: FLAIRS Conference 2013
9. Wang, S., Esfahani, E.T., Sundararajan, V.: Evaluation of SSVEP as passive feedback for improving the performance of brain machine interfaces. In: ASME 2012 International Design Engineering Technical Conferences and Computers and Information in Engineering Conference 2012, pp. 695-701. American Society of Mechanical Engineers
10. Esfahani, E.T., Sundararajan, V.: Classification of primitive shapes using brain–computer interfaces. Computer-Aided Design **44**(10), 1011-1019 (2012).
11. Lécuyer, A., Lotte, F., Reilly, R.B., Leeb, R., Hirose, M., Slater, M.: Brain-computer interfaces, virtual reality, and videogames. Computer **41**(10) (2008).
12. Göker, M.H.: The effects of experience during design problem solving. Design Studies **18**(4), 405-426 (1997).
13. Fiebig, D.G., Keane, M.P., Louviere, J., Wasi, N.: The generalized multinomial logit model: accounting for scale and coefficient heterogeneity. Marketing Science **29**(3), 393-421 (2010).
14. Khushaba, R.N., Greenacre, L., Kodagoda, S., Louviere, J., Burke, S., Dissanayake, G.: Choice modeling and the brain: A study on the Electroencephalogram (EEG) of preferences. Expert Systems with Applications **39**(16), 12378-12388 (2012).
15. Wolpaw, J.R., McFarland, D.J.: Control of a two-dimensional movement signal by a non-invasive brain-computer interface in humans. Proceedings of the National Academy of Sciences of the United States of America **101**(51), 17849-17854 (2004).

16. Pfurtscheller, G., Flotzinger, D., Kalcher, J.: Brain-computer interface—a new communication device for handicapped persons. Journal of Microcomputer Applications **16**(3), 293-299 (1993).
17. Goldberg, L.R.: An alternative" description of personality": the big-five factor structure. Journal of personality and social psychology **59**(6), 1216 (1990).
18. Lang, P.J.: International affective picture system (IAPS): Digitized photographs, instruction manual and affective ratings. Technical Report (2005).
19. Sourina, O., Liu, Y.: A Fractal-based Algorithm of Emotion Recognition from EEG using Arousal-Valence Model. In: BIOSIGNALS 2011, pp. 209-214
20. Ramirez, R., Vamvakousis, Z.: Detecting emotion from EEG signals using the emotive epoc device. In: International Conference on Brain Informatics 2012, pp. 175-184. Springer
21. Benlamine, M.S., Bouslimi, S., Harley, J.M., Frasson, C., Dufresne, A.: Toward Brain-based Gaming: Measuring Engagement During Gameplay. In: EdMedia: World Conference on Educational Media and Technology 2015, vol. 1, pp. 717-722

The Long Lasting Effect of Neonatal Handling on mGluR5 and Arc mRNA Levels in Medial Prefrontal Cortex of rat Brain

Maria Nikolakopoulou[1], Anna Abatzi[1], Panagiotis Giompres[2], Elias D. Kouvelas[1], Ada Mitsacos[1]

[1]University of Patras, Department of Medicine, Laboratory of Physiology, Patras, Greece
[2]University of Patras, Department of Biology, Laboratory of Human and Animal Physiology, Patras, Greece

Abstract. Neonatal handling is an experimental animal model of early life experiences known to affect the hypothalamic-pituitary-adrenal (HPA) axis. Metabotropic glutamate receptor 5 (mGluR5) and immediate early gene Arc/Arg3.1 are important for several forms of synaptic plasticity. This study aimed at identifying the effects of neonatal handling on mGluR5 and Arc mRNA levels in prefrontal cortex of adult male rat brain using in situ hybridization

Keywords: Neonatal handling, mGluR5, Arc, Prefrontal cortex.

Neonatal handling is an established animal model for the study of the effects of early life experiences on the stress response. This model consists of a brief, repeated maternal separation during the first three weeks of life [1]. It has been shown that neonatal handling affects hypothalamic–pituitary–adrenal axis (HPA axis) function.

The group I metabotropic glutamate receptor 5 (mGluR5) is a G-protein coupled receptor. mGluR5 activate Gq/G_{11} phospholipase C-mediated signaling and is important for modulating several forms of synaptic plasticity and excitatory synaptic transmission. mGluR5 has been implicated in various psychiatric disorders, such as anxiety and depression and it has been identified as a novel therapeutic target [2,3].

Activity-regulated cytoskeletal-associated protein (Arc/Arg3.1) is a member of the immediate-early gene family. Arc protein is localized post-synaptically and is involved in various forms of neuronal plasticity, in AMPA receptor endocytosis and LTD. Additionally, Arc is involved in actin polymerization an LTP consolidation [4].

This study aimed at identifying the effects of neonatal handling on mGluR5 and Arc mRNA levels in prefrontal cortex of adult male rat brain using in situ hybridization. Rats were subjected to maternal separation for 15 min from postnatal day 1 to 22. The induction protocol of Arc mRNA was based on the study of Guzowski et al. [5]. We used the same induction time (30 minutes), but we modified the period the rat stayed in the open field (10 minutes). Open-field behavioral responses were also evaluated.

We observed an effect of neonatal handling on the mRNA expression levels of the mGluR5, and the immediate-early gene Arc. This long lasting effect of neonatal handling was present in adult rat medial prefrontal cortex (mPFC). In particular, we found

© Springer International Publishing AG 2017
C. Frasson and G. Kostopoulos (Eds.): BFAL 2017, LNAI 10512, pp. 203–204, 2017
DOI: 10.1007/978-3-319-67615-9

an upregulation of both mGluR5 and Arc mRNA in anterior cingulate (Cg1) and pre-limbic cortex (PrL), ranging from 54% to 58% for mGluR5 mRNA and from 22% to 26% for Arc mRNA. These changes at the mRNA levels are most likely functionally relevant assuming that analogous changes occur at the protein level. In the open field we observed statistically significant higher moving duration, but no difference in time spent and number of entries in the center of the neonatally-handled rats.

A large amount of evidence points to a role of mGluR5 blockade in producing anxiolytic effects in rodents [3]. A recent study has shown that mGluR5 expression correlates to the degree of stress resilience and that the pharmacological activation or inhibition of mGluR5 modulates stress vulnerability [6]. In addition, previous studies have also shown that the translation of Arc is induced by the activation of group I metabotropic glutamate receptors. In particular, stimulation of neuronal cultures with glutamate elevated Arc mRNA expression and this increase was blocked by MPEP, a negative allosteric modulator of mGluR5 [7]. Moreover, Park et al, [8] using biochemical and genetic approaches have identified the intracellular signaling pathways involved in Arc translation mediated by the activation of group I mGluRs.

Taken together, the activation of Arc translation observed in the mPFC of neonatally handled rats may be correlated to the upregulation of mGluR5 mRNA levels. Knowing that neonatal handling is an animal model of stress resilience and in particular adult neonatally handled male rats exhibit a shorter duration of the stress response, our data suggest that a brief and repeated maternal separation during neonatal life alters the mGluR5-Arc pathway of adult mPFC and this may be implicated in the stress resilience of neonatally handled rats.

References

1. Levine S. Infantile experience and resistance to physiological stress. Science, 126(3270), 405 (1957).
2. Matosin N., et al. Metabotropic glutamate receptor mGluR2/3 and mGluR5 binding in the anterior cingulate cortex in psychotic and nonpsychotic depression, bipolar disorder and schizophrenia: implications for novel mGluR-based therapeutics. J Psychiatry Neurosci, 39(6), 407-16 (2014).
3. Spooren W.P., et al. Effects of the prototypical mGlu(5) receptor antagonist 2-methyl-6-(phenylethynyl)-pyridine on rotarod, locomotor activity and rotational responses in unilateral 6-OHDA-lesioned rats. Eur J Pharmacol, 406(3), 403-10 (2000).
4. Farris S., et al. Selective localization of arc mRNA in dendrites involves activity- and translation-dependent mRNA degradation. J Neurosci, 34(13), 4481-93 (2014).
5. Guzowski J.F., et al. Environment-specific expression of the immediate-early gene Arc in hippocampal neuronal ensembles. Nat Neurosci, 2(12), 1120-4 (1992).
6. Shin S., et al. mGluR5 in the nucleus accumbens is critical for promoting resilience to chronic stress. Nat Neurosci, 18(7), 1017-24 (2015).
7. Kumar V., et al. Activation of intracellular metabotropic glutamate receptor 5 in striatal neurons leads to up-regulation of genes associated with sustained synaptic transmission including Arc/Arg3.1 protein. J Biol Chem, 287(8), 5412-25 (2012).
8. Park S., et al. Elongation factor 2 and fragile X mental retardation protein control the dynamic translation of Arc/Arg3.1 essential for mGluR-LTD. Neuron, 59(1), 70-83 (2008).

Escalating Low-dose Δ9-THC Treatment in Adolescence Induces Spatial Memory Deficits in Adulthood

Nafsika Poulia[1], Foteini Delis[1], Alexia Polissidis[2], Nikolaos Pitsikas[3], Katerina Antoniou[1]

[1] Department of Pharmacology, University of Ioannina, Ioannina, Greece
[2] Laboratory of Neurodegenerative Diseases, Biomedical Research Foundation Academy of Athens, Athens, Greece
[3] Department of Pharmacology, University of Thessaly, Larissa, Greece

Clinical and preclinical studies suggest that delta-9-tetrahydrocannabinol (Δ9-THC), the main psychoactive component of cannabis, during adolescence, can trigger long-term behavioral and neurobiological alterations later in adulthood [1, 2]. Preclinical studies have focused on the effects of rather high Δ9-THC doses. Here, we evaluate the behavioral and neurobiological profile of adult rats that received escalating low-dose Δ9-THC during adolescence.

Adolescent, male rats received escalating low-dose Δ9-THC treatment or vehicle, twice daily, from postnatal day (PND) 35 to PND 45 (0.3 mg/kg PND 35–37; 1 mg/kg PND 38–41; 3 mg/kg PND 42–45). On PND 75 we assessed: a) spatial memory, using the object location and the Morris water maze tasks, b) neuroplasticity markers BDNF, TrkB, and p75 and c) dopaminergic activity, in prefrontal cortex (PFC) and hippocampus (HIPP).

The object location task included the presentation of two identical objects in two distinct areas of an open field arena (Trial 1), followed, 1hr later (Trial 2), by the presentation of the same two objects, one in the same location as in Trial 1, the other in a different, novel location. Location discrimination index was defined as time spent exploring the object in the novel location minus time spent exploring the object in the familiar location divided by total object exploration time.

The Morris water maze task included training of the rats to reach a submerged platform in a circular pool filled with opaque water, based on extramaze cues that are used by the rat to create a spatial map. Next, the platform is removed from the pool. Memory of the previous location of the platform was assessed by measuring time spent in the respective quadrant of the pool.

Protein expression levels were determined from preparations of fresh-frozen tissue that was excised from anatomically defined areas of the brain. Proteins were separated with SDS-polyacrylamide gel electrophoresis, transferred onto nitrocellulose membranes, and detected with specific antibodies that were visualized with HRP-chemiluminescence.

Tissue levels of dopamine and its metabolites (DOPAC and HVA) were determined using high pressure liquid chromatography with electrochemical detection, from fresh tissue that was excised from anatomically defined areas of the brain. Dopamine turnover ratio was defined as the ratio of tissue DOPAC over dopamine levels.

© Springer International Publishing AG 2017
C. Frasson and G. Kostopoulos (Eds.): BFAL 2017, LNAI 10512, pp. 205–206, 2017
DOI: 10.1007/978-3-319-67615-9

The applied treatment of escalating low-dose Δ9-THC induced significant spatial memory deficits, along with lower BDNF levels and impaired dopaminergic activity.

Discrimination index in the object location task was significantly lower than vehicle. Time spent in the target quadrant was significantly less in the Morris water maze task, compared with vehicle, while no visuomotor coordination deficits were observed. BDNF protein levels were lower in both PFC and HIPP, compared with vehicle. Dopamine turnover ratio was lower in PFC and higher in HIPP, compared with vehicle.

Overall, we show that low dose Δ9-THC treatment in adolescence induces long-term deficits in spatial memory, accompanied by impairments in neuroplasticity and neurotransmission of the adult brain.

Our findings add to previous studies showing that treatment with cannabinoid receptor agonists affects cognitive function. Long-term deficits in spatial learning and memory have been previously reported after adolescent treatment with high doses of synthetic cannabinoid receptor agonists or with high doses of Δ9-THC. Studies have also shown that treatment with high doses of synthetic cannabinoid receptor agonists in adolescence induces long-term decrease in BDNF levels in HIPP and PFC, that treatment with high doses of Δ9-THC decreases dendritic length and spine density in hippocampus, and that BDNF plays a critical role in cognitive function, including spatial memory. Finally, reduced dopamine metabolism in PFC along with hyperdopaminergic activity in subcortical areas are to be expected after Δ9-THC treatment [1, 2]. These cognitive and neurochemical impairments are also present in psychiatric disease. In particular, schizophrenia is associated with cannabis use in adolescence, with lower BDNF expression levels in PFC and HIPP, and with dopaminergic hypofunction in PFC and dopaminergic hyper-responsiveness in subcortical areas [1, 2].

Our findings extend the aforementioned studies by showing that (i) Δ9-THC treatment during adolescence impairs spatial memory and associated measures of neuroplasticity in adulthood and that (ii) these Δ9-THC-induced impairments can be produced by a low-dose regimen. The long-term vulnerability of brain and behavior to low Δ9-THC doses has two significant implications: First, that low-dose exposure to cannabis constituents in adolescence may have harmful long-term effects on cognitive function. Second, that this model of adolescent Δ9-THC exposure is an endophenotype of cognitive dysfunction in psychiatric disease that may be a valuable tool to effectively address mechanisms underlying residual effects of early cannabis use.

References

1. Andreasson S, Allebeck P, Engstrom A, Rydberg U (1987) Cannabis and schizophrenia. A longitudinal study of Swedish conscripts. Lancet. 2: 1483-6.
2. Rubino T and Parolaro D (2017) Susceptibility to Psychiatric Diseases After Cannabis Abuse in Adolescence: Animal Models. In: Endocannabinoids and Lipid Mediators in Brain Functions, M. Melis, Editor. Springer, pp 237-255.

Performance Comparisons of Classifiers Applied to Electroencephalogram Signals

Alisson Ravaglio Santos[1], Gabriel Chaves Becchi[2],
Emerson Hochsteiner de Vasconcelos Segundo[3], Viviana Cocco Mariani[1,3]
and Leandro dos Santos Coelho[2,4]

[1] Dept. Electrical Engineering, Federal University of Parana (UFPR), Curitiba, Brazil
[2] Computer Engineering, Pontifical Catholic University of Parana (PUCPR), Curitiba, Brazil
[3] Mechanical Engineering Graduate Program (PPGEM), PUCPR, Curitiba, Brazil
[4] Industrial and Systems Engineering Graduate Program (PPGEPS), PUCPR, Curitiba, Brazil

Abstract. There has been intensive research from academics and practitioners regarding models for neurosciences. This paper aims to compare different classifiers of the machine learning field to classify electroencephalography data obtained using an Emotiv neuroheadset. The motivation of this research is the brain-computer interface design to control an unmanned aerial vehicle (drone) by communication system between a human and a computer system based on machine learning framework with robust, efficient and fast classifiers.

Keywords: Brain-computer Interface, Machine Learning, Classifiers, Emotiv neuroheadset, Electroencephalogram.

1 Introduction

This paper aims to evaluate the performance of classifiers [1,2], such as extreme learning machine, k-nearest neighbors, fuzzy nearest neighbors, logistic regression classifier, extra trees, random forest, naïve Bayes and support vector machine to classify electroencephalography (EEG) signals collected using an Emotiv EPOC neuroheadset. The Emotiv wireless device is placed in the scalp in a non-invasive way, this device will capture electric potential differences with a frequency of 128 Hz between neurons, the voltage is amplified and transformed into electrical signals and sent to a computer in MATLAB-Simulink (MathWorks) environment, where the signals will be classified according to predetermined performance criteria using classifiers. A graphical representation of the developed research is presented in Fig. 1.

Several tests were realized with several people using Emotiv neuroheadset. The output signals are divided in 5 classes based in thoughts (for future use in the movement control of a drone, which relevant use and other subjects are discussed in [3]), being 0 for neutral, 1 for up, 2 for down, 3 for left and 4 for right. The results (mean values) for a person are summarized in Table 1. As seen in Table 1, three classifiers presented excellent performance results in terms of classification (5 classes) with a

C. Frasson and G. Kostopoulos (Eds.): BFAL 2017, LNAI 10512, pp. 207–208, 2017
DOI: 10.1007/978-3-319-67615-9

success accuracy (training and testing phases) of 100% (using all input features, i.e., 14 sensors signals) using desktop with Intel i7 5820K processor and 128 GB of Random Access Memory (RAM).

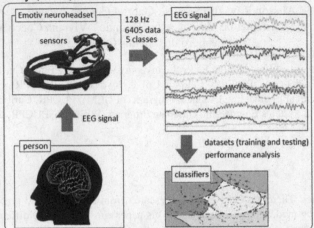

Fig. 1. Representation of the developed research using EEG signals and classifiers.

Table 1. Performance results using cross-validation (*k*-fold =10) and partitions (10% until 90% with step of 10%) of training and testing datasets. The best results are presented in bold font.

Classifier model	Training accuracy	Testing accuracy	Training time (s)
Extreme learning machine	0.391±0.002	0.392±0.012	**9×10^{-4}**
k-nearest neighbors	**1.000±0**	**1.000±0**	0.54
Fuzzy nearest neighbors	**1.000±0**	**1.000±0**	3.70
Logistic regression classifier	0.626±0.338	0.622±0.343	0.91
Extra trees	0.963±0.007	0.959±0.012	0.62
Random forest	0.999±0.001	0.998±0.003	0.24
Naïve Bayes	0.637±0.002	0.636±0.011	0.71
Support vector machine	**1.000±0**	**1.000±0**	15.51

Acknowledgements: The authors would like to thank National Council of Scientific and Technologic Development of Brazil - CNPq (Grants: 404659/2016-0, 303908/2015-7-PQ, 405101/2016-3, 303906/2015-4-PQ) for its financial support.

References

1. Hastie, T., Tibshirani, R., Friedman, J.: The elements of statistical learning: data mining, inference, and prediction. 10th edition. Springer, Heidelberg, Germany (2013).
2. Bishop, C. M.: Pattern recognition and machine learning. Springer, Heidelberg, Germany (2006).
3. Luppicini, R., So, A.: A technoethical review of commercial drone use in the context of governance, ethics and privacy. Technology and Society 46, 109-119 (2016).

Quadcopter Control Based on Electroencephalogram Headset and Hybrid Fuzzy Classifier

Alisson Ravaglio Santos[1], Guilherme Nack Cordeiro[2], Gabriel Chaves Becchi[2], Helon V. H. Ayala[3], Viviana Cocco Mariani[1,4] and Leandro dos Santos Coelho[1,5]

[1] Dept. Electrical Engineering, Federal University of Parana (UFPR), Curitiba, Brazil
[2] Computer Engineering, Pontifical Catholic University of Parana (PUCPR), Curitiba, Brazil
[3] IBM Research, Rio de Janeiro, Brazil
[4] Mechanical Engineering Graduate Program (PPGEM), PUCPR, Curitiba, Brazil
[5] Industrial and Systems Engineering Graduate Program (PPGEPS), PUCPR, Curitiba, Brazil
alissonrs@outlook.com, guilherme.nack@outlook.com,
gabrielbecchi97@gmail.com, helonv@br.ibm.com,
viviana.mariani@pucpr.br, leandro.coelho@pucpr.br

Abstract. The Takagi-Sugeno (T-S) fuzzy model has been applied widely to solve modeling, identification, forecasting, pattern recognition, control systems and machine learning problems. In this paper, a hybrid T-S fuzzy classifier combined with Bayesian Gaussian mixture model and quadratic discriminant analysis was proposed and validated to classify electroencephalography (EEG) data collected using an Emotiv neuro-headset. The results suggested that the developed T-S model has achieved good accuracy in EEG classification task. After, the proposed hybrid classifier was adopted to a brain-computer interface design to control an unmanned aerial vehicle, an AR-Drone quadcopter.

Keywords: Takagi-Sugeno fuzzy classifier, Machine Learning, Electroencephalogram, Unmanned Aerial Vehicle Control, Brain-computer Interface.

1 Introduction

Fuzzy logic provides human reasoning capabilities to capture uncertainties, which cannot be described by precise mathematical models. The Takagi-Sugeno (T-S) fuzzy model [1] is a system described by fuzzy if-then rules which can give local linear representation of the nonlinear system by decomposing the whole input space into several partial fuzzy spaces and representing each output space with a linear equation. Such a model is capable of approximating a wide class of nonlinear systems. A T-S fuzzy model with structure given by [2] combined in the ensemble machine form with Bayesian Gaussian mixture model (GMM) [3] and quadratic discriminant analysis (QDA) [4], an generalized Bayesian classifier, was proposed and validated.

In the other hand, a brain-computer interface (BCI) is a direct communication pathway between a human brain and an external device. The BCI design adopted in this research can be divided into three parts: (i) the procedure of electroencephalography (EEG) signal acquisition using Emotiv neuro-headset, (ii) the EEG signal classification

© Springer International Publishing AG 2017
C. Frasson and G. Kostopoulos (Eds.): BFAL 2017, LNAI 10512, pp. 209–210, 2017
DOI: 10.1007/978-3-319-67615-9

based on hybrid fuzzy model, and (iii) use of the classifier signal generated by hybrid fuzzy model implemented in Simulink-MATLAB environment linked with Emotiv neuro-headset used by a person to control an unmanned aerial vehicle of the type AR.Drone quadcopter platform manufactured by Parrot (a French enterprise) via wireless communication.

The Emotiv device is equipped with 14 electrodes (6405 samples for the classifier inputs) and the output signals (divided into 5 classes) are based in thoughts for the movement of the drone, being 0 for neutral, 1 for up, 2 for down, 3 for left and 4 for right. Results of the proposed hybrid classifier was 100% of accuracy in the training data (70% of dataset), and 99.9% of accuracy in the validation data (30% of dataset) using cross-validation with k-fold equal to 10. The fuzzy classifier without GMM and QDA presented 100% of accuracy in the training data, but only 93.2 of accuracy in the validation data. In this context, the proposed hybrid fuzzy classifier results can be considered satisfactory for EEG data classification applied to UAV control.

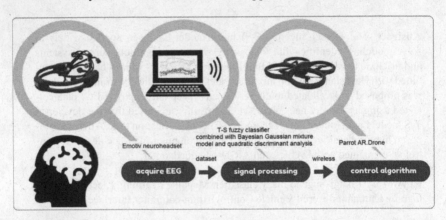

Fig. 1. Proposed project combining hybrid fuzzy classifier, EEG sygnals and UAV control.

Acknowledgements: The authors would like to thank National Council of Scientific and Technologic Development of Brazil - CNPq (Grants: 404659/2016-0, 303908/2015-7-PQ, 405101/2016-3, 303906/2015-4-PQ) for its financial support.

References

1. Takagi, T., Sugeno, M.: Fuzzy identification of systems and its applications to modeling and control. IEEE Transactions on Systems, Man and Cybernetics 15(1), 116-132 (1985).
2. Abonyi, J., Roubos, H.: Simple fuzzy classifier based on inconsistency analysis of labeled data, Chapter 12 in: CoIL Challenge 2000: The Insurance Company Case, Peter van der Putten and Maarten van Someren (eds), Sentient Machine Research, Amsterdam and Leiden Institute of Advanced Computer Science, Leiden, LIACS Technical Report 2000.
3. Kämäräinen, J., Paalanen, P.: GMMBAYES- Bayesian classifier and Gaussian mixture model toolbox v1.0 (2005), *http://www2.it.lut.fi/project/gmmbayes*
4. Srivastava, S., Gupta, M. R., Frigyik, B. A.: Bayesian quadratic discriminat analysis. Journal of Machine Learning Research 8, 1277-1305 (2007).

Support Vector Machine Approaches with Features Selection to Detect Cognitive States from Brain Images

Marco Antônio Boaretto[1], Emerson Hochsteiner de Vasconcelos Segundo[2],
Viviana Cocco Mariani[1,2] and Leandro dos Santos Coelho[1,3]

[1] Dept. Electrical Engineering, Federal University of Parana (UFPR), Curitiba, Brazil
[2] Mechanical Engineering Graduate Program (PPGEM), PUCPR, Curitiba, Brazil
[3] Industrial and Systems Engineering Graduate Program (PPGEPS), PUCPR, Curitiba, Brazil
marco.boaretto@hotmail.com, e.hochsteiner@gmail.com,
viviana.mariani@pucpr.br, leandro.coelho@pucpr.br

Abstract. Functional magnetic resonance imaging (fMRI) has been a relevant
instrument of study of human brain to determine mean activation in different
brain regions. In this paper, a support vector machine (SVM) approach using
radial basis functions (RBF) kernel and a least squares SVM with RBF kernel
combined with feature selection approaches are evaluated for discriminating
cognitive states of human subjects based on their spatio-temporal fMRI patterns. This paper summarizes the results obtained of fMRI data of six human
subjects. The results when compared with results using other machine learning
approaches demonstrate the feasibility of training SVM with features selection
to distinguish instantaneous cognitive states of human subjects based on their
observed fMRI data.

Keywords: Functional Magnetic Resonance Imaging, Brain Image Analysis,
Machine Learning, Support Vector Machine, Feature Selection.

1   Introduction

Functional magnetic resonance imaging (fMRI) is an advanced non-invasive technology based on the increase in blood flow to the local vasculature that accompanies
neural activity in the brain.

In this paper, a comparative study of support vector machine (SVM) and least
squares SVM (LS-SVM) [1] combined with feature selection approaches, such as
mutual information (MI), statistical dependency (SD) and RELIEF [2], applied to
binary classification to fMRI dataset of six human subjects. The classification results
of mean performance using cross-validation ($kfold$ = 10) were summarized in Table
1. The adopted SVM and LS-SVM show promise for the goal of automatically identifying mental states. The details about timing, imaging parameters, stimulus and behavioral data related to the fMRI experiments (Starplus fMRI data) with the six human subjects were described in [3].

© Springer International Publishing AG 2017
C. Frasson and G. Kostopoulos (Eds.): BFAL 2017, LNAI 10512, pp. 211–212, 2017
DOI: 10.1007/978-3-319-67615-9

Table 1. Mean performance results with partitions of training (75%) and testing (25%) datasets of six subjects human. The best results without feature selection and using feature selection in terms of F-score are presented in bold and italic fonts, respectively.

Classifier	Feature selection	Training (75%)	Testing (25%)
Naïve Bayes	No	0.939±0.021	0.712±0.067
	MI	0.866±0.029	0.706±0.102
	SD	0.869±0.031	0.712±0.095
	RELIEF	0.940±0.021	0.712±0.068
k-nearest neighbors	No	0.824±0.018	0.768±0.063
with k equal to 10	MI	0.862±0.022	0.755±0.086
	SD	0.863±0.030	0.750±0.082
	RELIEF	0.824±0.018	0.768±0.063
Random forest	No	0.942±0.018	0.708±0.070
with 20 bags	MI	0.943±0.018	0.677±0.087
	SD	0.943±0.020	0.682±0.102
	RELIEF	0.943±0.020	0.701±0.075
AdaBoost.M1	No	0.944±0.019	0.709±0.079
	MI	0.942±0.020	0.666±0.092
	SD	0.941±0.020	0.672±0.095
	RELIEF	0.944±0.019	0.709±0.079
Support vector machine	No	0.940±0.021	**0.966±0.038**
with radial basis function	MI	0.915±0.024	0.941±0.049
kernels	SD	0.913±0.028	0.946±0.039
	RELIEF	0.934±0.021	*0.966±0.039*
Least squares support vector	No	**0.947±0.017**	0.712±0.067
machine with radial basis	MI	0.937±0.020	0.665±0.107
function kernels	SD	0.937±0.019	0.657±0.107
	RELIEF	*0.947±0.018*	0.712±0.068

Acknowledgements: The authors would like to thank National Council of Scientific and Technologic Development of Brazil - CNPq (Grants: 404659/2016-0, 303908/2015-7-PQ, 405101/2016-3, 303906/2015-4-PQ) for its financial support.

References

1. Suykens, J. A. K., Van Gestel, T., De Brabanter, J., De Moor, B, Vandewalle, J. Least squares support vector machines, World Scientific Pub. Co., Singapore, 2002.
2. Kira, K., Rendell, L.: The feature selection problem: traditional methods and a new algorithm. 10th International Conference on Artificial Intelligence (AAAI), San Jose, CA (1992).
3. Starplus fMRI data, *http://www.cs.cmu.edu/afs/cs.cmu.edu/project/theo-81/www/*

Support Vector Machine Optimized by Artificial Bee Colony Applied to EEG Pattern Recognition

Diogo Schwerz de Lucena[1], Sinvaldo Rodrigues Moreno[1],
Viviana Cocco Mariani[1,2] and Leandro dos Santos Coelho[1,3]

[1] Dept. Electrical Engineering, Federal University of Parana (UFPR), Curitiba, Brazil
[2] Mechanical Engineering Graduate Program (PPGEM), PUCPR, Curitiba, Brazil
[3] Industrial and Systems Engineering Graduate Program (PPGEPS), PUCPR, Curitiba, Brazil
lucenadsl@gmail.com, sinvaldo.moreno@gmail.com,
viviana.mariani@pucpr.br, leandro.coelho@pucpr.br

Abstract. In this paper, a multi-class support vector machine (SVM) classifier optimized by swarm intelligence algorithm, known as artificial bee colony (ABC) , was adopted to perform patterns recognition tasks in a brain-computer interface (BCI) application. The proposed strategy involves two main approaches applied to a BCI case study in electroencephalography (EEG) motor imagery classification. The first is relate to apply clustering analysis by similarity in multi-class SVM and the later introduces SVM optimization procedures based on ABC algorithm. The objective of applying clustering analysis by similarity is to grouping different classes into a one, based on their proximity in the feature space. The performance enhancements achieved on classification task of EEG signals (Berlin BCI competition IV dataset) by the proposed SVM-ABC approach outperformed others SVM approaches found in literature.

Keywords: Brain-computer Interface, Support Vector Machine, Machine Learning, Artificial Bee Colony, Electroencephalogram.

1 Introduction

Usually noise is embed on the raw electroencephalography (EEG) signal acquired in non-invasively form. Mostly due to the acquisition process is performed by applying the sensorimotor cortex, during the motor imagery through by a brain-computer interface (BCI). Whereas due to transcranial nature of the data collection method, a limited spatial resolution also is observed, resulting in complex signal processing task. In the last years, machine learning (ML) and optimization approaches [1] have significantly improved BCI. ML has being used mainly to extract meaningful features from noisy signal of large dimensionality and to classify them into computer commands. Support Vector Machine (SVM) is a ML approach applied to perform classification tasks. It received lot of attention on the past few years, and still keeps increasing on popularity, since its introduction by Vapnik in 1990's [2]. SVM is a maximum margin model based on structural risk minimization rather than empirical risk minimization.

C. Frasson and G. Kostopoulos (Eds.): BFAL 2017, LNAI 10512, pp. 213–214, 2017
DOI: 10.1007/978-3-319-67615-9

In this paper, a multi-class SVM classifier, optimized by artificial bee colony (ABC), is applied to solve the EEG patterns recognition task considering the *Graz dataset A* available to the contestants in BCI competition 2008 [3]. This data set consists of EEG data from 9 subjects. The cue-based BCI paradigm consisted by four different motor imagery tasks, namely as the imagination of movement of the left hand (class 1), right hand (class 2), both feet (class 3), and tongue (class 4). The signals were sampled with 250 Hz and band pass filtered between 0.5 Hz and 100 Hz. The sensitivity of the amplifier was set to 100. An additional 50 Hz notch filter was enabled to suppress line noise.

The scheme representing the proposed SVM-ABC approach is depicted on Figure 1. The main difference in our approach, when compared to the classical SVM, is related to embedding the ABC algorithm into the optimization process of the SVM classifier. The proposed SVM also was modified to be able to performing the clustering analysis by similarity technique, in which the training data are applied into grouping step of two similar classes (in the feature space). By executing this procedure multiple times is possible apply multiple binary SVM classifiers into a multi-class problem. The method presented in this paper achieved results similar to the best algorithms in the BCI competition. Regardless, the proposed algorithm implementation is a quite simple task, also, it remains opened to receive further improvements (e.g. selection of the ABC parameters, and SVM algorithm).

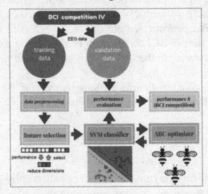

Fig. 1. Hybrid SVM with ABC optimization approach proposed in BCI case study.

Acknowledgements: The authors would like to thank National Council of Scientific and Technologic Development of Brazil - CNPq (Grants: 404659/2016-0, 303908/2015-7-PQ, 405101/2016-3, 303906/2015-4-PQ) for its financial support.

References

1. Ramadan, R. A., Vasilakos, A. V.: Brain computer interface: control signals review. Neurocomputing 223, 26-44 (2017).
2. Vapnik, V. N..: The Nature of statistical learning theory. New York, NY: Springer (1995).
3. Brunmer, C., Leeb, R., Muller-Putz,, G.R., Schogl, G.: Graz data set A. BCI Competition 2008, avaliable: *http://www.bbci.de/competition/iv/desc_2a.pdf*

Author Index

Printed in the United States
By Bookmasters